LIMITED EDITION OF 750 COPIES

OLDBURY
AND ROUND ABOUT
IN THE
WORCESTERSHIRE CORNER OF THE BLACK COUNTRY
BY
FREDERICK WM. HACKWOOD
AUTHOR OF
'SOME RECORDS OF SMETHWICK'
'HANDSWORTH OLD AND NEW'
'HISTORY OF TIPTON'
'A HISTORY OF WEST BROMWICH'
'WEDNESBURY, ANCIENT AND MODERN.'

ARMS OF HALESOWEN ABBEY
ILLUSTRATED

EDITED BY ALAN A. VERNON

Brewin Books

First produced in a Limited Edition
and printed and published by
Whitehead Bros. Wolverhampton and
Cornish Bros. Ltd., Birmingham

This edition of 750 numbered copies published by
Brewin Books Ltd., Studley, Warwickshire B80 7LG, 2002
www.brewinbooks.com

© Introduction – Alan A. Vernon 2002
All rights reserved

The editor's rights have been asserted

British Library Cataloguing in Publication Data
A catalogue record for this book is available from
The British Library

ISBN 1 85858 220 2

Made and Printed in Great Britain by
Warwick Printing Company Ltd.
Theatre Street, Warwick CV34 4DR

DEDICATED
TO ALL TRUE-BORN
NATIVES OF THE BLACK COUNTRY
WHO
PLAIN-DEALING AND BLUNT OF SPEECH,
ARE TRANSPARENT IN THEIR SIMPLE HONESTY;
AS STRENUOUS IN THEIR SPORT
AS THEY ARE UNFLAGGING IN THEIR TOIL;
REVELLING IN THE PLEASURES OF THE TABLE THEMSELVES,
THEY ARE AS EVER HEARTY AND PROFUSE IN THEIR HOSPITALITY TO OTHERS;
AND IN MANY OF THE MOST MARKED TRAITS
OF THEIR ANGLO-SAXON FOREFATHERS,
STILL PRESERVE THE ANCIENT SPIRIT AND CHARACTERISTICS OF
THE TYPICAL MERCIANS

PREFACE

With the publication of the present volume the Author makes his first incursion into the topography of Worcestershire, and at the same time closes a long list of local histories, every one long since out of print and unobtainable in the book market. From his pen have issued, during the past thirty years, separate works on Wednesbury, West Bromwich, Tipton, Darlaston, Willenhall, Sedgley, Smethwick, Handsworth, and Cannock – all Staffordshire parishes and all more or less within the limits of the famous Black Country. To the same populous region of coal and iron belongs, by actual situation and the tie of every material interest, Oldbury, which is essentially a Black Country town though geographically included within the confines of Worcestershire. As explained in the text the position of Oldbury has always been anomalous; how anomalous may be judged by the fact that when the first canal was cut through it the parliamentary sanction described it as being in Staffordshire, and a short amending Act had to be immediately passed to rectify the error.

    The Author has only to add that in the production of this book he has, from first to last, received the most ungrudging aid and the most hearty co-operation from Messrs. Whitehead Bros., who have spared no effort to issue it in the most presentable form possible. Whatever the attractiveness of "OLDBURY AND ROUND ABOUT" over its fellows, to them alone belongs the credit.

Published in a limited edition
of 750 copies

No: 162

FREDERICK WILLIAM HACKWOOD

F. W. Hackwood was born to Enoch and Sarah Hackwood on the 18th April 1851 at 69 High Street East, Wednesbury. His father, Enoch was a tailor, the family had settled in Wednesbury in the middle of the 18th century, the Hackwoods originally came from Stoke-on-Trent.

In 1868 he was admitted to St. Peter's Teachers Training College, Saltley and in 1871 he was appointed headmaster of St. Bartholomew's Church Schools at Wednesbury. In 1878 he was Headmaster of Dudley Road Board School, Birmingham and in 1888 he became Headmaster of Soho Road Board School, also in Birmingham where he stayed until 1916 when he retired.

In 1874 he married Sarah Phoebe Simkin and they had two children, a son, Harold and a daughter, Louisa. He lived with his family at Comberford Lodge, Bridge Street, Wednesbury, until a subterranean fire at a neighbouring colliery forced them to leave the house and move to Handsworth. During the course of his life Frederick Hackwood wrote 28 books about Staffordshire and the Black Country, a 'Oldbury Round and About' being one of them, and was published in 1915. Apart from writing on local history, he wrote books on a variety of other subjects including Natural History, Education, Church Lessons, Biography, Marriage, Sport and Food.

In addition to being a teacher and an author, he was also a magistrate, a town councillor, a footballer, and the founder of several clubs and societies and was involved in creating open spaces like parks, allotments and the re-afforestation of reclaimed colliery waste areas.

The last years of his life were spent at 2 Veronica Road, Balham near to his son, where he died on the 4th December 1926 aged 75 years.

BOOKS BY F. W. HACKWOOD.

Notes of Lessons on Moral Subjects.	1883
Darlaston.	1887
History of Tipton, in Staffordshire	1891
A History of West Bromwich.	1895
Some Records of Smethwick.	1896
Sedgley Researches.	1898
Handsworth Old and New.	1908
Annals of Willenhall.	1908
Oldbury and Round About.	1915
The Story of the Black Country.	1892
Chronicles of Cannock Chase.	1903
Staffordshire Curosities and Antiquities.	1905
Staffordshire Stories.	1906
The Birmingham Midlands.	1906
Staffordshire Worthies.	1911
Staffordshire Sketches.	1916
Staffordshire Customs, Superstitions & Folklore.	1924
Staffordshire Glimpes.	1925
Staffordshire Miscellany. [posthumously]	1927
Through the Midlands.	1905
Westward of the Wash.	1906
Story of the Shire.	1921
Olden Warwickshire.	1971
Notes of Lessons on Kindness to Animals.	1892
The Practical Method of Class Management.	1896
Natural History Reference Notes.	1897
Notes of Lessons on the Church Service.	1897
New Object Lessons. [Animal Life]	1898
Chatty Object Lessons in Nature Knowledge.	1900
Old English Sports.	1907
The Good Old Times.	1910
Inns, Ales and Drinking Customs, of Old England	1909
Good Cheer, The Romance of Food and Feasting.	1911
William Hone, His Life and Times.	1912
Life of Lord Kitchener.	1913
Dragons and Dragon Slayers.	1923
The Bridal Book. The Lore, History and Philosphy of Love, Courtship and Marriage.	1923
The Wednesbury Papers.	1884
Wednesbury Workshops.	1889
Olden Wednesbury.	1899
Religious Wednesbury.	1900
Odd Chapters in the History of Wednesbury.	1920
Wednesbury Notes & Queries 3 Vols.	1902
Wednesbury Ancient & Modern.	1902
Pocket Guide to Wednesbury.	1908
Christ Lore.	1902

ACKNOWLEDGEMENTS

I wish to thank the following for their help and assistance in republishing this volume. Firstly, to Alan Brewin, in agreeing to my suggestion to make this book available once more to a wider public. Sandwell Community History and Archives Service at Smethwick Library. Staff at Oldbury Public Library. Terry Daniels for writing the foreword to this book. Members of Oldbury Local History Group. Lastly but not least the people and the town of Oldbury whose history should not be forgotten but remembered for the contribution to the area known as the 'Black Country'.

FOREWORD

'Oldbury and Round About', published in 1915, was one of the last books on Black Country towns by Frederick Hackwood. It covers the Oldbury Urban District, which comprised Oldbury, Langley and Warley and was formed in 1894, and then 'rounds up' nearby places such Rowley Regis and Halesowen. By then, Oldbury had become an industrial town, whereas Warley had retained its farms, lanes, hamlets and rural character.

A thousand years earlier Oldbury, Warley and Langley Green had been tiny settlements within Halesowen manor, later coming under the influence of Halesowen Abbey until its dissolution in 1538. Oldbury and Warley became separate manors within Halesowen parish, and were largely agricultural until the late eighteenth century when the canal arrived in Oldbury. In 1841 Christchurch was opened and Oldbury parish formed.

The rich ten-yard seam is deep in Oldbury, and coal could not won here until suitable methods had been developed. Thus, mining came late, it reached its peak around 1850-60, and had almost vanished by 1915, as the flooded mines had to be abandoned.

Ironstone was found with the coal, leading to iron making and metal processing. Nails had been made by hand for centuries, but William Hunt's works at 'The Brades' was the first factory: it gained a world-wide reputation for edge tools. By Hackwood's time, Oldbury still had puddling furnaces, rolling mills, foundries, forges and stampings, although its blast furnaces had long gone. There were leading manufacturers of tubes [Accles & Pollock] and boilers [Edwin Danks]. Brick making followed mining, particularly near Rounds Green, and the area became scarred with marl holes.

The local chemical industry began with Chance Brother's Alkali Works in 1835 producing materials for their glass works at Smethwick. In 1850 Albright & Wilson started to make phosphorus for matches, and in the 1860s Lugwig Demuth opened a tar works. While these industries certainly blighted the landscape, they also attracted migrant workers, ensuring Oldbury's rapid growth in the nineteenth century.

The people of Oldbury were naturally non-conformist and radical, for they had to live with poor housing and the disadvantages of their industries. Gradually social improvements were made bringing better health and more opportunities for education and leisure. By 1915 Oldbury had four new council schools and a technical college and various benefactors had given public parks. It was surrounded by canals, situated on the Birmingham to Dudley tramway and served by two railways, had its own gas works, sewerage farm and cemetery – overall, it was a bustling town,, full of chapels, shops and pubs!

Living conditions continued to improve, although the biggest changes would come after Hackwood's time, particularly through council housing. Oldbury became a borough in 1935, but its hard-won independence was to last only thirty years until it was swallowed up in 'Warley' and 'Sandwell'. However, these changes were well into future for the Oldbury that Hackwood describes.

Terry Daniels
Vice-chairman, Oldbury Local History Group

INTRODUCTION

When Elihu Burritt wrote his book 'A Walk in the Black Country and its Green Borderland' in 1856, the title might have been referring to Oldbury. When Frederick Hackwood produced his book 'Oldbury and Round About in the Worcestershire corner of the Black Country' in 1915, Oldbury still had rural surroundings even though the parish was rapidly becoming industrialised, he described Oldbury as 'a pleasant and pretty place nestling at the foot of the green slopes of the Rowley Hills'.

'Oldbury and Round About' as the title indicates, covers an area larger than just the township of Oldbury, until 1844 it was part of the parish of Halesowen. There are references to Rowley Regis, Netherton, Brierley Hill, Pensnett, Kingswinford, Cradley, Dudley, Frankley, Hagley and Clent in the text

When Oldbury like many neighbouring towns became absorbed into the County Borough of Warley and later into the Metropolitan Borough of Sandwell, it lost its connection to the County of of Worcestershire, previous to this it had been part of Shropshire, today, like its neighbours it is part of the defunct county of the of the West Midlands.

Oldbury owes its existence to its location near to coal and ironstone seams, but its continuing presence in the Black Country as manufacturing town is due to the men and women who live and work in the area, and now even though its natural resources have long since disappeared, the people that made Oldbury what it is today, still produce goods which are sent to all over the world, and long may this be so, for if the history of Oldbury teaches us anything, it is to survive you have to change and Oldbury has changed many times and in many ways.

Alan A. Vernon											October 2002
A. & B. Books											©

CONTENTS

I.	INTRODUCTION	1
II.	PHYSIOGRAPHICAL AND GEOLOGICAL	5
III.	HISTORY IN LOCAL PLACE NAMES	9
IV.	HALESOWEN PARISH CHURCH – THE FABRIC – MEMORIALS – BELLS.	14
V.	HALESOWEN PARISH CHURCH – PAROCIAL RECORDS.	19
VI.	THE MANOR OF HALESOWEN – ITS EXTENT	22
VII.	THE MANOR OF HALESOWEN – ITS GOVERNMENT – PARISH CONSTABLE – MILLS – MANORIAL CUSTOMS	26
VIII.	HALESOWEN ABBEY – THE MONKS – THE BUILDING – POSSESSIONS – SHRINE OF ST. BARBARA – FARMING ...	30
IX.	MONASTIC LIFE IN HALESOWEN – VISITATIONS – THE ABBOT – OFFENCES	37
X.	THE DISSOLUTION OF THE ABBEY – THE DUDLEY FAMILY – THE SPOILATION THE REFORMATION – ST JAMES PRIORY, DUDLEY SANDWELL PRIORY.	41
XI.	EARLY HISTORY OF OLDBURY – PORTWAY – PART OF SHROPSHIRE AND HALESOWEN BLAKELEY HALL	46
XII.	DESCENT OF THE MANOR OF OLDBURY – ROBERT DUDLEY – ARTHUR ROBSART – CORNWALLIS FAMILY – LORDS OF THE MANOR ...	50
XIII.	THE CHAPELRY OF OLDBURY – CHAPEL OF EASE – NONCONFORMITY CHRIST CHURCH	55
XIV.	NONCONFORMITY IN AND AROUND OLDBURY...	58
XV.	THE RISE IN LOCAL METHODISM – JOHN WESLEY	64
XVI.	THE DAWN OF INDUSTRIALISM – NAILMAKING	71
XVII.	THE COMING OF CANALS – THE GRAND JUNCTION CANAL – JAMES BRINDLEY TRANSPORT OF COAL – THOMAS TELFORD ...	76
XVIII.	THE OLDBURY MINING DISTRICT – BROMFORD COLLIERY – ROUNDS GREEN COLLIERY – RAMROD HALL COLLIERY	81
XIX.	MINERAL RESOURCES AND MINING ENTERPRISE – SOUTH STAFFORDSHIRE COALFIELD – 'THICK COAL' – FAULTS AND FLOODING – IRONSTONE AND FIRECLAY	83
XX.	THE BRADES WORKS – BRADES TROWEL – ELIHU BURRITT – MANUFACTURE OF STEEL	87
XXI.	THE CHANCE INTEREST – SPON LANE GLASS WORKS – CRYSTAL PALACE – LIGHTHOUSE LANTERNS – ALKALI WORKS ...	91
XXII.	IRON – WORKING AND IRON – WORKERS – PUDDLING SHINGLING – WROUGHT IRON – PIG-IRON – 'BLISTER STEEL' – ARTISANS ...	99
XXIII.	DIVERSITY OF EMPLOYMENT IN OLDBURY – CROSSWELLS BREWERY RAILWAY ROLLING STOCK – TUBE MAKING – CHEMICALS – BRICKMAKING – BOILER MAKING	103

XXIV.	Oldbury : Early Forms of Local Government – Halesowen Salop – Worcestershire – Upper Halfshire – Board of Surveyors – Local Board of Health	106
XXV.	Oldbury Municipal Progress – Housing – Water Supply – Gas Lighting – Public Offices – Public Parks – Municipal Institutions – Urban District Council	109
XXVI.	Oldbury: Administration of Justice – Parish Constable – County Constabulary – Petty Sessions – Court of Requests County Court	111
XXVII.	Oldbury :Educational Institutions – Free School – Primary and Secondary Schools	116
XXVIII.	Warley and Langley – Wernlegh, Ruggacre, Cakemore, Wallaxhall, Brendall – St. Katherines Chapel – Warley Abbey – Brinsnell Hall – Moat Farm – Free Library	118
XXIX.	Oldbury and the Prospect Around – Walter White – Stour Valley Line – Telford – Brindley – Soho – Phosphorous	122
XXX.	Rowley Regis:its History and Industries – Kings Rowley Turner's Hill – The Hailstone – Rowley rag – Dud Dudley Nailmaking – Blackheath – Old Hill – Bassano Family	127
XXXI.	Rowley Regis Ecclesiastical History – St. Giles – Clent- destruction – Alms Houses …	132
XXXII.	The Cobbler Poet of Rowley – James Woodhouse – William Shenstone – Leasowes	138
XXXIII.	Netherton, Brierley Hill and Pensnett – Wrens Nest Hill Turner – Ruskin – Kingswinford – Enclosure Act	141
XXXIV.	Cradley: Its Early History – Domesday Book – Barons of Dudley – Cradley Heath – Pensnett Chase – Kingswinford	145
XXXV.	Cradley : Its Industrial Record – Iron Trade – Dud Dudley Chain making – Anchor Making	149
XXXVI.	A Green Borderland of Much Romantic Interest – Howley Charles II – Frankley – Hagley – Dudley	155
XXXVII.	The Leasowes and the Poet Shenstone – Great Barr Hall River Stour	161
XXXVIII.	Hagley, Clent and St. Kenelms – Hagley Hall – The Lytteltons St. Kenelm of Clent	166
XXXIX.	Some Old Families and Notable Personages – The Pastons Groves – Riders – Peter Ward – Henry Adock – William Caslon – Robert Hancock – Bridges …	173
XL.	Habits and Customs – Lore and Bibliography – Fairs and Markets – Burial Practice – Sports and Pastimes	180
	An Index	184

ILLUSTRATIONS

No.		Page
1.	Portrait of the Author *(Kemp)*	*Frontispiece*
2.	Map of Halesowen (1830) as part of Shropshire	10
3.	Church Lane, Halesowen *(Kemp)*	16
4.	Ruins of Halesowen Abbey	32
5.	The Infirmary, Hales Owen Abbey, in 1777 *(Bickerstaff)*	34
6.	Ruins of Halesowen Abbey *(Kemp)*	44
7.	Cradley Old Forge *(Sir Frank Short, P.R.E.)*	74
8.	Portrait of Sir James T. Chance, Bart *(J. C. Horsley, R.A.)*	92
9.	Rowley Hailstone, 1845	126
10.	Rowley Regis Church in 1907	128
11.	Dudley *(J. M. W. Turner, R.A.)*	142
12.	The Leasowes in 1830 *(Calvert)*	160
13.	St. Kenelm's Church, Romsley	171
14.	Portrait of William Caslon	175
15.	Portrait of Sir Frederick Bridge, Knt., C.V.O., M.V.O.	179

Portrait of the Author (Kemp)

OLDBURY
AND ROUND ABOUT

BY

Frederick Wm. Hackwood

I.—Introduction.

FEW TOWNS in England present greater difficulties to the Muse of History than those with which Oldbury confronts the most amiable advances of the recording Clio. For Oldbury is a township which never was a parish—that is, in the legal sense that it was an area of civil administration imposed on an ancient ecclesiastical foundation.

When the English Constitution was taking root in the land, and the old form of tribal government was waning before the dawn of Christianity and the domination of clericalism which accompanied it, the country was gradually divided into dioceses by the missioner bishops, who presently, having quite dispelled the mists of paganism, organised their sees into local government units called parishes. Oldbury was then, and for long afterwards, included in the parish of Halesowen.

Now it is nearly always possible to dig out the history of a parish from the various ancient parochial records; but of a fraction of a parish, which was not always a separate entity, the task is by no means so easy.

The first constitution of Oldbury into a distinct entity came at a later period, when its area was organised for civil and military government into a feudal manor. But, unfortunately, few of the old manorial records have survived, and again the historian is at a loss.

To complicate matters still more, the mother-parish, Halesowen, was not always included, for its wider government and superior civic administration, within the County of Worcester, to which it geographically belongs, but formed for several centuries a detached and outlying portion of Salop. The reason for this detachment will appear later.

Nor was the whole of Halesowen included in Salop. It is a large parish of several townships, one of which was already in Worcestershire, as is testified by its name, Warley Wigorn. And it did not consist of one piece; it was cut up into small patches and scattered among the townships of Oldbury, Langley, and Warley Salop, which were in Shropshire; some of these pieces were mere fields, some were larger and themselves enringed portions of Shropshire, so that on the small scale ordnance maps it was scarcely possible to distinguish the boundaries of the two counties. These anomalous dislocations and confusing boundary lines, after existing for centuries, were rectified by statute a few years after the passing of the great Reform Bill of 1832.

And when, at last, this detached piece of Shropshire was eventually taken into Worcestershire, it formed a tongue of Wigornian territory, which thrust itself like a peninsula of foreign soil into Staffordshire—an intrusion which the precisians have said ought to be rectified by merging it into that county.

So a movement was set on foot for transferring the town of Oldbury from Worcestershire to Staffordshire. At the reform of the Poor Laws in 1834, Oldbury, for some occult reason or other, had been included in the Poor Law Union of West Bromwich, an important administrative area on which the Local Government Board focussed all its official papers, so that for years and years this poor little slice of Worcestershire was administered and overshadowed in a government unit that comprised a wide area of Staffordshire parishes—West Bromwich, Wednesbury, and Handsworth.

The promoters of the movement for transference urged that Oldbury was already in the West Bromwich Union, and that on three sides out of four it was hemmed in by Smethwick, West Bromwich, and Rowley, all Staffordshire areas.

The Oldbury governing authorities, however, resisted the proposed transfer, feeling that it was in every way preferable to remain one of the larger towns of Worcestershire, than to be tacked on to one of the great urban districts of populous Staffordshire.

An opportunity to revive the project occurred in 1906, when Oldbury joined with Smethwick in a scheme for the provision of a joint Infectious Hospital. This time strong opposition was offered by the Worcester County Council, which naturally objected to losing one of its most important industrial towns, which was the centre of one of its largest Parliamentary divisions, and which comprised a rateable area of considerable value in a county so largely agricultural.

The proposal has not been allowed to die. Public movements have fanned it into life at various times; as when Smethwick was constituted a county borough, and again when the development of the Black Country tramway system linked it up into closer communication with the adjacent Staffordshire towns. It has almost seemed to onlookers at these contentions that the rights of self-government in the township might be invaded, if not denied, and the place regarded merely as a prize for which two powerful bodies might contend at will, without any reference to the wishes of the inhabitants themselves.

How came it that this outlying portion of Halesowen should have developed into a busy industrial centre, while the heart of that ancient parish scarcely outgrew its pristine rurality? The reason is not far to seek. Oldbury not only possessed great mineral resources (of which more will be said later), but when the period of industrialism first dawned it was found on the important coach-road between Birmingham and Shrewsbury and the north.

The importance of this factor in developing a locality, though comparatively insignificant when compared with wealth in natural resources, is not always recognised. These old roads, as arteries of traffic, are deserving of passing notice.

The "Britannia Depicta," published in 1753, says that the old road from Birmingham *via* Dudley and Bridgnorth if is now disused "by the coaches and wagons, and goes on to recommend the newer and better road through West Bromwich, Wednesbury, and Wolverhampton, which was turnpiked in 1721. This, however, is evidently a quotation from "Owen and Bowen's Road Book," published in 1731, containing the earliest mention of these local highways.

Far more ancient than the recommended road from Birmingham leading to the north and north-west through Sandwell and West Bromwich, is that connecting Birmingham with Dudley and its dependencies, going through Oldbury, or by the still more direct line passing a little to the right of Rowley Regis, which gives evidence by its "hollowed ways" of having been used for regular traffic at a very remote period. Oakham, it may be noted, was originally "Hollow-combe."

Probably the oldest coach route in this direction lay through Oldbury, Dudley, and Wenlock.

Daily postal communication between Birmingham and Dudley, Halesowen, Stourbridge, Kidderminstcr, and Bewdley was first, established in 1769.

Paterson's "Roads of England and Wales," issued by T. N. Longman, of Paternoster Row, in 1794, gives the London and Shrewsbury road through Birmingham and Wedgbury, which by that date had superseded the older one; adding as a "branch or cross road" the portion from Birmingham to Dudley and Kinver, thus:—

Smethwick, 4 miles—from London, 110

Oldbury,   3 ,,   — ,,   ,,   117

Dudley,   3 ,,   — ,,   ,,   120

Kinver,   8 ,,   — ,,   ,,   128

On left of Smethwick is Hales Owen, seat of the late Lord Dudley.

Near Dudley is Dudley Castle, Viscount Dudley. and Ward, who has a seat at Himley.

In passing through Oldbury a century ago, the traveller obtained a fine view of the surrounding country—of the Rowley Hills, the ruins of Dudley Castle, and the fine woods of Sandwell Park. But the pristine rusticity of the place was already beginning to fade.

. The road from Birmingham to Dudley through Oldbury is about nine miles, or nearly a mile shorter than the one through West Bromwich, Carters Green, and Great Bridge. Yet in that short space, the traveller formerly passed through four different counties; Birmingham being in Warwickshire, Smethwick in Staffordshire, Oldbury in Shropshire, and Dudley in Worcestershire. The eccentricity and arbitrariness of English political boundaries could scarcely further go than this.

Another stimulus to the growth of Oldbury was given in the latter half of the eighteenth century by the construction of artificial waterways in this high midland region where navigable rivers are unknown. When the rapidly growing traffic in coal, iron, and other heavy produce first called into being the canals, it was a fortunate thing for Oldbury that the new waterway between Birmingham and the ancient coalfield in the heart of the.Black Country—the original mining region round Wednesbury, Bilston, and Sedgley—ran directly through this developing township. Though the canals came first in 1769, a decade or two elapsed before they had their inevitable effect on the development of this fortunately situated village.

From a contemporary writer we obtain a glimpse of the place in its industrial infancy. Charles Pye, in his "Modern Birmingham," written in 1829, describes the road from that city to Dudley, as it then appeared. After details of the road through Smethwick, he goes on:—

"Leaving Smethwick, you proceed towards Oldbury, upon which road the trustees are making great improvements, by widening the road and turning the course of a brook, over which they are building a bridge, which, when finished, will be a great accommodation. This village is situated in the County of Salop, and is a chapel-of-ease to Halesowen.

"A new Court House was erected here in 1816, where the Court of Requests is held once a fortnight."

Thirty years later, namely, in 1846, the growth of Oldbury received a little fillip when the County Court was set up here. By this reform England and Wales was divided into sixty districts, or circuits, in which Courts were established for the recovery of debts (to supersede the ancient Courts of Requests), and that at Oldbury had jurisdiction over the surrounding district, including the larger town of West Bromwich-which was a distinct advance.

Returning to Pye's description of Oldbury in 1829, we read:—

"The Protestant Dissenters have here a neat place of worship, as have also the Methodists.

"Close to the village are several coal mines, and a blast furnace belonging to Mr. Parker.

"About a mile distant, on the left of the road, is the Brades, where Messrs. William Hunt and Sons have established a manufacture of iron and steel, which they form into scythes, hay knives, trowels, and every kind of hoe now in use."

Thus we see Oldbury fairly started on its career. of industrial expansion.

II.—Physiographical and Geological.

All the foregoing adventitious aids to evolution would have been barren of material result had not Oldbury possessed within itself those natural resources, which, properly handled, invariably lead to commercial prosperity.

But, first, to glance at the surface and its natural drainage system.

The river Stour, a tributary of the Severn, rises in two main branches; one near Wolverhampton, the other from several springs on the north-east side of the Clent Hills. It is the latter which runs through Halesowen, and in olden times fed the Abbey pools; it is asserted that no other river of its size in England turned so many water-mills before the era of steam as this used to work. Another branch, rising on the south side of the Clent Hills, passes through Belbroughton, and joins the Stour near its confluence with the Severn. By this river system Halesowen, is included within the basin of the Severn, and its drainage Waters, therefore, flow to the south-west into the Bristol Channel. But the superfluous rainfall of Warley and Oldbury is mostly carried away in the opposite direction, towards the north-east, by the Tame and Trent into the Humber. For Oldbury is situated on the edge of the plain near the headwaters of the river Tame; it is sheltered by the Rowley Hills, which form part of the midland watershed.

The area under notice in these pages is covered with a number of low hill ranges. The first of these, a northerly extension of the Lower Lickey Hills, are the rolling heights of Halesowen, then the conspicuous mound of Rowley Regis (820 feet), the line being continued by the wooded heights of Dudley Castle (730 feet), and afterwards by the Wren's Nest and Sedgley Hill. To the south-westward is a range of slightly higher elevation, stretching through Upper, or Bromsgrove, Lickey Hills (900 feet) to Hagley, where it is known as the Clent Hills (1,028 feet).

The Tame has two main heads, the southern one here, and the other, the western, between Wolverhampton and Cannock Chase. The southern head takes its origin from springs and brooks in the districts of Warley, Blackheath, and Rowley Regis, most of them, particularly those on the confines of White

Heath, being foul malodorous ditches. From the gathering ground between Cakemore on the cast and Rowley on the west, these streams, which are partly in Worcestershire and partly in Staffordshire, converge on Oldbury; and the brook which leaves this town then becomes the boundary between the two counties, and, incidentally, between Oldbury and West Bromwich.

Though Oldbury is on "the green borderland of the Black Country," and within easy reach of the pleasant orchards of Worcestershire, its destiny was sealed by the immense fact that it lay within the same mineral area as the prolific Staffordshire Coalfield.

The town of Oldbury stands on two geological formations, the red rocks—Permian—and the grey rocks, with clays, shales, ironstones, and coals. Further, the former formation is let down by the eastern boundary fault, the Permian rocks being on the east and the coal-bearing rocks on the west. The London and North-Western Railway crosses the "fault" at right-angles. A mile to the west, overlooking the town, are the. Rowley Hills, stretching some $2\frac{1}{2}$ miles in length and being $1\frac{1}{2}$ miles across at their northern extremity. This is the largest remaining sheet of lava in the Midlands, and must have had at an earlier period of the earth's history a much greater spread than it has to-day. By geologists it is called a sill of Dolerite, but in the commercial world it is known as "Rowley rag," and by highway surveyors is in great demand for road making. This volcanic rock is placed by Sir Archibald Geikie as first in withstanding breaking-strain, and when fresh it is undoubtedly the best road metal to be found anywhere in the district.

Situated near the south-eastern end of the South Staffordshire Coalfield, the town of Oldbury owes its existence to the anticline of carboniferous rocks which extend from Beaudesert, on Cannock Chase, to Halesowen. This main anticline, however, is broken up into three minor anticlines; and between one of these, running from Barr through West Bromwich and Oldbury, the town lies in a syncline which proceeds through Bilston to Cannock. All round the neighbourhood lie worked-out collieries, remains of blast furnaces, dismantled ironworks, abandoned claypits, all attesting to the wonderful mineral wealth of the place some sixty years ago. Several seams of coal, ironstone, and limestone (the last-named lying over towards Dudley) were all found close at hand and easy for the feeding of furnace, forge, and ironmill. Added to these were also enormous deposits of brick-earth and clays, which formed no insignificant part of the industrial resources of the Oldbury district; and if there is any town which can claim to owe its industries and the outward aspect it presents to the world to its geology, it is surely Oldbury.

Our earliest, or remotest, knowledge of a place is obtained from the unwritten history which geologists read "for us. If the scientist picks up a piece of limestone in one of the caverns at Dudley, and on examination finds it composed almost entirely of corals, he "reads" that, although in the centre of England, this place, once had the sea flowing over it, for to no other agency than the labours of these marine creatures could the origin of the limestone be attributed. The surface of the earth has undergone many changes, and the accompanying variations in its climate, before the present zones were fixed, are demonstrated by the geologist, who finds within the boundaries of the Arctic Circle the remains of luxurious vegetation, which could not possibly grow in that desolate and icebound region as it is now—a warm and genial climate must have prevailed in that now frigid region, when several species of Sequoia (one of the very largest trees in the world) grew there; when the magnolia blossomed there; the chestnut, the walnut, and the plum-tree bore fruit, and the vine brought forth grapes; and the glades of the forest were filled with waving ferns; where now vegetation of any kind would be sought in vain.

Contrariwise, there was an Ice Age, when the temperate zone, of which this midland district was a portion, was a cold and frozen land of grim Arctic aspect. When such conditions prevailed in Great Britain, and its mountains were covered with snow, its valleys filled with glaciers, and its seas ploughed by icebergs, relics of these primeval severities were left in the shape of boulders scattered about by ice-action. These stones are too numerous and too enormous to have been carried by any river, and so angular that they never could have been rubbed against each other in river beds; they were carried in precisely the same way as the glaciers of Switzerland may be seen moving down from the mountains to the valleys, carrying along blocks of stone embedded in the ice, and dropped when the ice melts.

A few years ago it was reported in a local newspaper that some drifted rocks, relics of the Glacial Period, some of them local and some erratic, had been found in this neighbourhood:—

A discovery of considerable interest to Midland geologists (said this report, published in 1905) has been made at Oldbury, where excavations were being made for an extension of the works of Messrs. Chance and Hunt. About sixteen feet below the surface the workmen cut into a mass of boulder clay, embedded in which were a large number of stones of various kinds, which bore exceptionally strongly-marked traces of the action of the ice floe. The stones are unmistakably of local origin, including specimens of clay-ironstone, shale, and basaltic rock, some of which are deeply scratched by the ice. The supposition is that they were ground off by the ice-sheet as it travelled over the country. Basaltic rock occurs locally at Rowley, but one specimen of the basalt found was declared to have travelled either from Scotland or from Cumberland.

Clee and other hills come into sight from the summit of Clent; and thence the spectator looks into a broad vale westward (which geologists once regarded as an ancient strait of the sea till the absence of any constructive coast-line compelled the abandonment of the theory), a channel for a great torrent, traces of which remain in scattered granite boulders similar to these erratic specimens. One, drifted far from its native bed in Scotland, is to be seen by the roadside just beyond Clent.

The operations of a beneficent Nature, it will be seen, have contributed, during a succession of geologic ages, to endow the Oldbury area with those valuable economic resources by which it has risen to an industrial eminence beyond the rest of Worcestershire. The earliest formation, evolved when low forms of marine life alone could find sustenance on the earth, stored up the limestone of the Dudley and the Sedgley Hills; the carbonate of lime now employed as a building material, as a flux for iron smelting, and in other industrial pursuits, being but a vast accumulation of the skeletons of creatures who lived in fairly deep water when this region was submerged beneath the Silurian sea.

Next in order came the laying down, also under water, of the old red sandstone, which may be seen exposed at the canal cutting north of Netherton. Then we have the coal measures, consisting of alternate beds of clays, with ironstone, sandstone, and coal; the last-named being the fossilised vegetable remains of ancient submerged forests, transformed under enormous earth pressure acting through long periods of time, and converting it into inflammable carbon compounds.

After the formation of the coal measures, there were intruded into and through them those masses of igneous rock we call Rowley Rag; it boiled up from the earth's centre as liquid lava, broke through the coal measures vertically, and then spread itself horizontally along their bedding planes.

A pamphlet published by Mr. Blocksidge, of Dudley, entitled "Rowley Rag," gives a most interesting account of the geological formation of the local basaltic deposit, and of the methods employed in quarrying it. The little work is copiously and admirably illustrated with local views, all informative and a few not unpicturesque.

In the Oldbury area there are not found above the coal measures the usual rocks known as the Permians and the Trias, which must have been denuded, or washed away at some time in the earth's long history, because they are both found covering the coal measures in West Bromwich, and also in that part of Oldbury lying east of the London and North-Western Railway Station; it is at this point that the eastern boundary "fault" makes the dividing line between the coal measures and the Permian sandstone already mentioned. In the Carboniferous period flourished enormous quantities of low plant life, as ferns, and conifers, but as yet no flowering plants. With the Triassic period came abundant reptile life, but no birds.

The Glacial epoch was the last stage in the deposition, great mounds of sands, clays, and other unstratified material being laid down in confused heaps, which have been subsequently rounded off by meteoric agencies.

By each of these formations some advantage has been conferred on the district, in the Carboniferous strata the clay ironstone being closely adjacent to the coal with which to smelt them. The sand and the clay, too, have not failed to stimulate the commercial activities of this thriving industrial region, as will be demonstrated in a later chapter.

III.—History in Local Place-Names

The study of place-names is of considerable historical importance. In an examination of the name of Oldbury, and in that of its parent-parish, Halesowen, not the least interesting points in their origin and history are to be gleaned.

Oldbury is a name with a fine ancient ring in it. It is the "Old burh," so named by the Anglo-Saxons because they found it an ancient, and perhaps deserted, British settlement that had been in existence centuries before their arrival on the scene. In the Anglo-Saxon tongue it was Ealdanbyrig, and in Middle English, Aldebury.

As might be expected in such a descriptive appellation, there are a number of places bearing it. There is an Oldbury in Kent~ near to Sevenoaks, and another one close to Tunbridge Wells; an Oldbury in Shropshire, a mile or so outside Bridgnorth; one in Warwickshire, where was once an ancient nunnery, not far from Atherstone; and one really an ancient earthwork—in Wilts. Gloucestershire boasts an Oldbury-on-the-Hill, and an Oldbury- upon-Severn.

Nash, the historian of Worcestershire, retails some local gossip he collected at the end of the eighteenth century, to the effect that, in a certain field in Oldbury, known as the Castle Leasow, old inhabitants had handed down a tradition of the existence of fragmentary ruins as those of a town that had once existed and gradually passed away. "I.find," he says, "a general tradition among the inhabitants that a great town anciently stood here, and extended from the present village, to the Castle Leasow, lying under the Bury Hill, which is near half a mile." The learned Doctor himself scarcely gave much credence to the tradition. There can be little doubt that the name Old-bury discloses the origin of the place as having been a human settlement in those far away times, when the raising of an earthwork fortification round it was simply a matter of necessity. But a great mound, or a rampart of earth enclosing a cluster of rude huts, would certainly not leave "ruins," or remains of any tangible kind, that could be traced one or two thousand years afterwards. On the other hand, it is

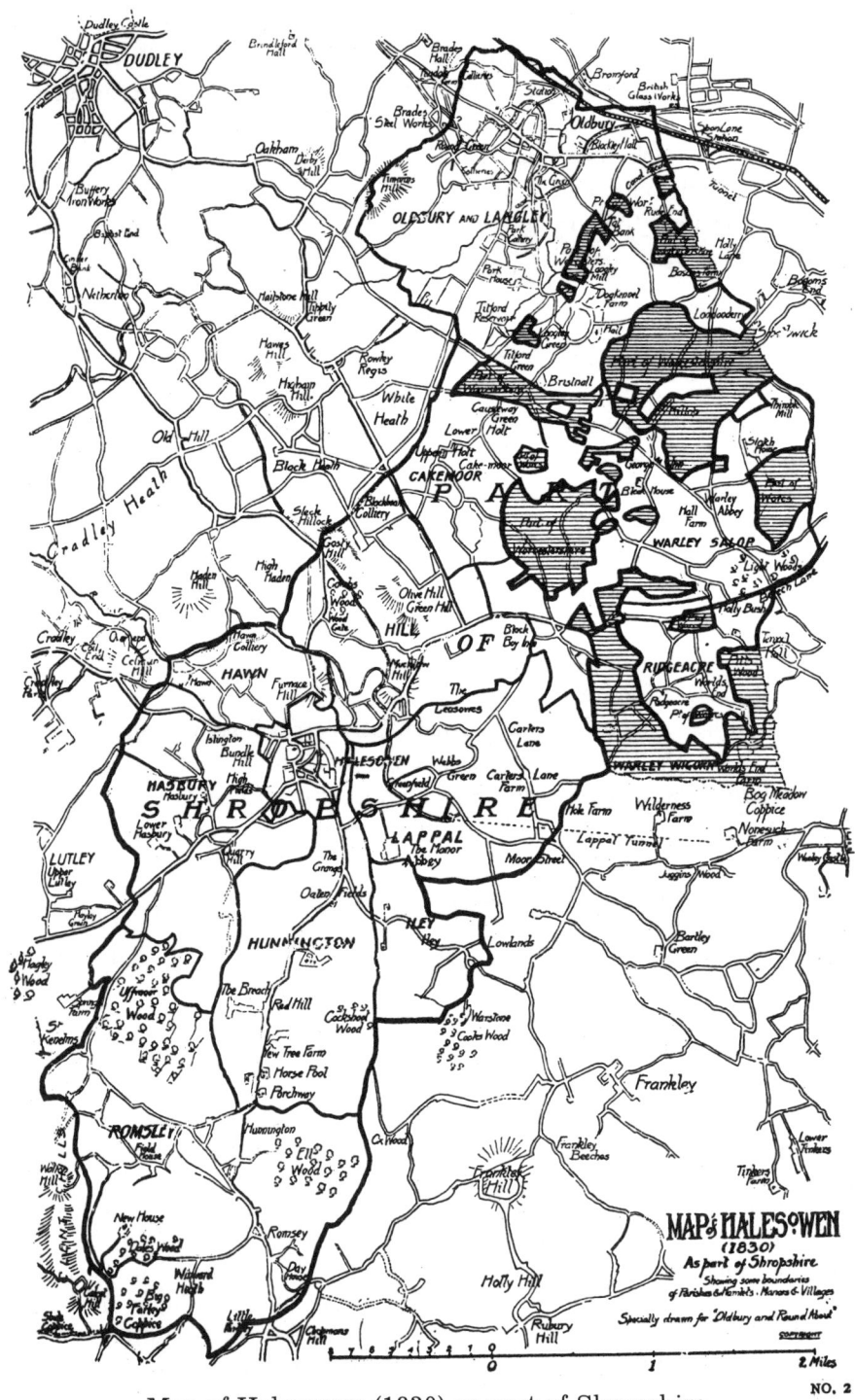

Map of Halesowen (1830) as part of Shropshire

quite possible that the place-name, "Castle Leasow," was a true word-relic of that existence, because the term castle, as applied to ancient entrenched forts of a like character, is found in use in many parts of England to this day. For instance, there is Castle Rings, on Cannock Chase. Even burial tumuli have for centuries been known as, and are still called, castles.

On the flimsy foundation of this place-name a piece of modern fiction, a quasi-ballad, entitled "The Legend of St. Brade." has been built up, the plot of which was evidently inspired by the old tale connected with Guy of Warwick and Guy's Cliff. In the Oldbury version the heroine is the fair Lady Brade—why called Saint Brade is not quite clear—who is supposed to reside in a mediæval Bury Castle (of course, built of stone like the Dudley Castle of the same period), and in the end to marry her long-lost lover, the young lord of Dudley, on his return from the Crusades. It is all very romantic and perhaps interesting; but it would be at least equally interesting to learn the derivation of the place-name, Brades. Many similar proper-names are derived from brad, signifying broad or spacious, as in Bradley. In others, however, a personal name, Brada, is known to survive; thus, Bradnope, in Staffordshire, is the hupp, or sloping plain, which Brada conquered from the Britons. The prose introduction to the Legend does satisfy the curiosity by associating the name Rood End with the existence there of a Holy Rood, or wayside cross; and also the name Crosswell, the well of healing waters near the said cross. Spon Lane, by the way, derived its name in a precisely similar manner—it had a holy well, above which was a wayside cross, the word Spon signifying the splint of the True Cross, which was preserved as a sacred relic in the shrine.

A score of places in England bear the name Hales, Hailes, or Hale in some form; thus we have Sheriff Hales, on the borders of Staffordshire and Shropshire. In the Worcestershire Subsidy Rolls of 1275 and 1327 there were over thirty place-names recorded as de-la-Hale,—atte Hale,—en la Hale,—in the Hale, all meaning "in the hollow," or "in the meadows." In the present case such description accords with the low-lying situation of the manor of Hales Owen. The terminal Owen was added in 1177, in consequence of the marriage of Emma, sister of Henry II., to David ap Owen, Prince of North Wales; this manor of Hales, which then belonged to the Crown, being given by the King to his sister in frankmarriage. She was succeeded by her son Owen, and ever since the place has been known as Hales Owen. The first mention of the suffix Owen—spelt Oweyn—occurs under date 1271.

Though Hales Owen was only a portion of the Princess Emma's dowry, it seems to have been the only livelihood left to her son, Owen, when for a time he was driven from Wales by his kinsmen, on the death of his father, David—in the usual struggle for a Welsh princeship. His other lands lay chiefly in the Vale of Clwyd.

It is probable that Hales Owen was David's English manor, which, in some way, was at the bottom of his foray into England when lie burnt Coventry.

Exception has been taken to this derivation of the name Halesowen, or, rather, to the first part of it. It has been pointed out that, though the country surrounding Halesowen lies in a basin-like depression, the town itself is on a hill-side, and therefore the root *hale*, "hollow," does not apply. The contention is, that the name Hales comes from the Celtic root *hal*, "salt," which is synonymous with the Teutonic *sal*.

This means that the name of the place is British and not Saxon, and it is argued out with no little elaboration thus. From Domesday Book it is known that, so far back as Edward the Confessor's time, a salt-pan belonging to the manor of Hala was worked at Droitwich. There is also historical evidence that salt-works existed in this country before, the advent of the Teutonic race, so that it is possible Halesowen owes its name to its early salt-pans, because, although Halesowen itself stands above the coal measures, the red sandstone formation occurs within the radius of one mile to the northward, and the origin of the red sandstone and that of rock salt (the reservoirs of brine springs) are intimately connected. The theory is ingenious, but should be taken—not inappropriately—*cum grano salis*.

Naturally, the name has assumed many forms as it came down through the centuries, when orthography was purely a matter of taste. Properly, it should be two words, but the economy of space and time dictated by the rush of modern life has compressed it into one, and both the Post Office and the Railway Companies favour the form Halesowen. Among the forms in which it has presented itself are Hala, Halas, Hales, Haleshowen, Halesowaign, Halesowyn, Halesoweign, Halesoweyn, Halez, Halisowen, Halseowen, Halsowen, Hayles, and Haylesowen. During the period the place was Crown property it may have been known as Hales Regis.

A further inquiry into the significance of the names of some of the surrounding localities will repay attention.

A very common terminal in local names is "ley." It is of Anglo-Saxon origin, and appears in a variety of forms, as ley, ly, lay, lea, and leigh, and always bears the same signification—a stretch of unenclosed and untilled land used as pasture; or open land of any kind, grassy or woody, upon which untended cattle could pick up a living. In the name of Lye Waste we have it in its Middle English form. In Leasowes we find the original form of the Black Country dialect name for meadowland, "lezzur." The name Hawn, on the other hand, signified a fenced-in place.

Some of these lands were called after their earliest holders; thus Dudley was Dudda's ley; Coseley was Cole's ley; Cradley, Cridda's ley; Frankley, Franca's ley; Illey, Ylla's ley; and Warley appears to have been Wœr-wulf's ley, corrupted first to Werueleye and then to Werneley. Rowley was the rough ley, when the word was not pronounced ruff, but as in this name; Langley was, of course, the long ley, and Blakeley, the black ley; Romsley was the rams' ley, and Melley the mill ley. Lutley, in Halesowen, was written anciently Ludeley and Lodeley, as if Lode were some personal name; otherwise Lutley might be a changed form of little ley. In the name Weolegh—Weolegh Castle was near Northfield—we trace the "lea of the deep pool."

The most venerable place-name in the locality is that of Penncricket Lane, which forms the boundary between Oldbury and Halesowen, and was an ancient county boundary when Oldbury was detached from Salop. The "et" must be discarded as intrusive—it was introduced when, to the ordinary mind, the word crick was unintelligible—leaving the name Penncrick, given by the British probably two thousand years ago, and meaning the head or end of the boundary.

The Three Shires' Oak, near the "Bear Inn," at Smethwick, was where Worcestershire, Warwickshire, and an isolated portion of Salop—since transferred to Worcestershire—came together.

Warstone Farm, in Frankley, derives its name from Hoarstone, meaning a boundary stone; it was the line of demarcation between Frankley and Halesowen, and also formerly between Worcestershire and a detached piece of Salop.

The first part of the name Lightwoods represents the Anglo-Saxon hlith, a slope or hill side; Clent is a name of Scandinavian origin, probably given during the Danish occupation, and denotes a peaked or craggy hill. Mucklow Hill was named from Muca's low, or burial ground; Offmoor Wood was at Offa's moor, and Walloxhill was originally Wealuc's meadowland. Similarly, Wassall Grove, derived from the personal name Wær, was Warsfelde, and then War's field. Walton (at Clent) was Wale town, or the town of serfs; and Quinton was the woman's town, from the Saxon word cwena, a woman. Hunnington was Huna's town.

The name Belbroughton has passed through many curious phases ; in 817 it was Belne et Brocton, the last portion being manifestly Brook town, though the signification of Belne cannot be guessed. In the thirteenth century the place was called Belne-Bruyn, or sometimes Belne-Simonis; one Simon de Bruyn being then the holder (1275). In the following century the name was written Bellenbrokton. Lifford was named from an owner called de la Ford. Another name which originated when the courtly Norman-French was spoken is Lappal, which in 1347 belonged to Thomas de Lappole, who in his turn took his surname, "la pool," from one of the several large sheets of water near the Stour there.

The Stour, which falls into the Severn at Stourport, rises at Halesowen. The name was anciently written Sture, and is probably connected with the

English word stir, and so denoted a turbid or rapid stream. The name of the Tame, on the other hand, indicates a slow and placid current. Contrasts are sometimes noted in names; there is the Rowley (rough ley) and the Smethwick (smooth village site).

Cowbach was the cow valley; Howley was the resort of owls; and Hasbury was the hazel hill; all these terms being of Anglo-Saxon origin. Ridgacre was the ridged acre, or the field on the ridge; and Reddall Farm was the farm (one of the Abbey granges) at the red well. Rood End, as already noted, obtained its name from the rood or wayside crucifix set up there in pre-Reformation times.

Tividale is said to be an importation—and a corruption—of Teviotdale.

Some names invite the invention of tales to explain them. In Frankley there is the Lower Tinkers and Tinker's Farm. It was no tinker who lent his name to these places; the appellation is merely a corruption of the name of one Richard Synekar, who, in the centuries of long ago, held this estate.

Of the place-name Cakemore, it can only be said that there is a Cakemuir in Scotland; but what the fore-part of the word connotes it would be rash to hazard a guess.

The compound name Warley Wigorn indicates that section of Warley which lay in Worcestershire,—Wigornia being the old Latin name for Worcester; and Rowley Regis indicates the King's Rowley, this manor in early times being part of the Royal demesne.

Much history and not a little geography may often be gleaned from a place-name.

IV.—HALESOWEN PARISH CHURCH: THE FABRIC.

The recorded history of Oldbury begins with that of the mother parish, Halesowen. As for at least some half-thousand years the inhabitants of Oldbury, in common with those of the other outlying townships, had to attend Halesowen for public worship, this ancient centre of the religious, moral, social, and also, in olden times (to an extent seldom realised), the political life of the place, demands a notice adequate to the weighty functions it has fulfilled.

The parish, from its extensive area, was probably formed at a very early date, and there is believed to have existed a church from the first introduction of Christianity into Mercia.

The present church, which is dedicated to St. Mary, stands in a spacious churchyard at the east side of the town. It is constructed of sandstone in successive styles of architecture, presenting several features of interest. The tower, commenced about 1390, was completed in 1440. The church is of good size, being 120 feet long, with a breadth of 60 feet. It was enlarged in 1839, and again restored in 1884.

From any point of observation the exterior is pleasing. Though Halesowen is getting fuller of factories and smoke-stacks every year, old houses remain in quaint, irregular clusters, one above another, their picturesque lines broken in summer-time by the foliage of umbrageous trees, and their colour relieved by just one touch of black and white in the half-timbered architecture of an ancient cottage; and to crown the vista the church piles up in the background from chancel to nave, and from nave again to massive tower and tapering steeple. The fine steeple is a dominating feature; the tower is unbuttressed, but there is a bold square staircase turret at the north-east corner, which rises well above the parapet and adds enormously to the effect. There are some grotesque gargoyles, and over the east window some interlaced blind arcading. It is an exterior that satisfies the eye.

The interior is perhaps more imposing than the outside, and offers a study of the various styles of ecclesiastical architecture, starting from the heavy Norman, through the tentative Transitional, to the latest phase of Gothic, the thin but graceful Perpendicular. Typical "bits' of Norman, Early English, Decorated, and Tudor may be discerned, telling in graven stonework the story of constructive evolution.

The south and west doorways, which obviously occupy their original positions, are good Norman work, the arches being enriched with zigzag and other typical mouldings, on shafted jambs.

The pointed arches of the nave arcading spring from octagonal pillars with poorly-moulded capitals; they are lofty and of good proportions, and with the four Massive and tall arches that support the tower, give an air of dignity to the interior. The chancel arch, transitional in character, is also lofty. Concerning this the late Archdeacon Hone supplies an explanatory and interesting note. The chancel arch was brought into its present form, as to height and width, before Sir Gilbert Scott took charge of the restoration. Till 1838 it had been a low arch pretty much corresponding in height with those at the west end of the church. In that year it was raised by many feet, the stones of the arch, and all the details that were found, being used again. In 1873 it was raised still higher, the arch was made wider; the cord ornament was added; and instead of a ruddy plastered surface above the arch, the wall was faced with good sound stone. But the plan of the original arch was carefully followed, and the greater part of the stones which form it are those of the old Norman structure.

On the north side of the chancel is a twelfth century window. On the piers of the arcades are face shafts, upon which rested either groin ribs or the principals of the aisle roof. There is nothing to show the width of the original aisles, but from the position of the south door, and part of the adjoining wall

Church Lane, Halesowen, 1915.
Specially drawn for this Work by Mr. Robt. Kemp.

and buttress, the aisle at this point seems to have been very wide. There are really two south aisles.

A problem is presented by the interior in the very peculiar ground plan which it discloses. There are two Norman bays at the western end of the church which present details seldom found in the arcades of a small Norman church. It has therefore been suggested that this was built as a narthex, or large western porch, and that the nave extended eastward from it, or that a Norman tower existed here with the nave beyond. This would have left room for a chancel and nave of about the usual proportions if the eastern end and chancel stood where, they do now.

The Norman font, probably as old as any part of the fabric, is square with rude carving on the sides, and rests on a large central dwarf column and four corner shafts with scalloped capitals.

There are some interesting monumental memorials. One is an elaborate monument erected to the memory of Major Halliday, who at one time resided at the Leasowes. Its height from the floor to its apex is twenty feet; the figure of the Major and Lady Jane, his wife, are life-sized, and the whole is excellently proportioned and beautifully carved. This piece of sculpture was executed by T. Banks, R.A., and cost upwards of a thousand pounds.

Several members of the Lyttleton family are interred within the walls of the church, though the memorials that remain of them are not numerous. The names occur of John Lyttleton, 1530; Edward, son of John and Muriel, 1614; Sir John, Knight of Frankley, 1589-90; and Gilbert, his son and heir, 1599.

The monument to which the greatest interest attaches is that of the poet, William Shenstone, whose body lies in the adjacent churchyard, on the south side of the edifice, and near to the remains of his brother. An elegant urn standing on a pedestal bears the following graceful tribute:

> Whoe'er thou art, with rev'rence treade
> These sacred mansions of the dead;
> Not that the monumental bust,
> Or sumptuous tomb here guards the dust
> Of rich or great; (let wealth, rank, birth,
> Sleep undistinguish'd in the earth)
> This simple urn records a name
> That shines with more exalted fame.
> Reader—if genius, taste refined,
> A native elegance of mind,
> If virtue, science, manly sense,
> If wit that never gave offence,
> The clearest head, the tend'rest heart,
> In thy esteem e'er claim'd a part;
> Ah! smite thy breast and drop a tear,
> For know thy Shenstone's dust lies here.

The significance of the phrasing of this epitaph will be gleaned in a later chapter, in the thoughtful words of John Wesley.

The families of Peshall (or Pearsall), Fernando Dudley Lea, and Lord Dudley have also intra-mural sepulture here. Memorials of the local families of Green, Underhill, Powell, and others are to be found on the walls.

Formerly some beautiful specimens of stained-glass armorial bearings adorned the windows of this church. The arms of that eminent lawyer, judge Lyttleton, Knight of the Bath, and justice of the Court of Common Pleas in the reigns of Henry VI. and Edward IV., impaled with those of Joan Burley, his wife, were accompanied by their portraitures so perfectly executed that Lord Coke, in the preface to his first Institute, observed that the countenance of that great man may be seen as represented in the churches of Frankley and Hales Owen. The windows have been removed to the Middle Temple, London, where (if anywhere) the law may be said to be enshrined.

The bells of Halesowen are a musical set of eight in the key of E with three flats, justly admired for the clearness of their tone. Six of these were placed in the steeple in the year 1707, and not improbably the old bells were re-cast at the same time. Some half-century after this, a gentleman named Skittleton, on a visit from London, while admiring the sweetness of tone in the bells, at the same time lamented that they were not a perfect octave, and generously offered to rectify the fault by presenting the first and second bells. The offer was accepted, and on the arrival of the new bells they were welcomed by a public demonstration. At first they were fixed on a frame over the other bells, but this arrangement being found inconvenient, they were afterwards fixed in a range, which was ingeniously effected by raising the carriages of the two largest bells. The inscriptions on the bells are as under:

1. Thomas Lestor and T. Peck, London, Fecit 1753.
2. At proper times my voice I'll raise
   And sound to my subscribers' praise.
      Thomas Lestor and T. Peck, London, 1753.
3. Jesus be our speed. 1707.
4. God bless the town of Hales Owen.
5. Be it known to all that doth me see
   That Joseph Smith in Edgbaston made all we.
6. Samuel Clinton and John Foley, Churchwardens.
      R. Wells, Aldbourne, Fecit 1778.
7. Sir Charles Lyttleton, benefactor, 1707.
8. When sound of bells doth pierce the ear
   Come to the church God's word to hear.
   My mournful voice doth warning give
   That here men cannot always live. 1707,

Impressions from coins adorn most of the bells; on the fifth bell is a very perfect one of a William III. shilling.

Six of the bells appear to have been re-cast at Edgbaston; the seventh bell was the gift of the lord of the manor at that time, Sir C. Lyttleton.

There is a curious episode in connection with the history of this peal. It was an old custom on Shrove Tuesday, immediately the hour of eleven in the forenoon had struck, for the ringers to imitate the sound of "Pan on" by striking the bell with a hammer, as well as ringing it. On one occasion the bell was cracked in this way, and it remained in this imperfect condition for a length of time until at last a woman, named Susannah Box, indicted the churchwardens for having a cracked bell. They then had it re-cast, with their own names upon it, in the year 1778, as the inscription shows.

A famous local bell-founder was Joseph Smith, whose name appears on No. 5. He lived opposite the Swan Inn at Edgbaston, and his name appears on the bells of many Midland churches, with dates ranging from 1701 to 1732.

A peculiar old custom in connection with this parish was on Shrove Tuesday to shrive not only the parishioners, but the bells in the steeple—perhaps because they, too, had tongues to speak with!

V.—Halesowen Parish Church: Parochial Records.

At Halesowen parish church the festivals of St. Stephen (December 26th) and St. Katherine (November 25th) were kept with great solemnity, for in succeeding yearly accounts a considerable sum, though not always the same, is charged to those days for lights or wax tapers. Till recent times the High Bailiff of the Manor held his annual dinner of St. Stephen's day. To St. Katherine a side chapel was dedicated.

Here are given a few extracts of interest from the church accounts:—

1497.	Paid to Sir Robert. Chaunce for	£	s.	d.
	singing St. Katherine's Mass … … … …	0	0	6
	For ringing to the same … … … …	0	0	3

The courtesy title "Sir" was then used in place of our modern prefix "Rev." It is interesting to note the surname Chaunce, which is doubtless that of the Chance family now connected with Oldbury, who were yeomen farmers in Bromsgrove at that time.

Church Ales were much in vogue in Halesowen, and for the better support of these friendly and charitable meetings (the money collected by the sale of ale thereat being given to the poor) there appears to have been a stock of pewter pots, spittoons, and other utensils. On one side of the accounts of the year 1497 appear:—

	£	s.	d.
Paid for a pewter dish lost at the Ale in this town...	0	0	8
For ditto that was lost at Cradley	.	.	.

Rather quaint are the terms in which some of the items of expenditure are expressed:—

		£	s.	d.
1514.	Paid for lea of yarn that hangeth the cloth afore our lady	0	0	2
	(This refers to the altar cloth.)			
1518.	Paid the bell founder of Nottingham five marks. A mark was of the value 13/4.)			
1529.		£	s.	d.
	Item for mending the face of St. Katherine's image	0	0	4

and on the other side of the accounts:—

Received at the Church Ale at Easter	2	6	8
Among the payments of that year are:—	£	s.	d.
Paid for repeyling the organs to the organ maker at Bromycham	0	10	0
Item for making a candlestick for St. James ...			
Paid for scouring St. Katherine's lamp	0	0	2

Here is accounted for a votive offering to the altar of the Virgin Mary:—

Received from Nicholas and John Taylor for lamp oil which they find for their lady's image at their own cost	£ 0	s. 10	d. 0

The first Register of Halesowen parish commences with the year 1559, the second year of Elizabeth's reign, and that in which the Protestant religion was re-established after the Marian re-action. The abodes, or places of residence, of the parties registered are not shown till 1623, and then and afterwards but intermittently; but most of the surrounding parishes and villages are mentioned, particularly Birmingham, Oldbury, and Cradley. No. 6 Register (1736–1761) on vellum, appears to have been "lost" for many years; it was discovered in Birmingham, purchased, and restored to its rightful place. From April, 1754, the marriages are entered in a separate book.

A few notes, rather than copious extracts from the Halesowen Parish Registers, are only possible here.

In 1657, during the Commonwealth, a civil marriage by Justice Greaves is recorded. There are no records from 31st October, 1671, to 25th March, 1676—

but this was a period of laxity. Marriages at St. Kenelm's are recorded at Hales Owen. No. 5 Register (1700-1716) has its early leaves obscured to page 14.

Among the clergy named are the Revs. John Westwood (in 1660), Fran. Pierce (in 1677 and 1681), Wm. Hume (1685), Tho. Jukes (1697, and his burial in 1719), John Amphlett: (1719), Josiah Durant (1731), Pynson Wilmot (1732, and his marriage to Joyce Frankcombe in 1748), all Vicars of the parish. In 1773 Hy. Sanders, "Minister," and in 1788 J. Parke, Curate, are named.

Of course, the names of the churchwardens appear from time to time. Among them are:

1677.	John Foxall and Wm. Grove de Town.
1681.	Tho. Pearsall de Haune.
	Edwd. Bibb d le Moatt.
1683.	Wm. Hollmer, Cradeley
	Wm. Round, Oldbury.
1685.	Rd. Gosling.
	Thos. Brentham.
1688.	John Parkes and Wm. Robinson.
1689.	Wm. Hassold and Thos. Haden.
1690.	John Lea and Thos. Darby.
1692.	Thos. Haden and Ithiel Lloyd.
	Rich. Mucklow and John Shenstone.
1693.	Georg Darby and Joan Lowe.
1694.	Thos. Harper and Jona Carpenter.
1696.	John Hill and Humfrey Baylies.
1697.	Zachar. Downing and Thos. Palmer.
1699.	Edwd. Hare and John Tunks.
1700.	Samuel Butler and Josiah Packwood.
1702.	Wm. Gosnell and John Mucklow.
1703.	Rd. Higgins and Thomas Wright.
1712.	Sam. Hickman and Thos. Lea.
1713.	Wm. Grove and Saml. Butler.
1714.	Richd. Pryn and Thos. Cooper.
1715.	Wm. Lea and Thos. Pearsall.
1716.	Tho. Wight and John Low.
1718.	Robt. Robinson and Thos. Bissell.
1719.	Wm. Howell and P. Dudley.
1720.	Joseph Brettel and Saml. Fariner.
1721.	Wm. Smith and John Perkins.
1722.	Joseph Townshend and Thos. Partridge.
1723.	Thos. Shenstone and Jacob Smith.
1724.	Richd. Perks and Thomas Toy.

1727. Robt. Bloomer and Walter Woodcock.
1728. Wm. Robertson and Wm. Knowles.
1730. John Lea and John Shenston.
1731. Paul Lowe and John Hill.
1732. Francis Lea and Jno. Bosworth.
1733. Jno. Alinson and Edward Boolton.
1735. Saml. Powel and Joseph White.
1736. Saml. Powel and Wm. Freeth.

Among other personal names in the Register that strike the eye are:—(1658) Wm. Bloomer, "commonly called Goate-beard"; (1670) Wildsmith Badger, a Halesowen name in use for several generations; (1704) Edward, son of Clement and Mary Acton de la Furnice, was baptised—he afterwards became stepson-in-law to the great Dr. Johnson; and (1757) the Rt. Hon. Fernando, lord Dudley, of the Grange, buried.

Of place-names, we may note in passing the first mention of th^t. locality "de Blackheath' in 1679; Colley Gate is called Coley Yeat in 1695; and Iverley is written Overley in 1701; Cradley Forge, which had been worked many centuries, had its tenant, John Merryhurst, buried in 1713; and though the Registers contain much more of interest, these scrappy and desultory notes must suffice.

The Halesowen Parish Registers have been printed and published by the Parish Register Society for the County. They contain a list of Incumbents and Patrons, compiled by the Rev. W. Davis-Winstone.

Halesowen and Oldbury, although in Salop, were in the diocese of Worcester, and wills were proved there. The Worcestershire Historical Society has published a Calendar of Wills and Administrations recorded at Worcester to about 1650.

VI.—THE MANOR OF HALESOWEN: ITS EXTENT.

Originally the manor of Halesowen was co-extensive with the parish. It was a Saxon manor, and possibly as a political division it was co-eval with the ecclesiastical parish.

By permission of Viscount Cobham the early Court Rolls of the manor of Hales (1270-1307) were printed and published in 1912 by the Worcestershire Historical Society. They were carefully edited by Mr. John Amphlett, M.A., assisted by Mr. Sidney Graves Hamilton, M.A., and have proved a valuable contribution to local history. Not the least useful adjunct to the volume is a map, taken from the Ordnance Survey, showing the boundaries of the parishes and hamlets, and by its colouring distinguishing more clearly the configuration of the manor and its vills; though in the case of Warley Wigorn and Warley Salop in the north of the manor, many of the detached portions were so minute and intermixed that this could not be done in every instance. The Lyttleton family are first mentioned in the Rolls in 1293.

That Halesowen was originally in county Worcester is apparent from Doomsday Book (1086), which says:–"In Clent Hundred Earl Roger holds of the King a manor called Halas." The place appears to have been given by the Conqueror to one of his Norman favourites, his kinsman Roger de Montgomery (Mont Cymri), Earl or Count of Shrewsbury (and Salop), and it was thus Hales became absorbed in the latter. In 1102 the Earl of Shrewsbury adhered to the side of the unfortunate Robert, Duke of Normandy, when he tried to wrest the Crown of England from his brother, Henry I. On the failure of that attempt, the Earl was deprived of his estates, and in this way Hales passed into the holding of the Crown.

Although the manor remained a detached portion of Shropshire for many centuries, the parish of Halesowen has always included part of Worcestershire.

The descent of the manor of Hales appears to have been in this wise. From Roger Montgomery, Earl of Shrewsbury, to whom it had been granted by the Conqueror, it went on his death in 1094 to his second son, Hugh. When Hugh was slain some four years later it passed to his elder brother, Robert Belesme, who had inherited the paternal estates in Normandy. He, however, in succeeding to these English estates, had to pay the King, William II., a fine of £3,000 for the Earldom of Shrewsbury, to which the manor of Hales belonged. The Earl's other landed estates included Bridgnorth, Arundel, and Blythe. All these possessions were confiscated in 1102, when the Earl, as already intimated, espoused the cause of Robert Curthose, the Conqueror's eldest son, against Henry I. It then remained Crown property for 75 years, till a grant of it was made to David ap Owen (see p. 11).

In the reign of Edward the Confessor the manor, then valued at 24 pounds, was held by Olwine, who also held a house in Worcester, valued at 12 pence, and had a salt-pan in Droitwich, worth 4 shillings.

At the Domesday valuation it was assessed at 15 pounds; and the other economic conditions were expressed in feudal terms, which the following pages will attempt to elucidate.

The unit of assessment was the hide, consisting of 120 acres, and of these Hala, or Hales, contained 10. In demesne were 4 ploughs, 36 villeins, 18 bordars, and 4 radmans; there was a church, with 2 priests, and the estate had on it work for $41\frac{1}{2}$ ploughs. There were also 8 serfs and 2 bondwomen. By subinfeudation, the tenant-in-chief, Roger, Earl of Shrewsbury, granted $1\frac{1}{2}$ hides to Roger the Huntsman, under whom were 6 villeins and 5 bordars, with 5 ploughs. This portion, valued at 25 shillings, is conjectured to have been

Romsley, because this vill was found to have had a perfectly constituted Manorial Court from a very early period (1278).

Romsley, with its diversity of surface, including hill and dale, not a little of which afforded excellent covert for beasts of the chase, was well suited to the pursuits of the hunter. Its woodland tracts included Great Farley, Little Farley, Ell Wood, the Dales, and Uffmoor; the last-named being so considerable a stretch as to give rise to a local saying that "Uffmoor has an acre for every day in the year."

By demesne land may be understood that portion of the manor which was not let out to freeholders, but retained in the lord's own hands, and cultivated for him by means of villein service; or, as we should say in modern parlance, it was the home farm. Of course, the "demesne" varied in extent from time to time, increasing as lands escheated to the lord, or were forfeited to him for some manorial offence; and decreasing as new holdings were granted to new tenants. But it is easy to arrive at the approximate acreage of the arable land in the manor. The method of computation is by the number of plough-teams required to work it.

Thus, say the Editors of the Court Rolls, there were 4 ploughs on the lord's demesne, $41\frac{1}{2}$ in the employment of the freeholders, 1 in the use of Roger the Huntsman, and 5 in the service of the villein tenants, or $51\frac{1}{2}$ in all. Multiplying $51\frac{1}{2}$ by 120 gives us 6,180 acres, the amount of land under cultivation in the census year 1086. And as the entire extent of the manor is known to be 10,136 acres, there remained 3,956 acres of meadow or uncultivated land, most of it probably "waste."

At this period Hales was in Worcestershire, and the ecclesiastical parish, which was important enough to engage the services of two priests, contained also the Worcestershire manors of Frankley, Lutley, and Warley Wigorn.

Frankley, in Carne Hundred, the Saxon holder of which Wulfine, was held under the Norman Conqueror by William, son of Ansculph, baron of Dudley, by whom it was sublet to Baldwin. The figures relating to it are given as 1 hide; in demesne 1 plough; and 9 bordars with 5 ploughs and 2 serfs. The woodland extended to a league in length by half a league in width; and the value had fallen from 40 shillings after the devastations of the Conquest.

Warley Wigorn (or Werwelie), in Carne Hundred, was also held of the King by the same William Fitz-Ansculph, under whom the actual occupier at the time was Alelm. The statistical return gives the extent as $\frac{1}{2}$ hide in demesne 1 plough; also 2 villeins and 8 bordars with $4\frac{1}{2}$ ploughs; there were 2 serfs. In the Confessor's time, when it was held by Æthelward, it was worth 17 shillings a year, but had now fallen to 10 shillings in annual value.

It seems probable that at one time Warley Wigorn along with Warley Salop made up one vill, the two together containing 1 hide of land. So that when

Hales became part of Shropshire half a hide remained in the Worcestershire manor, which was retained by the lord of Dudley. From Fitz-Ansculph's heirs Warley Wigorn passed, with the barony of Dudley, to the Paganels and the Somerys, and presently is found in the occupation of the Fokerham family.

Lutley, in Cresselau Hundred, was held at Domesday by the priests of Wolverhampton, who had held it in Saxon times. Its extent was 2 hides; there were on it 2 villeins, 2 serfs, and 1 bordar, with 5 ploughs; and it was set down as worth 15 shillings.

The villeins, it may be explained, were tenants who held land by servile tenure, ploughing and harrowing, sowing and reaping, and performing other farm services for their lord so many days in each year. They were the customary tenants, performing the duties customary to the manor; in later times they were the copyholders of the manor. The bordars, or boors, were inferior villeins, mere squatters on the land, who had been allowed to build their own cottages outside the village and to cultivate a small patch of outlying land, in return for which they supplied the manorial magnate with eggs, poultry, vegetables, and similar small foodstuffs. Radmans were socmen, or tenant husbandmen, paying a free (that is, non-servile) rent, but subject to the lord of the manor's court. The, serfs and bondwomen were probably household servants, and therefore landless.

The several vills into which the manor of Hales was divided numbered eleven in all: (1) Oldbury, with which was included Langley, though the latter may have had a separate existence prior to the year 1270 ; (2) Cakemore; (3) Warley, cut up into an extraordinary number of small holdings in the hands of villein tenants, scattered over the common fields of the manor; (4) Ridgacre, or Quinton (recently annexed by Birmingham and so taken out of Worcestershire into Warwickshire); (5) Hill, which appears to have possessed a court of some kind; (6) Lappall; (7) Halen, now called Hawn; (8) Hasbury; (9) Illey; (10) Hunnington; and (11) Romsley, of which some of the manor rolls are still extant.

These subsidiary vills came into existence after the Domesday record was made; and about 1271 the borough of Hales was constituted by the Abbot and Convent, probably out of a portion of Halen; the special court attached to which seems to have been known at first as the Court of the Hundred.

In the thirteenth century manor rolls presentments are occasionally met with from other localities, which are termed vills, such as Wallokshall, Hampstead, and Shirlet; but these were probably only groups of houses.

VII.—THE MANOR OF HALESOWEN: ITS GOVERNMENT.

Though, by historic inference, the vills of Hasbury and Hill may very possibly have had manorial courts in ancient times, it cannot be inferred that Oldbury ever boasted a court of jurisdiction separate from that of Hales. The Editors of the Rolls suggest that the "curia," which has been somewhat faintly identified with this (as with the other less independent vills), may indicate the headman's office, a central place in the village where manorial business of a routine character might be transacted.

In an Oldbury matter which came before the manorial court at Hales in 1270, the jurors, who were acting as judges, were drawn not from Oldbury vill alone, but from the whole manor, which stretched away for as much as eight miles from the northern limits of Oldbury.

So wide and extensive was the manor of Hales that for administrative purposes in at least one department of local government, it was divided into two parts. This was for the Assize of Ale, administered through officers known as Ale-conners, or Ale-tasters, who were charged with the duty of seeing that all the ale and beer sold within the manor was of standard strength and in good measure. The two divisions were known as "Near Stour" (*citra stour*) and "Beyond Stour" (*ultra stour*), although it is not apparent that the stream had anything whatever to do in dividing these two administrative areas. Oldbury was subject to the ale officers of "Beyond Stour."

A constable appears to have been appointed for each vill—in 1293 a peace officer was certainly appointed for Oldbury, and another for Romsley. It was the duty of such to preserve the peace and to arrest offenders, especially when the "hue and cry" was raised. Here is a typical case of the state of mediæval society. One day John Wallokshale's daughter lent Thomas Miller of Oldbury a little brass pot, and after the time for which the utensil was lent had expired, she went to his house to get it back. Two boys who were there gave her the pot quietly enough, but as soon as she reached the boundary between Hales and Bromwich, at which point the authority of a parish constable would cease, they set upon her with knives and drew blood. She escaped from her assailants, and very properly raised the hue and cry, by which the felons could be pursued with voice and horn from one end of the country to the other. Whether these offenders were eventually arrested is not recorded; when their felonious conduct was brought before the manorial court all that transpires appears to be that they could not be found. Their names, however, were known—one was Walter and the other Adam; probably they were never allowed to enjoy the "liberty" of the manor again.

One of the most jealously guarded rights in a feudal tenure was that of the lord of the manor compelling his tenants to use and support the manorial mill.

In a large and far-reaching manor like that of Hales, it became necessary as the population increased to establish several grist mills, for which the Abbot would obtain the usual franchise by royal grant, if he could; otherwise, tenants on the outskirts, dwelling a long way from the central corn mill, would fall back on the use of the domestic hand-mill, or more probably resort to some "foreign" mill, and so give rise to litigation between the obstreperous tenant and the outraged lord. There are ancient references to a number of corn mills along the banks of the local streams.

In 1272 Bromwich mill was let to "Henry the Miller," at the annual rent of ten shillings. There was a mill at Blakeley, one at Balewick (or Walwick), and another at Warley called (after the name of the miller, about the year 1300) "Bird's mill." In 1294 a new mill appears to have been erected at "Abbeley near Oldbury," when the tenant was allowed the deduction of a penny a year from his rent for permitting a watercourse to be made down the centre of his meadow. All water rights were regarded as valuable in those days, even on the most insignificant streams. There was another mill at Oldbury called Greet mill, the miller of which a man named Thomas Wednesbury, made a practice of opening the sluices of the Oldbury mill, higher up stream, and drawing away the water to turn his own wheels. This led to litigation in 1301, and a local jury in the manorial court returned a verdict against the said Thomas Wednesbury, residing at Greet mill, declaring that he had unlawfully opened the water-gates, and taken the water from the Oldbury mill, to the hurt of that mill, and for the use and convenience of his own mill at Greet. In the following year (1302) there appears to have been some activity in local mill building, and yet another was put up in Oldbury, as well as a new one at Romsley.

Manorial customs, though common in their main features throughout the country, varied in some of their minor features according to locality, and these small local variations of custom gave rise to endless disputes between the lords and their tenants, which had to be settled in the manorial courts before a local jury well acquainted with the usages of the manor. Everywhere it was customary for villeins to render such services as ploughing and harrowing the lord's demesne lands, and to perform other forms of farm labour for the efficient cultivation thereof, in return for the land they held under him. It was the exact nature of such services, and the precise extent of them which varied in different manors. In Hales it seems to have been the custom for a villein tenant to go upon the abbot's land to do the ploughing and the harrowing at the Lenten season, working six days for every virgate of land (say, thirty acres) held by him. Also it was customary for the villein to sow the lord's oats and corn, and to mow the grass, and to render all lawful services of a like nature. It was about 1326 that money payments were substituted for personal services, but not till after much disputation and legal wrangling.

There had always been certain feudal fines and dues payable; and when (if ever) the Abbot had acquired the mill franchise, each tenant would have to take his corn to the manorial mill and pay for the milling of it, generally in a percentage of the meal. The Abbot would also have preferred his tenants to do all their buying and selling in the market which he established, with royal warrant, in Hales; but this he does not appear to have been able to enforce with any show of legality.

All tenants were subject to the Abbot's Court; and he could tax them at such times and to such extent as it was usual to take tallage in the kingdom. For a *heriot* due on the death of a tenant it was customary in Hales for the lord abbot to take the best beast, except a mare; and for the heir to pay a *relief* of two years' rent before he could succeed to the possession of his father's holding.

In pre-Reformation times it was practically impossible for inland districts to obtain a supply of sea fish, except of the dried and salted variety. Inasmuch as there were many fast days which had to be observed on a fish diet, means were taken to provide some sort of a supply of fresh-water fish. Where there was a river or a good stream the difficulty was solved, but in an elevated midland region, such as this, artificial means were resorted to, and pools were constructed, called "vivaria." It is manifest that the monks of Halesowen and Sandwell would be compelled to provide themselves with reliable fish-stews to keep up an adequate table supply, for even a broad river with a fish-garth specially constructed for angling purposes, as there were along the Severn and the Trent, did not always yield when required. Hence the monks' wail in the song—

"To-morrow will be Friday, and we've caught no fish to-day."

In 1275 a new pool was made between Wallockshale and Oldbury, at which period there were two pools in Oldbury fairly close together, one the Vivarium, and the other known as the Waspol—that is, the "Washpool," doubtless a little lower down the stream and used for sheepwashing.

With so many diverse. interests involved, disputes and law suits were of frequent occurrence. The customs of the manor were formally set forth in the year 1275, though in the following year an inquiry had to be instituted into certain grievances, of which the abbey's tenants still complained. The disputes between the abbey and its tenants appear to have been finally adjusted in 1326.

Halesowen was erected into a borough in 1271, and in 1306 the Abbot was certified lord of the township of Halesowen. In 1344 Edward III. granted a Fair to the town, to last four days at the Feast of Barnabas, with weekly markets to be holden on Monday. The Fairs came to be held at Easter and Whitsuntide;

and by the early nineteenth century the market was held on Saturday, with a smaller one on Wednesday, but neither was much attended, except in the evening.

In a later chapter it will be shown how the manor, on the dissolution of the abbey, passed first to the Dudley family, and subsequently to the Lyttletons.

The Market Cross in Cornbow was erected in 1540, the year Halesowen market house was built. At that time the weekly markets were held on Sundays, by proclamation of the town authorities, and possessed real commercial value and significance. The Cross—said to be an old-time symbol of honest trafficking—has had to be repaired several times within living memory.

The population of Halesowen in 1563 was recorded as 280 families; estimating on the average of five to a family, this would yield 1,400; in 1690 the population of Birmingham was under 4,000.

In some Chancery proceedings of the time of Elizabeth certain manorial customs of Halesowen were disclosed. Gilbert Littleton, Esq. (who died in 1599) was then lord of the manor. The plaintiffs were Laurence Piersall and several other tenants of the said manor, and they showed that from time immemorial such tenants had held their messuages, lands, and tenements by the names of messuages, and half-yard land., and nooke land; and upon admittance they used to pay fines certain, viz., for the first, £1 6s. 8d. and not above, and one heriot; for the second, 13s 4d and not above, and one heriot; and for the third, 6s 8d and not above. The plaintiffs also claimed a right, by custom, to demise their lands from three years to three years without licence.

Another suit refers to "concealed monastic lands." It was to recover possession of "a messuage, land, and fulling mill at Swyndon, some time belonging to the dissolved monastery of Our Lady at Halesowen, since found to have been concealed from the Queen, and afterwards sold by her, and now vested in the plaintiff," whose name was Walter James.

It is shown in another case that the manor of Halesowen was held, after the death of Sir John Dudley, Duke of Northumberland, by his widow, the Duchess; and that on her decease it was conveyed to Sir John Littleton, from whom it passed afterwards to his son, Gilbert. At another time in the same reign Thomas Blounte and George Tuckey, Esquires, are named as "lords of the said manor of Halesowen." These two men appear to have been, in some sort, trustees to the Dudley family. Anyhow, many titles were created by them in the Halesowen district by settling lands, for *a consideration,* on leases for 1,000 years at a peppercorn rent, there evidently being some doubt as to their power to convey the *fee simple.*

Halesowen Grange became the seat of the family of Lea Smith, representative of the senior co-heir to the barony of Dudley. The barony, after remaining with the Ward family over a century, became vested in the Leas of Halesowen Grange, and on the death of Fernando Dudley Lea in 1757 it fell into abeyance among his lordship's sisters.

The Rev. Edward Best, M.A., Vicar of Wednesbury and Bilston at that time, kept a diary, in which is found this interesting entry.—

"1758. February 28. On this day I attended (by ye appointment of Mr. Thomas Steward of Birmingham) being nominated a Commissioner in ye business of proving ye Will of ye Fernando Dudley Lea, Lord of Dudley, of Dudley Castle, etc.

"1758. April 3. On this day I again attended this Commission at Hales Owen on ye business of proving ye Lord Dudley's Will, when we examined Wm. Shenstone Esq., one of ye subscribing witnesses," etc.

This is manifestly an allusion to Shenstone the poet. It is also interesting to learn the romantic turn of events subsequently.

One of his lordship's sisters, Frances, became the wife of Walter Woodcock, Esq., and to their descendants Dame Fortune seemed most chary in the distribution of her favours. Their daughter, Anne, married William Wilmot, and another daughter, Mary, became the wife of Benjamin Smart. About 1840, says Sir Edmund Burke, one of our greatest authorities on the Peerage, "the traveller on the Dudley Road, upon reaching the toll-gate at Coopers Bank, and depositing the usual fees of the pike in the hands of the toll-keeper, little dreamt that the individual following this lowly occupation was next brother of one of the co-heirs of the barony of Dudley. But so it was. George Wilmot, the toll-keeper of Coopers Bank, was a descendant of the very Lord Dudley whose proud castle towered in the distance. A nephew, Daniel Sinclair Wilmot, was a Custom House officer at Bristol, while another of the co-heirs of the barony, John K. Wilmot, was in 1859 residing in very humble quarters in Cleveland Street, Mile End. As to the senior co-heirs, one was Joseph Smart, a small farmer, then living at Oatenfield Farm, near Halesowen; another, Robert Smart, carried on the business of a butcher and grazier at Halesowen.

Of the later history of the town a most entertaining and informative account of Halesowen was written and published in 1854 by John Noake, in his RAMBLES IN WORCESTERSHIRE, Series III., p. 258.

VIII.—HALESOWEN ABBEY.

The most notable event in the history of Halesowen was the founding of its Abbey. The presence of an institution of this magnitude and importance, dominating as it did the religious and social life, not only of the parish but of the surrounding parishes—and in some cases quite eclipsing the parochial activities—could not have been without many and far-reaching influences on the life of the locality in its varying human phases. That the original name of New Street in the city of Birmingham was Halesowen Street is not without significance.

In 1215, the year of Magna Charta, King John granted to Peter des Roches, bishop of Winchester, the manor and advowson of Hales, with the chapels of St. Kenelm's and Frankley as the endowments of a new abbey. This King favoured the Premonstratensian order; and his royal gift of the manor of Hales was a right princely one, for it included five subordinate ones, namely, the manors of Cradley, Warley (Salop), Romsley, Ludley, and Oldbury, together with the townships of Hasbury, Hawn, Cakemore, Hill, Warley, Ridgacre, Lappell, and Illey, all owing suit and service to the Abbot's manor court of Halesowen. The monastery was actually the manor house, a civil appellation it retained to the last.

So under this cheap form of royal patronage a band of monks make their appearance in Hales one bright day in the year of grace 1218, and selecting a pleasant valley about one mile to the south-east of the church, commence building operations on one of their usually elaborate plans for the erection of an abbey stately and beautiful as befits the order to which they belong. As a "reformed" order of Austin Canons, they were founded in 1120 by St. Norbert at Premonstratem, in Picardy. There is a legend to the effect that St. Norbert, having obtained permission to institute his new order in the diocese of Laon, the spot for the first religious house was pointed out to him in a vision; and he named the site Pre Montre, or *Pratum Monstratum* ("the meadow pointed out").

The monks were sometimes called Norbertine Canons, but more commonly White Canons, from their habit, which consisted of a white tunic, a rochet, a white cloak worn over these, and a white cap. The White Canons first came to England in 1143, settled at Newhouse in Lincolnshire, and thence sent out branches at Welbeck, Croxton, and other places.

The colony of builders who came to establish themselves in the valley of the Stour, proceeded steadily and carefully with their task, never hurrying or scamping their work, and at the end of some two or three years the edifice was ready for the occupation of their brethren. When a further band of white-robed Canons came from Welbeck Abbey and took possession of their new home at Hales, they found it in every respect entirely to their satisfaction. How good was that thirteenth century design, and the craftsmanship by which it was carried into execution, may be judged to this day. An examination of the ruins will disclose that, although at the Reformation it had endured three centuries, the Early English work had not been replaced. The visitor to-day may gaze upon its tall lancet windows and groined roofs, and admire a fine

Ruins of Halesowen Abbey.
Specially drawn for this Work by Mr. Robt. Kemp.

row of deepset coupled lights in the massive fragments of the refectory walls. The graceful lines of this older part contrast with the later conventual buildings. One of these newer erections, now used as a barn and a cart-shed, is low and squat; it was originally of two storeys, the dormitories showing its purpose as either a guest-house or an infirmary. From the adjacent conventual burial ground, where bones are sometimes turned up, has been recovered the stone coffin of one of the abbots; the carving divides the lid into two trefoil headed panels; in the upper one is the crucified Christ between the two thieves, and in the lower is the kneeling figure of the Virgin, one of the symbols which appeared in the official seal of the abbey.

Outside may be traced the remnant of a moat, for at one time the abbey sought and obtained powers to fortify itself, although there is no record that the turmoil of war ever raged around its sacred walls. There is, however, a record that one abbot was once sued for diverting the Stour between Cradley and Rowley, taking the water to keep his moat fed, and therefore in a state of defence.

The completion of the habitable fabric in 1221 had by no means ended the building operations of the monks. The extension and embellishment of the monastery was a labour of love that occupied several generations of monks, though it is evident that the conventual church was finished, as it was planned, in the thirteenth century. Money came freely from the royal coffers, and the work was done well.

For two reigns at least the convent of Halesowen basked in kingly favour. Some of the early abbots were mitred nobles, and sat in Parliament between 1294 and 1314.

Writs of summons to the abbot of Halesowen are extant for eight years between 1295 and 1313. In 1300 the abbot was summoned to military duty according to feudal tenure; neither bishops nor abbots who were King's tenants-in-chief being exempt, except very occasionally by special grant. Liability to military service was the result of contract. By Common Law every inch of soil belonged to the Crown, and the King demanded and accepted from Crown tenants that military service which was recognised as equivalent to a money rent—the holding of land meant compulsory military service, from which neither cleric nor layman could safely be allowed exemption. Some ecclesiastical barons actually took the field in person at the head of their retainers, but the practice was not of very frequent occurrence.

Military tenures were not destroyed till the Statute of 12 Charles II., long after monastic establishments had ceased to exist. The abbey had assisted Edward I. in his first war against the Welsh by maintaining a body of men-at-arms; yet at the assizes of 1292 the Charter of King John was produced to prove that the house was exempt from this service of sergeantry. The wily

The Infirmary, Halesowen Abbey (Kemp)

monks won their case, probably by a legal quibble; for the tenure of sergeantry by which they held Halesowen manor certainly implied the rendering of military service, or at least the provision of some munitions of war, whenever the King took the field.

From the first the abbot and his monks sought to amass as much wealth as they could possibly acquire. The manor of Halesowen, of which the abbot was lord (holding the land by the feudal service of sergeantry) was in itself an extensive property, including the subordinate manors and tithing towns already enumerated. Also, in addition to the chapels of St. Kenelin's and Frankly, they held the great tithes of Walsall, Wednesbury, and Clent.

But rich as the foundation became, the monks were for ever pleading poverty in the hope of acquiring more wealth. They complained that, being on a great high road, they were called upon to extend much hospitality to travellers and wayfarers. The abbey had certainly granted (probably under moral compulsion) a pension to the Prior of Worcester and also to the bishop.

To Lichfield it had granted, no doubt as a sort of sop, a yearly pension out of the fruits and profits of Wednesbury and Walsall churches for the support of two choristers in the cathedral. Yet in the year 1505 we find the monastery exceedingly prosperous, enumerating amongst its household stuff such luxuries as feather beds with silken coverlets.

In the same inventory are set down "vessils, basyns, ewers, and great chargers of silver," besides salts, bowls, cups and goblets of silver, and processional crosses of silver gilt. Then there was the precious "Schryne of St Barbara's hede of sylver and gilte, with crosses and beadds upon it."

A fruitful source of income was this silver-gilt, bejewelled shrine, in which was preserved a most precious and holy relic, to which most lavish offerings were brought by the devout—nothing less, in fact, than the head of St. Barbara. Now, good St. Barbara was a martyr who perished in the tenth and last of the Roman Persecutions. The strongest tower, chamber, or bath erected for her always miraculously acquired a trinity of windows, although her implacable pagan of a father cut off her head for it; and when she was flogged by her heathen persecutors the whips all turned to feathers—which was all very marvellous. But what the saintly Barbara's head was doing in Halesowen, a thousand miles or more from the scene of her Christian martyrdom, and a thousand years after her death, only those skilled in the monkish mysteries of hagiology can explain. It was sufficient for the abbot and his monks to possess a relic which—in the earlier centuries of their history, at least—brought much money into their treasury.

Of the wide possessions of the abbey there were a number of farms let out to tenants; there were also a number of demesne farms, cultivated by the monks themselves, but exactly how many of these it would be difficult to say.

The number probably varied from time to time, as the demand for land fluctuated. There were nearly always monastic demesne farms at Warley, Hill, Owley, Farley, Whitley, Uffmore, Rudhall, Blakeley, and New Grange, all within the parish of Halesowen. The were called Granges, that is, granaries, and were fully equipped with barns, stables, stalls, and all the necessary agricultural offices and outbuildings.

Grange Farm in Lutley belonged to the abbey, and what came to be known as Blakeley Hall and Warley Abbey were originally monastic home farms. Reddall Farm, at Warley Wigorn, was originally Radwell Grange.

In 1291 the abbot's granges included Pircote, at Oldswinford; Warley, Hill, and Owley; Farley and Uffmoor in Romsley; Witley, or Whitley, between Hill and Hasbury; Rudhall, or Radewell, in Ridgacre; Blakeley in Wallockshall; apparently two more at Hampstead, close to Wallockshall; New Grange, and one other at Hales.

Mention is also made in the Court Rolls of the existence at Oldbury in 1280 of a "great grange," which seems to have been somewhere on the Rowley side; and again in 1297 allusion is made to the grange of one Philip Wagstaff, but this may have been merely a tenant's barn.

In 1414 the granges at Blakeley, Owley, Radewell, Uffmoor, and Farley had passed in the hands of the Vicar of Kidderminster, apparently on a sixty years' lease.

There were other lands owned or controlled by the abbey in surrounding parishes, one as far as the Lenches, where forty acres of forest land had been reclaimed by monkish effort. Monks, as a rule, were generally well advanced in the practice of agriculture. They always attended to the drainage, keeping the watercourses clear to prevent floods; they strove to bring waste land into cultivation, in many ways setting their tenants and neighbours a useful example, which, unhappily, was too seldom followed.

From an Inquisition taken in 1276, in the time of Abbot Nicholas, it appears that the tenants of the manor held land by the payment of forty pence yearly for every yardland (an area varying according to locality from fifteen to thirty acres). Also the tenant owed suit to the manor court of Hales, and if in any court anyone made default he forfeited sixpence, and after judgment given, twelvepence. On the decease of a tenant, the abbot as lord of the manor claimed the best beast (except a mare) as a *heriot*; also the lord claimed half the goats, hogs, and bees, and horse-colts. On coming into possession of his lands, the heir had to pay two years' rent as a *relief*. All tenants were obliged to plough the lord's demesne lands six days in each year for a whole yardland, and three days for half-a-yardland; to sow the lord's corn and oats for ten days in each year, for each holding of a yardland; and to render freely one day's service besides, for which the tenants were wont to have a repast at the manor hall. Also the tenants were called upon to mow the lord's grass, and to mend his fences when necessary.

The fee payable to the abbot when a tenant's daughter married was twelve shillings; but if she married out of the manor it was two shillings. As there was no manorial grist mill, the tenants might grind their corn wherever they pleased. Undoubtedly there were mills in the parish, one of them the property of the abbot—but the usual manorial franchise of compelling his tenants to patronise it was not attached thereto.

Whether the abbey was a blessing or a curse to the neighbourhood; whether the rapacity of the fraternity benefited or impoverished the community; whether the hospitality of the house relieved distress or encouraged mendicancy and bred vagrancy; whether these white-robed monks were ministering angels or a brotherhood of sensual and vicious men are questions which can only be answered from a full knowledge of the facts.

Some of the facts recorded in history will be placed before the reader in the next chapter.

IX.—Monastic Life in Halesowen.

That the existence of monasteries in olden times obviated the collection of poor rates and the provision of workhouses is incontrovertible. But that they were the nurseries of dishonest mendicancy, and exercised an indiscriminating charity that was utterly demoralising, is also not to be contested. But sentiment has looked with a lenient eye upon this social and moral delinquency of the mediæval monastery, seeing only in its lavish almsgiving the picturesqueness of a bountiful hospitality. The immunity from taxation it enjoyed, the unconscionable methods by which so much of its vast wealth was accumulated, even the barefaced robbery of the parish churches, all escaped censure, if not criticism.

The Premonstratensian order claimed exemption from episcopal control or interference, and only once in the thirteenth century did a bishop of Worcester make a visitation of this abbey. This was by Bishop Gifford, a man of forceful character and great episcopal dignity. By the rule of the order visitations could be made only by the abbot of Premontre, but as he was a foreigner this function had to be exercised here by an English representative. Towards the close of the fifteenth century Richard Redman, abbot of Shap in Westmoreland (later he became in succession bishop of St. Asaph and of Exeter) filled the office of Abbot-general Commissory of the English Province, and as such he made eleven Visitations of Halesowen, at intervals of about three years between 1475 and 1506.

A circuit of Visitations was made, starting from the north, through Welbeck and Halesowen in the Midlands, passing on to the southern counties, and back through Lincolnshire on the eastern side. The Commissory held his Visitation in the chapter house of the abbey, surrounded by his secretary, the registrar, and the various other officials of his suite. The religious life and monastic discipline of the house was inquired into, the finances and economic arrangements were passed under review, the buildings were examined and their state of repair commented upon; in theory nothing in the religious, moral, or material life of the convent was supposed to escape critical investigation. But it cannot be said that in practice these courts of inquiry were not often hoodwinked.

The Visitations of 1485 and 1505 were marked by the elections of an abbot. The brotherhood of Halesowen seems to have been kept up by a purely local supply of initiates, if the monastic names identifying a brother with the place of his nativity be any indication—nearly every brother in the confraternity being known by his baptismal name prefixed to some such cognomen as Nechells, Burton, Bromsgrove, Kinver, Tong, or the name of some other place within easy radius of Halesowen and its sphere of influence.

There does not appear to have been any regular period of noviciate, and a brother's progress probably depended upon his good behaviour and general aptitude. Thus we find Roger Wednesbury a novice in 1488, a deacon in 1491, and a priest in 1494; while Thomas Dudley served as an acolite before becoming a deacon in 1494, and was not a priest till 1497. Again, Richard Hampton was a subdeacon three years between his noviciate and his priesthood, while Thomas Kinver is described as a novice in 1494, in 1497, and yet again in 1500.

The greatest number in residence at any one time appears to have been twenty-one in 1491; in 1488 and again in 1500 there were but seventeen, from which numbers must be deducted four, as the lists included the names of the vicars of Hales, Walsall, and Clent, and the prior of Dodford, who, of course, would be stationed in their respective cures, and not resident in the abbey, though they might sometimes be recalled to undergo monastic discipline for some fault, and allowed to return to their charges, having thus formally purged themselves of their offences,

An abbot was elected from within the fraternity, and the choice of the house was then approved by the abbot of Welbeck. The election involved appointments of committees, private conferences, and meetings in the chapter house also processions and the singing of the Te Deum, a ceremonial installation, the placing of bell-ropes in the hands of the newly-elected, and the presentation to him of the great seal of the abbey. Then each canon knelt, placed his keys of office at his feet, and vowed obedience. The form of oath which the new abbot took to the diocesan in 1306 was thus worded, and shows how completely the abbey had been brought under episcopal control:—

"In the name of God, Amen. I, Walter, abbot of the monastery of Hales, of the Premonstratensian order, in the diocese of Worcester, profess to the Church of Worcester canonical subjection, reverence, and obedience; and to thee,

Father, Lord William, by the grace of God bishop of Worcester, and to thy successors canonically entering, I promise faith and canonical subjection, and this I subscribe with my own hand."

The revelations of the Assize Rolls in 1272 and again in 1292 do not throw a pleasant light upon the internal life and discipline of this secluded abbey. The abbot's servants seemed to use lethal weapons without hindrance or rebuke, and murderous assaults appear to be quite common occurrences in Halesowen. They were lawless times, however. In a case of robbery committed at one of the abbey granges, the robbers were caught by a monk and the abbot's bailiff; these two accepted a bribe and allowed the malefactors to escape. Then the monk, fearing detection, himself turned robber, escaped, and was outlawed. This is a fair sample of the disclosures concerning Hales abbey and the conditions prevailing in its vicinity.

A case of a different complexion was that in which the abbot was cited before the courts for obstruction. It was charged against him that he had caused the King's highway to be ploughed up at "Portmarchelde toward Cleithford," to the length of a furlong and in breadth thirty feet, and that he had included in his park within the manor of Hales fifty feet of another public road. The abbot acknowledged the obstruction, but pleaded that the said road was deep and useless, and that it lay on his own proper soil; and that he had made a new road, straighter, and more to the advantage of the county. Evidence in support of this contention was offered, and the abbot's plea was allowed.

The monastic life was monotonous if not at times exasperatingly dreary to one with the feeblest spark of the social instinct burning within him. There were the rising at midnight, the long services, the coarse food, much fasting, many hours of silence, the isolation and repression of the cloister, and the many little sins of omission and commission into which the unwary canon was liable to fall. There were specified pains and penalties for every offence against the rules of the order, even for wrong cutting of the tonsure, for failing to attend midnight mattins, for taking food too soon, for breaches of silence or of cloister. Canons were forbidden to eat or drink in any house within a league of the monastery.

In 1478 charges of incontinence and immorality were brought against two brothers, one of whom cleared himself. In 1491 Marjory Coke and other suspected women were ordered to be removed and not allowed to hang about the monastery. For neglect of mattins the punishment was one day's fast; for breach of silence, or for taking food before chapter, a day on bread and water was imposed; for breach of cloister Roger Wednesbury and Richard Hales were, in 1491, ordered to say by turns the Psalter through once, "after hours," in the cloister.

For graver offences the punishment was banishment and imprisonment. In 1497 there was serious internal commotion within the monastery, in which five mutinous monks were concerned. At that time there were eighteen of the white-robed canons in residence, exclusive of those living out upon their vicarages—the parochial livings of which it must be remembered, were permanently impoverished by their appropriation of the great tithes. The five culprits were Roger Walsall, Roger Wednesbury, Thomas Dudley, Richard Bacon, and Richard Hampton—the last-named doubtless a native of Wolverhampton. The ringleader of this conspiracy against the abbot was Roger Walsall. He and his friends in the house, supported by some of the "bloods" of the town, mutinied against the abbot and the vicar of the parish, and a sad state of things was revealed when the matter came to be investigated. Every sin in the monastic decalogue appears to have been committed; there was immorality, breach of cloister, disobedience, breach of silence, neglect of mattins. Further—though whether this could be laid to the charge of the offenders is more than doubtful—there was a debt of £50, the house was out of repair, and it was not so well stocked as it ought to have been. The deficiencies were material as well as moral. Probably the management was extravagant and wasteful. In 1489 it was returned that the annual consumption of the establishment amounted to 60 beeves, 40 sheep, 24 calves, and 30 swine; that 1,110 quarters of barley were used (presumably for brewing), and that the weekly requirement for bread was 20 bushels of wheat and rye.

A minatory Visitation of the abbey by the bishop of Worcester was followed by the imposition of punishment. Roger Walsall was sent to Croxton Abbey, there to be imprisoned ten years; Bacon was sent to a Yorkshire monastery for three years, with 40 days' imprisonment; Roger Wednesbury was consigned to Newhouse Priory, in Lincolnshire; Dudley to a Norfolk convent; and Hampton to another Lincolnshire house of the order. Yet such was the easy rule of this sinister monachism that most of these punishments were soon afterwards remitted; in 1517 Bacon is found occupying the honourable office of Sub-prior, while the other four are complacently reported to be "worthy canons." The episode is dated 1481 in Bagnall's HISTORY OF WEDNESBURY (p. 130), which appears to be an error; the same authority gives (plate 2) the arms of one "Roger Weddesbury," who was Prior of Worcester in 1507, but these two Rogers could not be the same because their orders were not identical and their vows different.

The arms of the Abbey of Halesowen were:—"Azure, a chevron between three fleurs de lys argent." Here we have the Virgin's colour, blue, from "Mare" the sea, and the white lilies of the Annunciation.

Halesowen abbey, like every other institution of the kind in England, whether it existed for good or for evil, was overtaken by the earlier flood-tides of the Reformation and swept away in what manner will be shown in the next chapter.

X.—The Disolution of the Abbey.

The dissolution of the monasteries by Henry VIII. was not an isolated act in history, but the last stage of a process which had been long in progress, dating perhaps from the suppression of the Knights Templars in 1312. That the climax arrived at this particular period but demonstrated the power of the monarchy in Tudor times. Although in the great quarrel between Henry VIII. and the Pope Halesowen subscribed to the Royal Supremacy in 1534, this did not save the abbey from the fate of all the others a few years later. It was despoiled at the dissolution just like all the other religious houses.

The last abbot, William Taylor, delivered up possession in 1538, and in the following year a grant of the abbey property was made over to Sir John Dudley, a royal henchman, who was subsequently known to history as the notorious Duke of Northumberland. It was in this way that the nobles were appeased and compromised—they shared with the King in the plunder of the church property.

Dudley assigned the property (the manor of Halesowen and all its appurtenances—the site of the abbey, the advowsons, and everything) to his wife Joan, and it remained in her possession after he was beheaded. Subsequently Sir Robert Dudley, partly by inheritance and partly by purchase, succeeded to the ownership. Ultimately it was sold to two moneyed speculators in real estate, named Blount and Tuckey. At the dissolution the manor was held by the service of the twentieth-part of a Knight's fee, and a yearly rent of £28 1s. 6d. Blount and Tuckey sold the manor of Halesowen to the Lyttleton family, in whose possession it still remains.

The spoliation of the Church was condoned by others besides the nobles. It must be understood that a deadly enmity often existed between the monks and the parochial clergy, owing to the insatiable rapacity of the former. The rivalry between the "regular" clergy, as the inmates of a monastery were called, and the "secular" clergy who ministered to the parishioners, was likened, in the sly humour of the age, to the game of "fox and goose" being played between them; and in some ancient parish churches may still be found quaint carvings of a marauding fox running away with a fat goose—the fat goose symbolising the great tithes they appropriated from their secular brethren.

The monks of Halesowen contrived at various times to get hold of the tithes of Walsall, Wednesbury, St. Kenelm's, Clent, Frankley, and other places in the neighbourhood. Here is a case which affects the parish of Hales itself, and seems, outwardly, to wear an aspect of satisfied agreement.

In the year 1270, Godfrey, bishop of Worcester, made a settlement between the abbot of Hales and the perpetual vicar of the church of Hales, that the said vicar should have and receive from the abbot ten marks yearly, a house, with outhouses, orchard, garden, and vesture of the churchyard, and that the canons should find another priest to be under the vicar, and to bear all ordinary and extraordinary charges.

The appropriation of the great tithes of Wednesbury had left a beggarly pittance for *vicarius* appointed to do parochial duty there. The same injustice accrued when Walsall rectory was similarly reduced to a vicarage.

Unseemly squabbling and costly litigation over these matters was of constant occurrence. In the law courts the advantage nearly always fell to the regular clergy. Among the exceptions, however, which prove the rule, was a case in 1278—a suit between the abbot and the dean and chapter of Lichfield over the advowson of Harborne, which the abbot lost.

As the monks were the creators of the law's intricacies, they knew best how to manipulate the law courts, and the balance of judgment was always heavily loaded in their favour. When the dissolution of the monasteries arrived, no section of the population took this great national revolution so complacently as the parochial clergy, whom they had so systematically impoverished. The benefice of Wednesbury, for instance, had been left with an income one-sixteenth of its original amount.

When the great crash came at the abbey, vast quantities of ornaments, images, relics, and other ecclesiastical stuff were transferred to the parish church. The old parochial account books disclose some of the particulars.

		£	s.	d.
Thus: -				
1539.	Item, paid for carrying the tymber, wyndes, lead, and other stuff from the abbey	0	2	0
	Fetching the rood and setting it up	0	2	10
	Expenses at carrying the relicks to the bishop	0	0	6
	(This seems to show that St. Barbara's head passed into the keeping of the bishop of Worcester.)			
	Paid my lord abbot for the organs four marks. Mending and setting them up	0	40	0
	Fetching the tabul or picture of St. Kenelm from the abbey, and setting it up	0	0	6
	Mending the legend book	0	5	0
	Carriage of three lodes of stuff from the abbey	0	0	6
	Expenses in setting up all the tabulls and all the images in the church	0	8	3
	Received at an ale at the beryng [bringing] the church cross	4	0	0

The following year a number of relics were disposed of

		£	s.	d.
1540.	Item, received for the box that the relicks were in	0	26	8
	Item, received for the rood that was sold ...	0	5	10

This was the year in which the market house was erected, connected with the cost of which is entered:

		£	s.	d.
	Paid towards making the new street and market house	3	12	0

In a later year we find:—

1547.	Paid to the writers of the Scriptures for writing on the pillars under the stepul	0	4	0

About this period, the Reformation having been enforced by legal enactment, most of the altars were pulled down and the images removed, as the following extracts will show:—

		£	s.	d.
1547.	Item, spent in drink in taking down the images	0	0	4
1548.	Paid at delivering our vestments at Brugenorth	0	0	4
	Item, for riddling away the stones at Jesus' altar	0	0	8
1549.	Paid for carrying away the taybulls from the church .	.	.	.
	Item, for polying down the hye altar and St. Mary's altar	0	1	2
1552.	Paid for taking down the cross in the church yard	0	0	10
1556.	Paid for mending the cross	0	0	2
	Paid for polying down the altars and the rood loft	0	0	22

The cross which was mended during the reaction in Mary's reign, was evidently the one in Cornbow.

A few years later came the Reformation, and, of course, such things as "graven images" and similar "idolatrous" appointments could riot be allowed, by the zealous reformers, to survive in an Anglican parish church.

The fabric of the abbey was neglected and fell gradually into decay, till it has become the picturesque ruin of the present time. Local tradition says that when Hagley Hall was rebuilt by the Lyttletons a couple of centuries ago, many loads of stones from the abbey ruins were carted away to be utilised in the reconstruction.

Of the other monastic houses in the locality, to share the common fate, the two nearest were those at Sandwell and at Dudley.

Ruins of Halesowen Abbey, 1915.
Specially drawn for this Work by Mr. Robt. Kemp.

St. James's Priory, Dudley, was built by Gervase Paganel, baron of Dudley, in 1161, in fulfilment of his father's pious intention. It was a cell of the great Austin Priory, of Wenlock, in Salop, and its prior, at the Visitation of the Government Commissioners, sent round to make preliminary investigations, was John Webley. It was found that the greater portion of its income was derived from places within the diocese of Lichfield, and the remainder from within the see of Worcester. Dudley Priory fell with its superior house at Much Wenlock in 1540, and its property was granted in the following year to the greatly favoured Sir John Dudley.

Sandwell Priory had come to grief earlier. In 1524 Cardinal Wolsey had set the example of suppressing certain of the smaller monasteries for the endowment of his colleges at Oxford and Ipswich. The priory of St. Mary, Sandwell, had long been on the verge of bankruptcy, with its discreditable canons (not the least of whose sins were the violent altercations in which they were frequently engaged with neighbours and rivals) and its wasteful and unbusinesslike management. All the buildings were in bad repair; everywhere at Sandwell dilapidation and neglect were in unmistakable evidence.

The deed for the dissolution of this establishment, a formidable vellum document of twenty-three pages, was dated February, 1524, and bore, among other signatures, those of Prior John, and Thomas Cromwell, Wolsey's secretary, who was afterwards specially employed by the King in this great national business of the Dissolutions. The Bull of Pope Clement VII. confirming the dissolution of this and a number of other monasteries was not issued till six months later. The house was not closed altogether; provision was made for the continuance of religious services in the convent chapel, while the servants arid inmates who had to be discharged were recompensed. The yearly income at the time was returned at £12 in spiritualities and £26 8s. 7d. in temporalities.

Just as the monks of Halesowen had got possession of Walsall church, with all its chapels, liberties and other appurtenances, including chapels-of-ease at Rushall and at Bloxwich converting its rectory into a vicarage, so had the monks of Sandwell got hold of the West Bromwich benefice.

Letters Patent were issued in January, 1526, granting to Cardinal Wolsey the sites of Sandwell Priory, and of another suppressed Staffordshire priory at Canwell, together with lands situated at Sandwell, West Bromwich, Wednesbury, Tipton, Dudley, Harborne, Wombourne, Barr, and a number of other Staffordshire parishes in which these convents held estates. When Wolsey fell from favour and came to be arraigned, the suppression of monasteries formed part of the charges laid against him; he was accused of forcing their wrongful suppression by "crafty persuasions." The rich endowments he thus acquired were supposed to have been applied by the Cardinal to the establishment of a new college at Oxford. A small portion of the Sandwell property passed to the college at Windsor and the prior of Sheen.

The remnants of the properties were ultimately sold off, realising £21. The bells at Sandwell were valued at £33 6s. 8d. On the other side of the account were certain charges made by Cromwell and his fellow-Commissioners for their labours in superintending the disposal of the conventual properties; for instance, one item set down the cost of their journey from Tickford to Sandwell, and their five days' expenses at the latter place.

In preliminary suppressions like this, with the tacit sanction of the Church, did Thomas Cromwell fit himself to become *malleus monachorum,* "the hammer of the monks," as he was called.

The dissolution of the monasteries was the precursor of the Reformation, and this great national upheaval, which marks so important an epoch in the history of the nation, is also the most momentous period in the annals of Oldbury; for it marks its emergence from the domination of the mother parish, Halesowen, and the commencement of its history as a separate local entity.

XI.—Early History of Oldbury.

The existing feature of Oldbury which goes farthest back into the recesses of antiquity is the old road known as the Portway.

To assume a Roman origin for Oldbury on the strength of its ancient Portway would be idle and unjustifiable conjecture. The probabilities are that Oldbury dates back to the British period, that it was an early Celtic settlement, and that the Portway was even then an approach to it, and a line of communication through it.

The term "portway' is applied to many ancient highways. The word "port" in Anglo-Saxon stands not only for a haven, but also for a town, particularly a market town, and hence many inland portways lead to and from old market towns. In Worcestershire alone there are eight or nine "port ways" or "port streets," connecting the market towns with the surrounding country.

Nor can the Oldbury Portway have been a British trackway, because these were always made along the higher ridges of the land for the avoidance of bogs and quagmires, when the country was undrained and the lower levels were consequently flooded every winter season. The most probable origin of this prehistoric line of communication was as a "salt-way," such as were often used in the remotest period of our history for the distribution of that highly necessary commodity. The salt "market" was at Droitwich, and the Portway in question came up through the hills to Oldbury, passed through Swan Village (alongside the site of the present gas-works there), and came out as Mollaston

Lane by the side of the Fountain Inn at Wednesbury Bridge. On the other side of the river Tame there it resumed the name of Portway, by which it is still known in Wednesbury, till it becomes Dangerfield Lane. Passing through Darlaston, Wednesfield, and Bloxwich, it eventually joins the old Chester Road, along which the salters in primitive times carried their loads of salt for distribution in the middle west. A similar salt-way branched off and went through Saltley towards the Lincolnshire and middle east districts.

Some writers, however, have called this ancient road a branch of the Icknield Street, the Roman road which passes through Birmingham and Sutton Park, on its way from Gloucestershire towards Chesterfield.

In the year 1804 a few Roman coins were found at Cakemore.

When the settlement of Britain was effected by the English, or Anglo-Saxons, in the fifth and sixth centuries, the southern edge of this midland plateau marked the meeting of the two main waves of colonising invaders; and though the ancient "mark" is not always discernible in the manorial, county, and diocesan boundaries, it is conjecturably certain that the line Oldbury to Dudley was part of that frontier of tribal outposts and defensible positions.

Nash, in his HISTORY OF WORCESTERSHIRE (Vol. I. p. 521), designates Oldbury "a manor situate in the Shropshire part of Hales parish." In discussing the signification of the name, he inclines to the opinion that Oldbury may have been a Roman station, because the Portway (which he evidently believed to be of Roman origin) passed through it. He claims that such a name as Old-borough points to an ancient fortified spot, the site of which is frequently marked by a barrow or earthwork. "No vestiges of this fort appear now at Oldbury," he continues, "but a very aged inhabitant informed me that in his father's time there were apparent ruins of a town near a certain pasture called the Castle-Leasow; and that a castle was said to have stood at the lower end of the said Leasow near the Well Hill. He added that a causeway still remained in the lands of one Harold directly leading to the Castle Leasow. . . . I find a general tradition that a great town anciently stood here, which extended from the *present village* to the Castle Leasow lying under Bury Hill. . . . . I could not discover any marks of buildings." This was written about 1774. The causeway here mentioned may have given its name to Causeway Green, which is situated in Warley parish and outside Oldbury manor. On an old map or parish plan is marked a road "To Gauser Green."

As in byegone times Oldbury, as a manor, was accounted as being in Salop, its name scarcely ever figures in the ancient chronicles of Worcestershire, as do the adjacent parishes belonging to that county. As part of Halesowen, it was Crown property in 1102, and from 1166 to 1173 there was paid yearly into the King's Exchequer the sum of 26s. 8d. for the "farm of Oldbury," which was probably the value of it when a few years later it passed into the possession of the new abbey.

Another county historian, Sampson Erdeswick, in his SURVEY OF STAFFORDSHIRE, written about the year 1597, quaintly says:—"Tame taketh its first beginning about Oldbury, being a mile or something more eastward from Dudley Castle. Whether a man might conjecture that place to be some principal seat of the barony, and the place where the first barons, in the Saxons' time before the Conquest, were seated of not, I stand in doubt; only the name of Oldbury of Burrough (an old Saxon word, signifying and old place, or town, of some account) would give some little light so it should be,"

In quoting this surmise of the old antiquary, it may be recalled that one of the lost roads of this locality was said to run from Dudley to Duddeston (in Birmingham), that is, from Dudda's ley to Dudda's town. If this legendary road ever existed it ran through Oldbury. The Tame, as previously mentioned, is pressed into service as a boundary (p 5 ante).

Erdeswick does not employ the terms "borough" and "town" in the sense in which they are now understood; but merely to express a group of dwellings, such as would constitute a hamlet. Oldbury was never a borough in the modern sense, nor was it even a market town. Markets were held by grant or prescription, and the inhabitants of mediæval Oldbury enjoyed the market franchise of the mother parish, Halesowen. The present-day market held in Oldbury is not an ancient chartered. privilege, but of the right acquired by custom in modern times.

If the conjectures of the county historian Nash be correct, Oldbury did not even become a manor till it had ceased to be a possession of the abbots of Hales. In striving to substantiate his surmise, he refers to a conveyance of the Oldbury estate, effected in the *4 and 5 Philip and Mary* (1559), to Thomas Blount and George Tuckey in consideration of 190 marks paid for Warley Wigorn and other adjacent lands—evidently one of the many transactions at that time whereby fat church lands were passing into the hands of rich merchants and plutocratic traders, whose ambition aimed at territorial aggrandisement. Many of our existing landed families were "founded" at that period.

From the time of Henry III. to the reign of Henry VIII. Oldbury does not appear to have been distinct from Halesowen, being generally described in the Court Rolls as a vill or township dependent upon Hales. As a separate manor it certainly had no existence till after the dissolution of the abbey. "Nor is it styled a manor in the grant to Sir John Dudley; but being excepted in the deed of conveyance from Sir Robert Dudley to Blount and Tuckey . . . . and likewise excepted in their deed of sale to Sir John Lyttleton, it remained," conjectures Nash (who was not particularly well-informed about Oldbury) "in the possession of the Dudley family, who in all likelihood procured a royal grant for holding a court leet there."

The full legal description of the lordship enumerates three separate places, calling it the manor of Oldbury, Langley, and Walloxshall, all in the county of Salop. The last- named member is now generally called Walloxhill; it was an ancient hamlet in Halesowen, and gave its name to a local family resident there. In a document of 1343 it is given as Walloxhale, the prefix (as already shown, P. 13) being a man's proper name, and the meaning of it "Wealuc's meadow land"

The lordship is fully described in a covenant of the year 1713 made between William Featherston, of Warwick, gentleman, and William Addington, of Lincon's Inn, gentleman. It.comprised the usual rents and services of the tenants; the right to hold a court leet and a court baron, with view of frankpledge (that is, taking surety for the good and peaceable behaviour of the freemen), and other liberties and franchises; it gave the lord the usual territorial rights over all waste or unoccupied land; the right to the goods of fugitive felons and outlaws; tithes or tenths of all corn, grain, and hay grown on the manor; certain customary gifts from the tenants due on particular occasions (as the passing of the land) and known as oblations or obventions, profits and emoluments. The "capital" residence, or manor-house, known as Blakeley or Blackley Hall, situated in Oldbury, had attached to it gardens and orchards, stabling and barns, and other appurtenances; meadow and pasture land and enclosed crofts, of which several are specified by name; to wit, the Barn Croft, the Moor Rough, the Grove Close. the Pool Tail Close, the Hill Leasow, Blackley, Lower Blackley, and the Great Meadow. Also the water corn mills, commonly called Oldbury Mills, and the Mill Pool thereto belonging.

Mills were important institutions and valuable properties in olden times. "Oldberrie mill," with its appurtenant land, was held by the Turtons of West Bromwich in Elizabeth's reign, when the rental was "xxd. a yeare." In 1592, it may be noted, William Turton the elder purchased two water mills from one Thomas Cooper, or Piddocke. One of them, known as "The Mill," was at Roway, where Messrs. Izon's works now stand; the other was the "Bromford Mill," then, or soon afterwards, worked as a Blade mill. Both had pools attached, that of the latter near the site of Bromford ironworks.

At Langley, near the Phosphorous works, is a dwelling still called Mill House, adjacent to what was probably the mill pool; another ancient mill pool, in Bradwell Road, is said to have been taken in by the Oldbury Carriage Works.

According to Reeves, who wrote a HISTORY OF WEST BROMWICH in 1836, Blakeley Hall, the ancient manor house of Oldbury, was a fourteenth century half-timbered building, with a moat round it, taken down about the year 1768. In his description, he says:—"The present building is near the site of the old, and is occupied by Mr. John Downing as the Farm House. On March 1st, 1829, I saw the moat complete and full of water."

The moat is shown on a plan of the estate, dated 1773 (after the canals had been constructed through it); even then it was one of the very few moated houses to be found in this district.

The present building known as Blakeley Hall is a plain modern three-storey house, near the site of the original Hall, which stood further back from the road, and had the moat round it. In 1340 the Hall appears to have had an oratory, or small private chapel, attached to it.

XII.—Descent of the Manor of Oldbury

Oldbury is first described as a manor in 1557, when Sir Robert Dudley settled it on himself and Amy his wife, with reversion to their right heirs, Arthur Robsart being one of the trustees. Thus was Oldbury associated with the romantic story of Amy Robsart, which has been immortalised by Sir Walter Scott.

Sir Robert Dudley, who afterwards figured in history as Earl of Leicester, the favourite of Queen Elizabeth, was the fifth son of John Dudley, Duke of Northumberland, and, like his unscrupulous father, a previous baron of Dudley, had acquired vast grants of land in and around that feudal holding, including Oldbury (see pp. 41 and 48).

The story of Amy Robsart is well known. It begins with the inveiglement of the beautiful girl from the home of her father, Sir Hugh Robsart, in Devon, and her secret marriage with Robert Dudley, Earl of Leicester. Then the tragedy slowly gathers to a head. She is placed in the keeping of Anthony Forster, a gloomy misanthropic man and a creature of Leicester's, at his residence, Cumnor Place, in Berkshire; while the gay earl attends the Court to disport himself before the Queen as a bachelor. That he was beloved of Elizabeth seems more than probable, and that he might have become Prince Consort but for his secret marriage is also shown to be well within the range of possibility. How Amy followed her faithless spouse to Kenilworth, there to be a witness of the brilliant festivities given by him in honour of his royal mistress, in July, 1575; how she was taken from thence and hurried back to Cumnor; how she was found dead at the foot of a staircase; and how this culmination of the tragedy occurred at the very moment when reconciliation with her husband, and recognition as his wife, were about to be made, are all incidents in the commonly accepted tale of romance. But unfortunately the facts of history do not fit in with the details of this popular legend.

Amy was the daughter and heiress of Sir John Robsart, of Siderstern, in the county of Norfolk. She was married to Sir Robert Dudley at Sheen in 1550, in the presence of Edward VI., with great pomp; so there was no secret marriage, so far as she was concerned, to begin with. Amy never was Countess of Leicester, for she died three years before her husband was created Earl; and she could not have been present at the princely pageants at Kenilworth, as her death had occurred fifteen years before they took place. Sir Richard Varney, the "villain of the piece," a relative of the Verneys of Compton Verney, has had his character, like that of Anthony Forster, gratuitously blackened by Sir Walter Scott, to meet the exigencies of the plot of his novel. There was, however, a secret, or pretended marriage—that of Dudley with Lady Sheffield, in 1573; and it was this which Scott seized upon to work into the design of his novel. The death of Amy, too, was actually a mystery, which has never been made clear. She died suddenly, nominally from the effects of a fall down stairs at Cumnor, while all the servants were away at Abingdon Fair (1560).

It was commonly believed that Dudley, if not Elizabeth herself, was accessory to the crime. Dudley showed great anxiety that no suspicion should attach to him; he sent his "good cousin," Blount, to inquire into the facts, and the said cousin worked to such good purpose, that the coroner's jury, after sitting from the 10th to the 13th of September, returned a colourless verdict of "Mischance," acquitting Forster and all the attendants of any acts of violence. The foreman of the jury wrote to Dudley, and there was evidently great perturbation everywhere. In the archives at Simancas is preserved a document which indicates that there had been a plot to poison this unhappy wife. Altogether it is a strange mystery, and has excited universal sympathy wherever the tale has been told. Over a room beyond the hall at Cumnor was an apartment which came to be called Lady Dudley's chamber; indeed, so great was the interest in the fate of the hapless lady, that Cumnor Place afterwards went by the name of "Dudley Castle." As a tale of mystery and romance it has never failed to capture the popular imagination.

The whole story is fully discussed in Timbs' and Gunn's ABBEYS, CASTLES AND ANCIENT HALLS, Vol. II., p. 46, under "Cumnor Place."

It appears that on Amy Dudley's death the aforementioned Arthur Robsart succeeded to the manor of Oldbury, and that he exercised manorial rights there in 1573, including frankpledge. He settled the manor on his son Robert, but as Robert died in his father's lifetime, it passed to his son George, who, in 1610, sold the reversion of Oldbury, after Arthur Robsart's death, to William Turton.

After the death of his grandfather George Robsart repented of the sale, and it was ultimately agreed that certain messuages in the manor should become the property of Turton, while the manor itself was settled upon George, his wife Anne, and their son Arthur.

Various other scraps of evidence are extant of the Robsart connection with Oldbury. During the reign of Elizabeth there was a Chancery suit by Arthur Robserte against Sir John Lytleton and George Tuckey to protect his title to the Oldbury lands, which had been conveyed to him by the Earl of Leicester. Sir John, who died in 1589, is said to have been knighted at Kenilworth by Queen Elizabeth on her visit in 1575. The first Arthur Robsart in 1597 acquired certain lands in "Westbromych" from Sir William Skeffington.

In 1601 a marriage was celebrated at Oldbury, by "Mr. Prichett, ye 14 day of Aprill," between Mr. John Francis and Mistress Anne Robsert. In the same year Robert Robsart and Dorothy his wife parted with lands in Perry Barr and Great Barr to Humphrey Wyrley, of Hamstead.

The Will of Robert Robsearte, of Oldbury, was proved at Worcester in 1620.

Nash is very vague as to the conveyance of Oldbury manor to the Cornwallis family. He says:—"How it passed from the Dudleys to the Cornwallis's I am to seek; but anno 1648 Charles Cornwallis, Esq., a younger branch of the lord Cornwallis of Suffolk, occurs lord of Oldbury, and as such held a court leet and baron here on the 29th of April that year. He died and left issue by Elizabeth his wife, the daughter of — Calmore, Esq., two daughters."

On the break-up of the Dudley barony, not only Oldbury, but Smethwick and other surrounding properties, passed into the hands of the Cornwallis family, members of which had taken up their residence at Blakeley Hall some years prior to the date mentioned by Nash. It is a recorded fact that Charles Cornwallis purchased Oldbury from Arthur Robsart and William Turton (son and successor to the before-mentioned William) in 1633.

Charles Cornwallis, of Broome Hall, Suffolk, who thus acquired the lordship of Oldbury, had already close connection with this locality. He was the son of Sir William Cornwallis, the essayist, and the grandson of Sir Charles Cornwallis. Sir Charles was knighted in 1603, and about 1614 was imprisoned for a year in the Tower by order of the Privy Council. Late in life (1618) he acquired from Lord Dudley the manor of Harborne, where he took up his residence, and where in 1629 he died. In the deed of conveyance the property is called "the manors of Horborne, *alias* Horbourne and Smithwyke." (SALT COLLECTION, Vol. VI., N.S. pp. 50–51.) Twenty years previously he had acquired also from the same owner "Ettingsall Parke, Parke Fields," and other lands in Sedgley.

That Charles Cornwallis was residence at Blakeley Hall between 1635 and 1640 may be inferred from the fact that his children were baptised and registered at Oldbury during that period. Also there would appear to have been living with him about the same time his sister Frances, who married Thomas Paston, at Oldbury (or at Halesowen).

One other land transaction may be mentioned. In 1661 certain properties of the manor of Oldbury were sold off by "feoffment made by Charles Cornewalyes, of Blackley Hall, in the parish of Halesowen in the county of

Salopp, esquire." But for a more interesting episode we have to go back a few years.

In a letter of Henrietta Maria, written from Walsall on Saturday, July 8th, 1643, that unfortunate Queen, who was then marching through this locality with a body of foreign mercenaries she had raised to assist her royal husband in his struggle against the Parliament, says she will start on the Monday and proceed—towards King's Norton and Stratford-on-Avon—"by the road which you told me by Fred."

This Fred who had inspired the royal confidence was Frederick Cornwallis, an amiable courtier, and one of those cheery companions whom princes delight to honour. He afterwards became Baron Cornwallis.

Two members of this family became bishops of Lichfield; namely, Frederick Cornwallis in 1750, translated to Canterbury in 1768; and James Cornwallis in 1781. See also Visitations of Nottinghamshire, 1589 and 1614, for the full family pedigree.

It may be difficult to realise, but such was the fact, that when Blakeley Hall was the home of the romantic Robsarts, or the courtly Cornwallis family, Oldbury was an attractive and picturesque spot, in the possession of all those pristine beauties which made it the equal of any of the most charming villages in the rural Worcestershire of to-day. The subsequent lords of the manor appear to have been non-resident.

It would appear that Oldbury was next possessed by "two joint lords of this manor," namely, Anthony Mingey, Esq. and William Featherstone, Esq., of Coventry, who had respectively married Anne and Frances, the two daughters of Charles Cornwallis. Presently, as Mingey had no issue, the whole devolved on Frances Fetherston, who left two daughters and co-heiresses, Anne, the wife of and Elizabeth, the wife of — Paston. No issue proceeding from the latter, Addington's two daughters next inherited Oldbury; Frances, who married Christopher Wright, of Coventry, gentleman; and Anne, who married Richard Grimshaw, gentleman; joint owners of the lordship.

Grimshaw left one son, who died unmarried; of him Christopher Wright purchased a moiety of the manor, and became sole lord of Oldbury, though he had no child to succeed to the property.

The Court Rolls show approximately the dates of the Grimshaw and Wright interest in the manor:—

A Court Baron of Oldbury Walloxhall, *alias* Langley Wollaxell, *alias* Langley and Wallaxell, 2 November, 1726, Elizabeth Paston, widow, Richard Grimshaw, gent., and Anne his wife, and Frances Addington, spinster, being lords and ladies of the manor, and John Grove, steward.

A Court record of 1752 shows Richard Grimshaw to be dead and his widow to be the lady of the manor; Thomas Fisher being steward.

A Court Baron was held 20 April, 1742, Richard Grimshaw, gent., and Anne his wife, Christopher Wright and Frances his wife, being lords and ladies of the manor, and John Gibbons, steward.

In 1773 a conveyance of cottage property within the manor of Oldbury shows Francis Wright of the city of Coventry, and Christopher Wright of the same city, gent, lady and lord of the said manor.

A special Court Baron of 19 August, 1788, shows Mary Wright, widow, to be lady of the manor, and Anthony Mainwaring, steward. The same names occur in the record of a Court Leet held 25 October, 1791. In June, 1799, the same lady of the manor has Ambrose Phillips Mainwaring for her steward.

Christopher Wright, on the death of his first wife, married Mary, the widow of Richard Parrott, Esq., of Hawksbury Hall, near Coventry. An account of the family of Parrott (or Perrott) will be found in THE MIDLAND ANTIQUARY; and in Vol. II., p. 65, it is stated that the Hawksbury estate "is now (1883) the property of Patrick Allan-Fraser, Esq."

At a Court Baron 12 March, 1812, Francis Parrott, Esq. is found lord of the manor, and A. P. Mainwaring his steward. In 1834, and again in 1840, another Francis Parrott is lord, and has John Carter for his manorial steward. The manor had evidently passed from Christopher Wright to the relatives of his second wife, the Parrotts. Elizabeth, daughter of Francis Parrot, M.D., of Birmingham, married Major John Fraser, of Arbroath, and from them Oldbury passed to their daughter Elizabeth, wife of Patrick Allan, who in 1851 assumed the additional surname and arms of Fraser.

In August, 1854, was held a Court Baron, when Patrick Allan-Fraser, Esq., and Elizabeth his wife were lord and lady, and Thomas Ball Troughton, steward. The same names are recorded in 1859, but in July, 1868, no names of proprietors are given, but T. H. Kirby is deputy steward. Since 1885 the name of Mr. Edward Caddick appears as steward of the manor, acting for trustees.

An insight into the copyhold customs of the manor was gained in a case which came before the public in July, 1898. An inquiry was held at the Talbot Hotel, Oldbury, at the instance of the Copyholds Department of the Board of Agriculture, arising out of an application by John and Edward Harper, of Dudley, to compel Edward Caddick, Robert Whyte, and James Muir, Esquires, lords of the manor of Oldbury and Walloxall, otherwise Langley Walloxall, otherwise Langley and Walloxall, to enfranchise under the Copyhold Acts certain lands situate at Rood End, to which the Messrs. Harper had recently been admitted tenants.

The object was to ascertain the amount and nature of the compensation due to the lords of the manor for the extinguishment of their manorial rights in the said lands, and for an Award of Enfranchisement of the lands as freehold.

Evidence was adduced by the steward of the manor as to the following customs:—That an arbitrary fine was payable by the copyhold tenant to the lords on every alienation of the lands and on the death of the tenant, but such fine could not exceed two years' improved annual value of the lands. That no fine was payable on the death of the lords. That a tenant could not demise the lands for more than a year without the licence of the lords, but such licence was granted on payment of a fine of £5 per cent. on the rental for seven years. That no leases were granted for more than 21 years. That the lords were not owners of the mines, and could not work them. That the tenants could not work the mines without licence of the lords, but such licence was granted on payment to the lords of one-fifth of the value of the mines. That the copyhold tenants were the owners of the surface of the lands and the mines, but the tenants would commit waste as against the lords by getting them without licence.

The lands in question were viewed, and ultimately an Award of Enfranchisement was made by the Board of Agriculture.

The manorial courts are now usually held at the Talbot Hotel. After the lords of the manor ceased to be resident, a house for the bailiff was built in a more central position. It stood near the Old Court House, and was known as the Manor House.

XIII.—The Chapelry of Oldbury

The history of Oldbury as a separate and distinct parish virtually begins with its erection into a chapelry, which was practically equivalent to its release from the domination of the mother parish, Halesowen. Its civil and ecclesiastical independence became then a mere matter of time, according as it showed fitness for self-government or otherwise. Worthiness in this respect may be measured in no small degree by a willingness to bear the cost of independence.

The expense of erecting the chapel-of-ease was borne by the principal inhabitants of Oldbury. The site appears to have been copyhold land, for " 24 Henry VIII., William Feldon, alias Carpenter, of Oldbury, entered into a bond of £10 penalty to Arthur Robstart, Esq., Laurence White of Rowley, John Parke of Langley, and Edmund Darby of Oldbury, their heirs and executors; that he will not henceforth make any claim or title to the Chapel Croft or any parcel thereof, by virtue of any copy of Court Roll touching the same; but only to hear God's service in the said chapel, as other tenants or inhabitants of Oldbury do."

As this was before the Reformation, "God's service" here referred to would be according to the rites of Romanism then practised throughout the realm. As it is also anterior to 1557 (see p. 50 ante), it is curious to note the name of Robsart connected with Oldbury at that date.

We are almost enabled to obtain a glimpse of how the Reformation came to this parish. It is on record that from the year 1490 till the Reformation the good people of Oldbury, as did also those of Frankley, contributed annually the sum of sevenpence towards the maintenance of the "hye light."

But in 1547, the year of accession of that most Protestant Prince, Edward VI., both Oldbury and Frankley bluntly declined to pay any more towards maintaining what had then become the "superstition" of altar lights. Next to the entry which records this new-born zeal for a purer faith is one which points its significance:—"Spent in drink in taking down the images, 4d."

The chapel-of-ease was licensed (though not consecrated) by Jerome de Ghinueus, bishop of Worcester, an Italian, who was subsequently deprived of his see by Act of Parliament for non-residence. It is said to have been in the hands of the Presbyterians till the Act of Uniformity, 1662, but the beginning of its recorded history appears in the Manor Rolls under date 1659, when it was surrendered to the Court, being on copyhold land, in due manorial form. Other formal surrenders took place at each renewal of the body of trustees.

Negative evidence goes to show that the people of Oldbury not only bore the initial cost of providing their own place of worship, but for long time also contributed to its regular maintenance.

Nash says.—"There being no fixed salary or endowment to this chapel from its first foundation till Queen Anne's Bounty was procured, the Dissenters got possession soon after the Revolution (1688) and held it till Bishop Lloyd's time [William Lloyd, a celebrated divine, one of the Seven Bishops committed by James II., and Almoner to Queen Anne, was bishop of St. Asaph's first, then of Lichfield (1692) and was translated to Worcester 1699] who ousted them, and notwithstanding the pretence of its standing on copyhold ground, he consecrated both the chapel and the cemetery" [or graveyard].

By the aid of Queen Anne's Bounty Fund lands to the annual value of £14 were purchased, and a Mr. Thorpe was licensed to the cure on the presentation of the vicar of Halesowen.

The "ousting" of the Nonconformists did not kill Nonconformity in Oldbury, for they proceeded to establish themselves in a small chapel of their own; and notwithstanding the bitter and active persecutions of those times, they survive in greater congregational strength to these more tolerant days, happily held in the respect and esteem of their neighbours.

The period of the Commonwealth is generally regarded as one of universal religious tolerance. There was tolerance assuredly, but as it did not comprehend the Church of England or the Roman Church, a large proportion of the people were excluded from its enjoyment. In February, 1657, the inhabitants of St. Kenelm's, Romsley, and Hunnington petitioned for the maintenance of a minister for them. If the prayer were granted it would mean the appointment of a Puritan clergyman, for the use of the Book of Common Prayer was strictly proscribed.

The strength of Puritanism in this locality is evidenced by the number of clergymen ejected from their livings by the Act of Uniformity, 1662. Calamy, the contemporary historian of Nonconformity, names and gives biographical sketches of Samuel Willes, rector of St. Martin's, Birmingham; Thomas Baldwin, junr., vicar of Clent; William Fincher, "a heavenly good man," vicar of Wednesbury; John Bassett, of Cradley; Richard Hilton, of West Bromwich, afterwards private chaplain to Philip Foley, Esq.; William Turton, M.A., of The Brades, ejected from Rowley; Richard Hinks, of Tipton; Thomas Byrdal, of Walsall; John Reynolds, of Wolverhampton; Thomas Badland, ejected from Willenhall, and who went to his native Worcester, where he was "a faithful and profitable preacher of the gospel for thirty-five years," and where he had as one of his assistants a "Mr. Hand, who had been ordained at Oldbury"; also of many other high-spirited, nobly-conscientious men in these two counties of Worcester and Stafford. It should not be forgotten that the great Nonconformist divine, Richard Baxter, was a native of Kidderminster, and had been schoolmaster at Dudley Free School. In 1671 the Rev. Ed. Paston, vicar of Halesowen, also suffered ejectment. At Cradley a Presbyterian congregation was started immediately after the "Black Bartholomew of 1662," and in 1787 an Independent Congregation was formed there.

The old church, or "chapel" of Oldbury—the edifice of which the Nonconformists had managed to retain possession from the Revolution to Queen Anne—which stood on the site of the present Free Library, was demolished, and a large piece of the churchyard was taken to improve the roadway. It was replaced by Christ Church, erected in the centre of the newly-grown town, in 1840, at a cost of £4,500, the Rev. George Sproston, who had held the benefice since 1836), being incumbent at the time. The value of the living, a perpetual curacy in the gift of Lord Lyttelton, was valued at £156 in 1850, and at £300, with residence, in 1873.

The parish curates of Oldbury have included:—

    Thomas Wright, 29th July, 1663.

    Charles Osborn, 29th November, 1665.

    John Muckross, 30th September, 1674.

    Thomas Stinton, 28th October, 1724.

    Jos. Hipkiss, 15th January, 1728.

The Parish Registers date only from 1714.

XIV.—NONCONFORMITY IN AND AROUND OLDBURY.

Oldbury, comparing its size with surrounding places, has an exceptionally interesting history as one of the strongholds of early Nonconformity. The interest, however, lies in the fact that its experiences were typical rather than exceptional—which seems somewhat paradoxical.

First, to give a number of historical references, unearthed by Mr. George Eyre Evans, the well-known historian of local Nonconformity, which not only add materially to our knowledge of the subject, but give it the backbone of authenticated contemporary evidence. The Record Office reference to these historic documents is "Domestic Entry Book."

Among the State Papers preserved at the said Record Office in London are a number in the Domestic Series which relate to the state of Nonconformity in this immediate locality at that period of religious intolerance, Here is the first (from Book No. 38A):—

> The house of Horton of Oldbery in Hales Owen, Shropsh. Pres[byterian] licensed 5 Sept.) 1672.

To understand the significance of this it must be understood that Episcopalianism was then dominant, and that Puritanism was under the ban of the law. But Charles II., on the fall of his bigoted Minister, Lord Clarendon, showed a disposition not to enforce the penal laws against the Nonconformists—among many repressions it was a dire offence to hold any religious assembly, even of very few persons, either in the open fields or in a private house, or for holding any service except according to the rites of the Established Church. In 1672 the King suspended these penal laws. At once 3,000 applications were made from all parts of the kingdom for licences to erect or use any edifice for public worship.

Here are three other local applications, also in Book No. 38A:—

> The howse of George Colborne in Royley Regis in Stafford. Pr[esbyterian] licensed 22nd July, 1672.
> The house of George Colborne of Rowleyregis in Staffordsh. Pr. licensed 5th September, 1672.
> The house of Wm. Russell of Rowley Reges in Staffordsh. 1672. [?] licensed.

It can be easily understood that after twelve years' relentless persecution many dissenters hesitated to declare themselves. Thus we have here (State Paper, Domestic, Car. II.) a letter addressed to one Mr. Robert Blany:—

Sr.

I am requested to p'cure Lycense, for Mr. Joseph Ecclesole, a non-conf[t] minister and Mr. —— Mr. William Turton alsoe to preach &c. in the house of Mr. William Keeling In Darleston in Staffordshire. I pray when ye goe up to Westm[r] get this done for one or both of the p'sons above named. I shall sattisfie for ye charges.

Yr. Assured Friend,

SA. FISHER.

I pray remember my father's business.

25 Ap. '72.

Mr. Joseph Ecclesole of Sedgley in Staffordshire.

Mr. William Turton of Rowley in Staffordshire crave Lycense for the House of Mr. Wm. Keeling in Darleston, Staffordshire, both of the presbyter p'swasion.

In a work on THE ORIGINAL RECORDS OF EARLY NONCONFORMITY (published in 1914) by Professor G. Lyon Turner, an interesting note is made on this letter. The Professor says (iii., 417):—"It looks very much as if lie [Sa. Fisher] were living in the provinces, and writes to Mr. Blayney to secure his good offices as of one well-known to his younger brother Charles, and to his father, on behalf of friends in Darlaston, Sedgley, and Rowley Regis in Staffordshire. The first-named ('Joseph Ecclesole') is Calamy's Joseph Eccleshall who, he tells us, was ejected from Sedgley, and who is described in a second application as Mr. Joseph Ecelsole of Sedgley in Staffordshire. In 1669 he was reported as preaching in Sedgley, holding Presbyterian Conventicles 'of above 200' in his own house. And also in Coventry as one of four who preached 'Att Leather Hall there at Conventicles of almost 1,000 every Sunday.' For him licences were obtained (in 1672) both for his person as a Presbyterian teacher, and for his house in Sedgley as a Presbyterian meeting-place. The second, William Turton, we learn from Calamy, was ejected from Rowley Regis, and is described in a second application as 'of Rowley in Staffordshire,' but to preach in the house of William Keeling in Darlaston. It is specially interesting, therefore, to find him reported in 1669 associated with six others as preaching to a Conventicle of '1 to 200,' 'att the house of Wm. Keeling at Darlaston' (as well as in the houses of Wm. Bayley and William Penson); and as preaching with two others at a Conventicle 'of 2 or 300' in Wednesbury. The application made for him in 1672 was granted, and both licences were issued on 1 May, 1672. Other friends, however, interested themselves in William Turton besides Mr. Samuel Fisher. One applied for him anonymously for the town of Stafford—'in Comitat. Staff. Mr. William Purton, Minister, to meete at Mr. John Wode's house in Stafford, Of ye presbiterian p'swation.' Though the document, in its semi-Latin form, bespeaks a legal training in the applicant, he curiously misspells Turton's name, calling him Purton. . . . Nor is this all. Four months later a licence is secured for the house of John Tuston of Rowley in Staffordshire, Sept. 5. Is the Christian name a mistake, as well as the surname misspelt? If it is meant for William Turton, it would confirm the statement that he was still living at Rowley Regis, although he had already been licensed both for Darlaston and Stafford. If there is no error in the Christian name, this may be a licence for William's brother. Quite probably Samuel Fisher was living at Birmingham with his father," etc., etc.

To resume the extracts from the State Papers (Entry Book 38A) relating to this district:

> Licence to Thomas Baldwin [ejected from Willenhall 1660, and from Clent 1662] of Rowley in Staffordshire.
> Presby[terian]. Sept. 5, '72.
> The house of John Tuston (? Turton) [brother? of William Turton the ejected rector of Rowley] of Rowley in Staffordshire. Sept. 5, '72.

Charles II.'s declaration of indulgence, which was dated 13th March, 1672, had specified that he would grant a convenient number of public meeting places "to men of all sorts that did not conform" provided they took out licences. Many of the applicants were ejected ministers who wished to be allowed to preach to their old congregations, or to gather new ones around them. But in July, 1673, the parliament voted that the King's declaration was illegal, and the persecution of the Nonconformists recommenced. In April, 1687, James II. issued his declaration to the Nonconformists, but they, having regard to their previous experience, were fearful of the issue. Soon after came the Revolution of 1688.

It may be mentioned that an old licence existed in respect of the Birmingham Old Meeting House, but it was lost, and after the Priestley Riots in 1791 a fresh one was obtained, which has since been very carefully preserved amongst the deeds of the Meeting. A licence appears to have been granted for the congregation who built the first Meeting House, made out to a member, authorising him to hold meetings or Conventicles in his own private residence. But this is somewhat of a digression.

Coming back to the region more directly under review, let us see what active part it took in the national struggle then being waged for religious liberty and constitutional equality.

This part of the country suffered severely in the Sacheverel Riots of 1715— Dr. Sacheverel was a local man, and once held the living of Cannock. The riots were part of a political agitation got up by the Jacobites and directed mainly against the Dissenters. The favourite cry was "No George!" and the treason-mongers who attended Wednesbury market did not hesitate to cry "Damn King George!" The Presbyterian Meeting House at Black Lake was the scene of great violence, where Cornet Lowe, a Whig gentleman, of Charlemont Hall, was shot on July 14th; while two of the "Tory jacks" who led the assault were also shot, namely, Francis Gibbons, of Sedgley, and Thomas Royston, of Wolverhampton. They were buried at Wednesbury amidst great excitement on the following Sunday.

"On Sunday, the 17th July (says a contemporary account of the proceedings, given in full in A HISTORY OF WEST BROMWICH, pp. 80-81, *q. v.*) the mob came again and fired the Meeting House at West Bromwich, and the Meeting House at Oldbury, and the Meeting House at Dudley." The chapels at Cradley and Bradley were also attacked and pulled down—that at Oldbury was destroyed by the easier methods of the incendiary, who deliberately applied the torch while the minister inside was preaching!

In those stirring times there was no room for the timorous evangelist in the ranks of the Nonconformist divines. The Rev. William Turton, M.A., the first minister of Birmingham Old Meeting, a man whose name is held in the highest reverence there, had enjoyed the benefice of Rowley Regis till ejected by the Act of Uniformity in 1662. Birmingham being a non-corporate town, he was enabled to establish a church of Presbyterian Nonconformists there in 1686, and continued to minister to the society he had founded till his death in 1716. He had previously laboured lovingly among the Dissenters of Oldbury, and continued during his ministry in Birmingham to preach there at regularly appointed times.

The published MEMORIALS OF THE OLD MEETING HOUSE, in dealing with the ministry of the Rev. Samuel Clark, 1757-1769, says:—"A connection at this time subsisted between the congregation at Oldbury and that of the Old Meeting House, the ministers of the latter officiating alternately at Oldbury."

The occasional Dissenting ministers officiating at Oldbury during this early period included the Rev. W. Turton, Paul Russell (an itinerant, afterwards of Coseley) and Tonks (? W. Tong, of Coventry). The settled ministers were the same as at Birmingham Old Meeting till the death of Mr. Clark in 1769; namely:—

    1700–1730—Rev. Daniel Greenwood.
    1714–1730—Rev. Edward Brodhurst.
    1732–1746—Rev. Daniel Mattock.
    1739–1756—Rev. Joseph Wilkinson.
    1746–1770—Rev. William Howell.
    1756–1769—Rev. Samuel Clark.

The overlapping dates indicate the working of ministerial colleagues, the duties most of the time being found too heavy for one man to accomplish satisfactorily. This supply arrangement continued till 1776, though the Rev. John Bradford, a Daventry student, was a settled minister at Oldbury from 1772 to 1775, after which he became a schoolmaster. The following year the Rev. William Proctor became the first permanent minister, and filled the office till his death in 1808. In this year the Oldbury Dissenting Chapel was erected on land given by John Turton, of The Brades. The last Trinitarian minister was the Rev. E. Brodhurst, who died in 1730, and the tendency to Unitarianism began with the Rev. Daniel Mattock, the Rev. W. Howell (1746) being a decided Arian, a sect which holds that Christ is not God in the same sense as the Father, but in an inferior degree, the body of the man Jesus being animated by a pre-existent created spirit. It was in consequence of Mr. Howell's appointment that the split took place at the Birmingham Old Meeting, which resulted in the establishment of Carr's Lane Congregation.

After Mr. Proctor, who died in 1808, the Rev. Herbert Jenkins and the Rev. James Fordyce frequently officiated at Oldbury, till the year 1811. From 1808 to 1812 the Rev. Samuel. Griffiths was minister in residence, having towards the end the assistance of the Rev. Samuel Goode on supply. Mr. Griffiths was educated at the Presbyterian College, Carmarthen, 1804-1808. He was succeeded by the Rev. Timothy Davis, born 15th January, 1786, who held the position from 1812 to 1845, and became quite an Oldbury man. Then came William McKean, who continued in the office till his death in 1869; his son, the Rev. Henry McKean, became his father's assistant in 1858, and in his later years was one of the best known and most active of Oldbury's public men. William McKean, a native of Paisley, came from a pastorate at Walsall to Oldbury, where for a quarter of a century lie was master of the Free School as well as the minister; his closing years were saddened by blindness.

It was the chapel of the Establishment, erected in 1529, which the Nonconforming congregation of Oldbury retained in their undisturbed possession till their "ousting" by the Episcopalians as already mentioned; a fabric in which were performed services according to the rites of the Roman Church for at least twenty years and till the first Uniformity Act in Edward VI.'s reign gave effect to the Reformation (1549); and afterwards the services according to the Anglican liturgy, and, as we have seen, the Nonconforming services of the Presbyterians. This historic little chapel stood in the market place till supplanted by the present parish church in 1840-1.

The original conventicle must have been very small, and it seems to have long remained small, for when the Rev. William Proctor was instrumental In getting the Meeting house rebuilt in 1806 the entire cost was only £300, of which the Oldbury brethren contributed but £13. This building was remodelled in 1862 at a cost of £300, and £200 more was expended upon it in 1889. The walls are chiefly those of 1806, and a small portion of the fabric of 1708 remains.

In 1728 the trustees acquired five and a-half acres of land near Oldbury, the income to be applied to the use of the poor, and towards the support of the minister of the Meeting house. In 1784 a building was purchased for a Free School, and in 1790 five acres more came to the trustees for the use of the poor. In 1817 Henry Hunt, of The Brades, presented to the trustees the house and garden adjoining the school, purchased by his father and others for the use of the minister.

There was instituted at Oldbury (as also at Dudley and elsewhere) a form of commemoration of those early Puritan divines who had been ejected from their livings by the Uniformity Act of 1662. The Oldbury Double Lecture, as it was called, was generally held in the week in which the 24th August occurred, that being the fateful day appointed by the Act of 1662 for these ministers to conform to the Book of Common Prayer, or to give up their benefices. It would seem that the chapelry of Oldbury had escaped the operations of this drastic measure, and that the Presbyterians had remained in possession here for a considerable time. Anyway, John Reynolds, a Puritan, upon leaving Oxford in 1699, was ordained with four others, in the chapel of Oldbury, by five of the recalcitrant clergymen who had been deprived under the Act. These men, who were looked upon by their followers as "fathers in Israel," were the Rev. Henry Oasland, M.A., of Bewdley; the Rev. William Turton, M.A., of The Brades; the Rev. T. Baldwin, of Chaddesley; the Rev. Mr. Mansfield, and the Rev. Mr. Bladen, all of them disciples of the great Richard Baxter, of Kidderminster. Reynolds resided for some time in the family of Mr. Philip Foley, of Prestwood, probably in the capacity of private chaplain; afterwards he held pastorates at Gloucester, Shrewsbury, Walsall, and other places, dying in the last-named town in 1727 after a sudden attack which took him while occupying the pulpit at West Bromwich. One of the "four others" ordained at the same time may have been the Rev. Mr. Hand, who went to a pastorate at Worcester. (See ANNALS OF WILLENHALL, p. 63.)

Jonathan Hand, says Urwick in his NONCONFORMITY IN WORCESTER, in dealing with the pastors of Angel Street Church in that city, was an assistant minister there for some years; . and his name occurs in the Baptismal Registers down to 1713. He was educated for the ministry at Sheriff Hales, and ordained in Oldbury chapel, Staffordshire (sic) on May 30th, 1699, with three others, John Reynolds, of Gloucester, Shrewsbury, and Walsall; Warren, of Coventry, and Bennett.

The Double Lectures, so-called because two were delivered in one day, were instituted to keep up the style of preaching, for which the Nonconformist divines were famous at a time when not a few of their Anglican brethren were veritable "dumb-dogs"—men admitted to holy orders without fitness or valid qualification of an kind.

The Oldbury Double Lecture did not always take place on or near the date of the "Black Bartholomew," as the Puritans called the ejectment Sunday of 1662; some-times it appears to have been celebrated at Whitsuntide, and at another period postponed to September, owing to the harvesting activities, a reason which connotes a rural Oldbury. Even the very purport of its institution was once in danger of being forgotten, and a local legend was put forward to account for it. This tradition related that a stack of chimneys at the Brades House suddenly fell down one day, by reason of which accident the Turton family resident there narrowly escaped with their lives. To commemorate their deliverance (so it was said) they invited the neighbouring ministers of their persuasion to assist them in keeping a Day of Thanksgiving annually; and being an influential and much respected family in close connection with the Birmingham and other Meetings in the locality, they established a form of commemoration at Oldbury. But this was scarcely the Double Lecture, the origin of which was national rather than local. There exists a list of lecturers, two eminent preachers for each year, who drew crowded congregations, from 1776 to 1865; when the "Double Lecture" was discontinued, and Oldbury was included as one of the regular places of the Monthly Meeting of Protestant Dissenters in the Midland district.

XV.—The Rise of Local Methodism.

The present-day strength of Nonconformity in this district almost persuades one to the Nietzschean idea of creative tragedy—which, applied in this sense, is but another expression of the theory that the blood of the martyrs is the seed of the church. After the persecutions of the seventeenth century it is not surprising that Methodism found a congenial soil here in the eighteenth. Nonconformity and Dissent, in the sunshine of tolerance, have since thriven mightily.

There is no evidence that John Wesley preached at or visited Oldbury, Halesowen, or Rowley, though he possibly passed through the first-named when journeying between Birmingham and Dudley.

In his JOURNAL Wesley writes: -

Monday, 19 March, 1770. I rode [from Wednesbury] to Craidley.

The entry, of course, refers to Cradley. Wesley's departure from accepted spelling is of frequent occurrence. He took local pronunciation at its face value, and spelt phonetically. Had any one spelt the name to him without pronouncing it, he doubtless would have made it rhyme with "badly," as do most strangers to the district unfamiliar with the place.

But to return.

Monday, 19 March, 1770. I rode to Craidley. Here also the multitude of people obliged me to stand abroad, although the north wind whistled round my head. About one I took the field again at Stourbridge. Many of the hearers were wild as colts untamed; but the bridle was in their mouths. At six I began at Dudley. The air was as cold as I had almost ever felt; but I trust God warmed many hearts.

No incidents of this visit to Cradley are preserved in the traditions of the place, nor can they be traced in any published writings, says Mr. W. C. Sheldon, who assisted in preparing the Standard edition of Wesley's JOURNAL. The historic site is the High Street next the present Baptist Chapel. It was originally called Dungeon Head, owing to a dungeon having being there, and he stood on a stone at the top. The stone, though still in Cradley, is not now *in situ*.

The history of Methodism in Oldbury apparently begins near the end of the eighteenth century, when a Sunday School was established for the express purpose, as a leaflet expressed it, of "educating in the rudiments of the English language, and promoting the moral improvement of the children of the poor." On behalf of this Sunday School a sermon was preached in 1802 by the Rev. Thomas Taylor, one of Wesley's preachers. He "travelled" from 1761 to 1816, and in 1796 and again in 1809 was elected President of the Conference. By the Conferences of 1801 and 1802 he was appointed Superintendent of the Birmingham Circuit, which at that time included Birmingham, Wednesbury, Darlaston, Walsall, Oldbury (in the order stated), and other places. The Circuit Account Book of 1798 shows that a quarter's contributions from Oldbury to the Circuit Board amounted to £1 7s. 0d.

As part of the Birmingham Circuit Oldbury would receive occasional visits from some of the leading Methodist preachers of the period, among whom were William Thompson, the first President after the death of Wesley in 1791, whose legislative mind stamped itself on the Conference proceedings in three critical years, and whose body rests in St. Mary's Church, Birmingham; Samuel Bradburn, one of the greatest natural orators and wits of the time; Henry Moore, Wesley's friend and biographer; and others.

A chapel was built at Oldbury in 1800, and two years afterwards a piece of land, "part of The Little Field," was purchased for a burial ground. According to "The Story of Oldbury Methodism" (an article by Mr. C. W. Keyworth, B.A., which appeared in THE METHODIST RECORDER of 20th October, 1904):—"On this land, in New Meeting Street, a chapel was erected and used till the present chapel was built. . . . But another building, now two cottages, in the same street, is spoken of as an earlier chapel. The burial ground is said to have been enlarged in 1828, and interments are registered from 1823 to 1891. The only building at present on the land is a small mortuary chapel rented by the local authority."

In 1828 Oldbury was third of twenty-four places, Rowley Regis and Tividale among them, on the plan of the Dudley Circuit; by which time there was a vigorous church in the place, and probably a resident minister.

In 1850 the Rev. George Curnock was appointed to the Dudley Circuit, and resided at Oldbury. He was the uncle of the Rev. Nehemiah Curnock, editor of the Standard edition of Wesley's JOURNAL, who was born at Great Bridge, 1840. He came at a critical time of chapel building, and it was by his influence that the present chapel, costing over £5,000, was erected on a good corner site instead of in a back street. The opening service, 25th October, 1853, was conducted by the Rev. John Lomas, President of the Conference that year. Mr. Curnock was at a later period Conference Precentor for many years.

In 1859 the Dudley Circuit was divided into three, and Oldbury became head of a new Circuit, although till subsequently to 1906 its number of members scarcely ever exceeded three hundred. The first ministers appointed were the Rev. J. Bramley and the Rev. W. L. Watkinson, at stipends that would appear remarkably meagre to modern ideas. The latter, now one of the most famous Wesleyan ministers living, came as a young man to his first circuit, and here he found a wife in the daughter of Mr. Samuel Swindley. Nine of the earliest years of his ministry were spent in the Black Country: Oldbury, 1859-1862; Tipton, 1865-1868; Wednesbury, 1868-1871. The new Circuit included five chapels: Oldbury, Tividale, Church Bridge, Brades, and Warley. There is now no cause at Church Bridge, but new societies were formed in the early sixties at Pope's Lane, Causeway Green, and Rowley, where chapels were subsequently built. In 1873 the Manse was provided, thus completing the set of premises, which includes chapel, schools, and minister's residence, with a frontage to two streets. In the cause of elementary education Oldbury Wesleyans did not fail to do their duty in the days of voluntary effort; their day schools, accommodating 600 children, date from 1853), and were the outgrowth of a humbler and earlier effort.

In 1884 the old chapel at Warley was replaced by a new one. For the chapel in the decayed neighbourhood of Pope's Lane has been substituted one in a situation of greater opportunities and of much pleasanter surroundings at Langley (1904). New ground has also been broken in the populous centre of Blackheath. For other details of much local interest to the members of the Methodist body reference may be made to the newspaper article quoted.

Clent Methodism is proud of the name of the Rev. John Thomas, a great missionary light, to whom a memorial chapel has been erected there. This worthy was born and brought up in the parish, where he became a blacksmith. Reading and writing, says Mr. W. C. Sheldon, were the sum of his school education, but of these he made the best. Meditative of temperament but none too robust of physique, he early came under the influence of Methodist teaching and became a local preacher. Then, fired with missionary zeal, he would walk long distances—to Dudley, to Wednesbury, or to Birmingham—to hear Newton, Watson, and other great advocates. His call (continues his biographer) reminds us of that early "Follow me," when they straightway forsook their nets and followed him"; for when Joseph Sutcliffe, then Superintendent at Dudley, sent his colleague in search of John Thomas, he was found at the smithy shoeing a horse. He left the job unfinished doffed his leathern apron, walked to Dudley, and took coach to London. There he was welcomed by George Morley, John Mason, and others, and arrangements were made for his early departure to Tonga in the following Spring. He went out, a young man of twenty-eight, with his wife, in 1825; and he laboured in that distant field for thirty-five years, broken only by a single visit to his native country. He ministered unceasingly with a sturdy devotion, and an unquenchable desire that the people who walked in darkness might see the light. The fascinating story of his missionary labours is told in TONGA AND THE FRIENDLY ISLANDS, by Sarah Farmer, published in 1885. It appears that eighty or ninety years ago a great chief, who afterwards became King of the entire group of islands, embraced Christianity. Other chiefs followed his example, and in 1834 a great conversion was effected, so that by 1865 practically the whole of the natives were professing Christians. They are a remarkable people, endowed by Nature with intellectual powers far superior to others in those Southern Seas; and it was upon material such as this that John Thomas laboured with so much loving devotion and met with such abounding success. In a population of 25,000 there were 8 native ministers, 811 local preachers, and upwards of 5,000 day scholars. John Thomas returned to his native land in 1860, and lived long enough to hear of the further remarkable progress effected in those southern islands by Dr. Egan Moulton. He died in 1881, in his 85th year. The Clent memorial chapel was erected on the site of his birthplace,

At Quinton the history of the cause goes rather further back into the annals of Methodism. There was living at "The Quinton" in the last years of the eighteenth century a Mr. Ambrose Foley, whose business or pleasure occasionally took him to London, where he heard Wesley. He was deeply influenced thereby, and his religious enthusiasm impelled him to action in his own neighbourhood. What he most coveted was a visit from the great Evangelist, and on 18th March, 1778, he wrote him thus:

> Rev. Sir,—Having long waited for an opportunity of conveying a line to you, blessed be God, the time has come; and as " I am a man that have seen affliction by the rod of His wrath," have engaged myself for some years past in frequently reading your sermons to a considerable company who wish well to your labour of love; and as they are some of them but babes in Christ, an instructive lesson might (with the Divine

blessing) greatly establish their faith, and much good be done to others. If you have an hour or two to spare, my house which is a good one, and my heart which is a bad one, are both open to you. Pardon, dear Sir, and Rev. Father in Christ, the importunate request of your humble servant.

AMBROSE FOLEY.

It does not appear that Wesley complied with the invitation until 24th March, 1781, when he wrote in his JOURNAL:

> I was invited to preach at Quinton, five miles from Birmingham. I preached there at noon, in the open air, to a serious and attentive, congregation.
>
> Some of them appeared very deeply affected. Who knows but it may continue.

Mr. Foley built in his garden a grotto, which became the meeting place of the villagers who came under the good man's influence. This was superseded in 1786 by a little chapel, opened by Wesley himself, which did duty for nearly a century. Wesley also visited Quinton in 1785 and 1790, and a letter is still treasured in the hamlet which he wrote to Mr. Foley in 1782. It is in the possession' of Mr. Horace Foley MacDonald, and runs:—

London,
26 February, 1782.

Dear Sir,

On Saturday, March 23rd, I hope to be at Birmingham in order to open the new chappel, and to spend a few days there. About the middle of the ensuing week I shall be willing to give you a sermon at Quinton. I am glad to hear that our labour there has not been in vain, and that you are not ashamed of the Gospel of Christ. It will be a particular pleasure to me to see Mrs. Foley, and I hope to see her happier than ever she has been yet. Peace be with your spirit.

I am, your affectionate brother,
J. WESLEY.

The "chappel" referred to was the one in Cherry Street, demolished in 1886. The Foley house, which was "a good one," was a farm just off the main road, and during his visits there Wesley showed his appreciation of the hospitality extended to him by making little presents to his hosts; among the most treasured of these gifts were pieces of china and earthenware, one a Staffordshire teapot being adorned with portraits of himself and other early Methodist divines.

The chair used by Wesley as his open-air pulpit at Quinton was kept as a relic in the vestry of the old chapel, but was deemed too shabby for the new one which replaced it in 1878, and was relegated to the cellar. Relic-mongers chipped it; one took off an arm; and a Black-countryman offered to buy it. The Quinton people " did not care to sell," but told him " he could have, it if he would do something handsome for a sick member in poor circumstances." He took away the chair, having given the invalid—half-a-crown! The chair was afterwards furbished up, taken to America, and deposited in a grand new church there, A fire broke out, which reduced the church to ashes, and with it the historic chair.

Wesley's eye was ever alert to the beauties of Nature and of Art, to the development and inventions of science and of manufacture. His observations on social problems and progress are acute and accurate, as well they might be, for added to the possession of a logical mind his opportunities for observing were unrivalled. For fifty years his travels were incessant, and embraced the entire kingdom from Kent to Connaught, and from Cornwall to Cumberland, and right on to Cromarty.

In July, 1782, he spent a few days in and around Birmingham, visiting `Mr. Boulton's curious works at Soho," and other places of interest, finishing with a visit to Hagley Park and the Leasowes. He writes, July 13th, 1782 (he was then in his 80th year):—

> . . . . Hagley Park, I suppose inferior to few, if any, in England; but we were straitened for time. To take a proper view of it would require five or six hours. Afterwards I went to the Leasowes, a farm so-called, four or five miles from Hagley. I never was so surprised. I have seen nothing in all England to compare with it. it is beautiful and elegant all over. There is nothing grand, nothing costly; no temples, so-called; no statues (except two or three which had better have been spared), but such walks, such shades, such hills and dales, such lawns, such artless cascades, such waving woods, with waters intermixed, as exceed all imagination! On the upper side, from the openings of a shady walk, is a most beautiful and extensive prospect. And all this is comprised in the compass of three miles! I doubt if it be exceeded by anything in Europe. The father of Mr. Shenstone was a gentleman farmer, who bred him at the University, and left him a small estate. This he wholly laid out in improving the Leasowes, living in hopes of great preferment, grounded on the promises of many rich and great friends. But nothing was performed, till he died at forty-eight, probably of a broken heart.

(Refer to p. 17 ante.)

The astonishing growth of Methodism in the eighteenth century is easily to be understood. Men of earnest thought and deep religious convictions, not satisfied by the superficialities of the ministrations offered them in the lethargic church of the Establishment, were ready to turn elsewhere in any direction that offered more copious draughts at the wells of spiritual life. Hence also the success, for a time, of the preaching of Joannah Southcott, who announced herself as the woman spoken of in REVELATION xii. She wrote and dictated many prophecies, some in verse, some in prose. Among those who accepted the genuineness of her message was the Rev. T. P. Foley, rector of Old Swinford church, near Stourbridge, and a member of the famous old Worcestershire family of that name. His preaching was such as drew large congregations to hear him, and he made himself conspicuous by strenuously upholding the claims of Joanna Southcott to be visited by the Spirit of Truth. About Christmas, 1801, he and four others journeyed from London to Exeter, to search diligently into the writings of the prophetess, and to prove whether her mission was true or false. As the result of the investigations, he returned fully convinced that she was divinely inspired, and he espoused her cause during the rest of his lifetime. The reverend champion wrote several books in support of his belief, two of which became fairly well known:—LETTERS AND COMMUNICATIONS, OR WHAT MANNER OF COMMUNICATIONS ARE THESE? and THE ANSWER OF THE REV. THOS. P. FOLEY TO THE WORLD FOR PRINTING THE BOOK, WHAT MANNER OF COMMUNICATIONS ARE THESE? Copies of these works are to be found in the British Museum, and in Public Libraries which collect Southcott literature.

As testimony to the appreciation the reverend gentleman's preaching met with, here is an extract from a letter dated from Leeds, 15th March, 1804:—"Since the 26 of Feb. that the Rev. Mr. Foley came to Leeds, he has been preaching in the country at different churches where he was invited by the clergymen. These churches were so crowded in the morning and in the afternoons they could not hold the people, the number was so large. At one of the churches the windows were opened for the people to hear in the yard, there being hundreds that could not get in."

The Rev. Thos. P. Foley, who has been called the "Apostle of Joannaism," died at a ripe old age in 1825, beloved and respected by a large circle of friends.

Joanna Southcott commenced her prophecies in 1792, and by 1810 she had 100,000 followers in the country. At one time she lived in semi-retirement at Blockley, in Worcestershire, and Joanna's cottage is still to be seen there, standing up above the road, a quaint little dwelling, something like a Noah's Ark, surrounded by a pretty garden. It is called Rock Cottage, and while there the prophetess, practically " driven into the wilderness " by the force of circumstances, kept the address as private as possible.

Joanna was a voluminous writer, and sixty publications came from her pen while she was living in this part of the country. Besides many that were printed in London, a number of her pamphlets bear the local names or imprints of James Light, Coventry Street, Stourbridge, and C. Bradley, Digbeth, Birmingham. A considerable sum of money was left by a lady named Essam to cover the cost of publishing Joanna's messages.

XVI.—The Dawn of Industrialism

The Oldbury of the eighteenth century was a pleasant and a pretty place, nestling at the foot of the green slopes of the Rowley Hills. It was also a primitive place—primitive in the simplicity of its unsophisticated inhabitants. Modern industrialism, in spite of its wonderful material achievements, debases the currency of humanity. And as no adequate attempt was made to arrest deterioration by the spread of education, it being the settled conviction of our forefathers that manual labour should be strictly divorced from intellectuality, the community of Oldbury (as of most industrial towns) found itself in a less enviable situation at the end of the first century of industrialism than at the beginning.

Most of our iron-working towns in their industrial infancy produced small wares which, for their marketing, were easy of transport. Thus Sheffield, which now produces the heaviest of armour plates, began with knives; and Wednesbury, which manufactures wheels and axles and other cumbrous forms of railway plant, at one time scarcely produced anything heavier than a door hinge. So it has been with Oldbury, and all the surrounding, Black Country parishes.

The oldest of the hardware trades in this region is nail-making. Its history is full of romance, and it still persists, though it has long since left the Wednesbury side, where it flourished in the fifteenth century, and is now practically confined to the Rowley district. The Pagets, whose descendants now enjoy the Marquisate of Anglesey, were Wednesbury nail-makers; Lord Dudley's descent is traced through the Parkes family, whose tombs are a feature of Wednesbury old church, and who also were in the nail trade there.

Another romance of the same type belongs to the Stourbridge side of the Black Country—the story of the founding of the Foley barony. Richard Foley was a small yeoman there in the time of Charles 1. He was an observant man, and noticed the immense loss of time and labour caused by the clumsy process then in use for dividing the rods of iron, in the making of the nails. The trade was fast being ruined by the competition of the Swedes, who were able to undersell the English market because, as Foley ascertained, they knew how to split the nail-rods by the use of machinery. Fired by his newly-acquired knowledge, Foley determined to find out the secret of this machinery. Suddenly he was missing from the neighbourhood of Stourbridge, and his own family did not know where he had gone; he remained away for several years. With little or no money in his pocket, it seems he got to Hull, worked a passage to Sweden, and eventually arrived at the Dannemora mines near Upsala, the only article of property in his possession being an old fiddle. Dick was a pleasant fellow and a capable fiddler, and he was not long in ingratiating himself with the iron-workers. Having in time acquired access to every part of the works, he keenly observed all the machinery employed for the process of iron-splitting, and when his mind had been fully stored, he suddenly disappeared from Sweden, and arrived back in England.

Supplied with funds by a Mr. Knight, of Stourbridge, he endeavoured to put his hard-gained knowledge to practical use; and the bitterness of his disappointment may be imagined when he found, after all his trouble, that his machinery would not work effectively. Richard Foley disappeared again—his neighbours said mortification at his failure had driven him away. But no. He was away back in Sweden, a simple-minded fiddler, being joyously welcomed by his old friends, the miners and the iron-workers. This time he was careful to discover the cause of his failure; made rough drawings and tracings of the machines; and presently returned to England to try again. A man of such purpose could not fail to achieve success. By his skill and industry he firmly established rod-splitting mills in this country, from which he in due time amassed a large fortune. Richard Foley was a man of benevolent disposition. He founded and endowed a school at Stourbridge; his son, Thomas, a great benefactor of Kidderminster, who was High Sheriff of Worcestershire in the time of the "Rump Parliament," founded and endowed the hospital at Old Swinford for the free education of poor children in the locality. All the early Foleys were Puritans, and the great Richard Baxter, in his "Life and Times," speaks highly of their just and blameless dealings in business. In the time of Charles II. the head of the family was ennobled with the title of Lord Foley of Kidderminster.

This romance of trade has been told by Samuel Taylor Coleridge, and retold with the usual moral by Dr. Smiles. And, like many other venerable legends, its authenticity has been challenged by the iconoclastic votaries of historic truth. The real hero of this trade romance is now said to have been a Bilston man named Brindley, who founded the Hyde Works at Kinver in the time of Charles II., and whose musical instrument was not a fiddle, but a flute as potent as that of the Pied Piper. Whatever element of truth there may be in this, it is tolerably certain that Brindley was not a Bilston man, for no such name can be traced in the Registers of that parish at that period.

Nail-making at one time or other has been common to every parish in the Black Country, and its tale has been told too often to need re-telling here. Volumes have been written about it—not so much about its romance as its abject sordidness, and the wretched return it brings the worker. Those few who got riches out of the trade, left off forging the nails and took to factoring them. We read of one Humphrey Hill, of Cradley who in 1625 is described as "a driver into the country with nails."

Here is an account written in 1786:—"The number of nailors within the county of Worcester *only* is small in comparison with the whole number in the counties of Worcester and Stafford ; by far the greatest part are in the county of Stafford, *viz.*, at Kingswinford, Wordesley, Brockmore, Brettel Lane, Gornal, Sedgley, Tipton, Corsley, Bromwich, Oldbury, Darlaston, Rowley, and other places, all bordering on the county of Worcester. There are different opinions respecting the number, but it is generally believed to be from 35,000 to 40,000; . . . the quantity of iron consumed weekly being 200 tons. The above comprises all ages and both sexes; both boys and girls begin to work by the time they are seven years old."

By the middle of last century women were still making nails for a penny an hour, conquered now by machines that poured out a stream of nails in tons upon tons every week.

The domiciliary workshop, in which the hours of labour are unregulated by the factory bell, has been a potent factor in the enslavement of the nailer. Yet the picturesque side of it has not gone undetected by the eye of the artist. In a fine etching, called "Wrought Nails," Sir Frank Short, P.R.E., has depicted some old nail shops at Cradley, near the historic site of Dud Dudley's famous "Cradley Forge," where he first "fined" his coal-smelted iron.

But neither art nor history has ever varied the sordid tale of this ill-paid form of industry. The inventive Dud tells us in his METTALLUM MARTIS that in 1665 there were "20,000 Smiths or Naylors at least dwelling near these parts, and taking of Prentices," who "have made their trade so bad that many of them are ready to starve and steal." And the artistic Sir Frank has written in the corner of his beautiful etching this pregnant inscription.

"By the sweat of their brow they—exist.
   Sunrise to them is over-late, and sundown but a lighting
     of their work-lamp.
As little sleep to them as may be, and not much, save
   smoke, to swallow.
Simple and sturdy hearts, men and women that work and
    make a nation,
   Where is your reward?
Great God! that there be nail-shops down in hell for other
   folk to try!"

74 OLDBURY AND ROUND ABOUT

Cradley Old Forge (Sir Frank Short, P.R.E.)

Nailing is one of the few derelict industries from pre-Factory Act days—an incongruous anachronism in these days of organised labour.

Another small item of production from the days when Birmingham was the toyshop of Europe is peculiar to this locality. At one time all the Jews' harps in the world were made in Rowley parish. The Barnsleys, of Cradley Road, were well-known makers. This instrument, for which the proper etymon is Jaws' harp, because it is played between the two jaws, is highly popular with the inhabitants of the lonely isle of St. Kilda. It is a primitive sort of musical instrument, the metal spring or vibrator producing only one note, and the variations to make the tune being effected by the player's mouth, the pitch of the note being determined by the size and shape of the mouth cavity, a skilful performer being capable of producing good musical intonations.

These days of small things could not continue for ever. Even corn, timber, wool, hides, and countless other commodities lost in value by the dearness of land-carriage. The advantages and cheapness of water-carriage where there were navigable rivers had become well-known. A cry was raised for the creation of artificial waterways, and nowhere more loudly than in this riverless plateau of mid-England. All over the country there were vast stores of natural wealth awaiting some form of cheap transit to make them really available—coal, salt, ironstone, lead, marble, limestone, and their various secondary products equally heavy for transport.

How canals widened the industrial horizon of the Black Country, and of Oldbury in particular, will be unfolded in the next chapter.

In each and every stage of the nation's commercial development, Oldbury was enabled to participate to the fullest extent in the general advance; first, with the improvement and turnpiking of the roads; then, with the introduction of the canals; and yet again at a later date with the making of the trunk railways. The exploiting of its mines had not to be attempted (as they had been at Wednesbury and Bilston, with the primitive appliances of the olden days) till it was possible to take advantage of the "multiplying" power of steam to facilitate their working.

Fortunate Oldbury may be said to have lain in the very heart of the coal and iron industries at the time when England was ceasing to be an ordinary self-supporting agricultural country, to become the only manufacturing country in the world. On the one side of it, at Soho, James Watt, in 1769, perfected the steam engine; and on the other, at Bradley, John Wilkinson, in 1768, successfully worked the first blast-furnace; enabled at last to employ the abundant mineral fuel of the district in the smelting of iron-ore. It was at the "mother furnace" of Bradley that the dream of Dud Dudley was eventually realised.

XVII.—THE COMING OF THE CANALS

The industrial evolution of this midland region, involving as it did the transport of coal, iron goods, and other descriptions of heavy traffic, now called for, and obtained, the provision of artificial waterways. The Grand Junction Canal was made to unite the ports of Bristol, Liverpool, and Hull; numerous subsidiary cuts followed. No place in England benefited more at the outset than the Potteries, earthenware as a freight being breakable as well as heavy.

Out of the Grand Trunk proceeded one branch to Fazeley, from whence was made a cut of $16\frac{1}{2}$ miles to Birmingham. The advent of canals on this side of Birmingham was heralded by an Act of Parliament in 1767, which authorised the making of a canal to connect that busy hardware town with the collieries at Wednesbury.

Till then the traffic of long trains of wagons laden with coals had ploughed up the roads. and made the highways a dismal spectacle. At a public meeting held at the Swan Inn, the famous engineer, Brindley, had produced plans and estimates for the construction of a navigable canal from Birmingham to "the principal coal works," recommending as the best route that over Birmingham Heath and Winson Green, through Smethwick and Oldbury, over Puppy Green, and through Tipton and Bilston, ultimately to join the Severn navigations beyond. The work was undertaken, and completed in 1769.

The route specified in the Act was "from New Hall Ring, adjoining to Birmingham, and from such other places near the same . . . to or near Smethwick, Oldbury, Tipton Green, and Bilstone, near several large Coal Mines and Stone Quarries, to go as near Wolverhampton as the level will admit of; or near Autherley, otherwise Alderley, there to join with the canal now making between the Severn and Trent: And also to make two collateral cuts as near to such Coal Mines as conveniently may be; one of which to be made through the Lands of —— Abney (widow) near Oldbury, and to be continued from thence by Girt's Green and Brickhouse Lane up, or near to, Wednesbury Holloway; and the other to near Toll End and up or near to Ocker Hill." No growing timber was to be cut down, and no manor house interfered with, though warehouses and watch-houses might be erected in suitable places.

On a plan, published in 1771, of the canal from Birmingham to "Aldersbury" near Wolverhampton, "with the collateral cut to the Coal Mines at Wednesbury," appear the following names of places along the route immediately after leaving Birmingham:—"(1) Sandpits, (2) Lodge, (3) Winson Green, (4) Pigmill Forge, (5) Mr. Robinson's, (6) French Walls, (7) Smithwick Hall, (8) Ruck of Stones, (9) Blugates, (10) Holt Hall, and (11) Spon Lane, where the collateral cut branches to the right." Evidently these were the names of places well-known, if they were not exactly landmarks, along the route. When the canal was improved a dozen years later, two streams at Smethwick, "called the Thimble Mill and the Blue Gate Streams, were turned under the said canal for the use of the mills of Abraham Spooner and Heneage Legge, Esqrs.," and to carry the water to the aforementioned "Pig Mill."

In 1782 public meetings were again held in Birmingham for effecting some very necessary improvements in the canal navigations, and for their further extension by collateral cuts. All the proposals were carried and the new works duly put into execution.

Among the new places mentioned in the Act of 1783 were "Dunkirk Farm" and the "Waste of West Bromwich" (*i.e.*, the heath, or common land); "Willingsworth Hall Pool" and "an Old Fire Engine at Broadwaters" (Savary's engine put down in 1739); the "lands of Bayley Caddick" at Toll End, and "the late John Wood's Engine Forge" (the Wood family were famous Staffordshire iron-masters of Wolverhampton and Wednesbury); the lands of Thomas Hoo "in Wednesbury Open Field" and the lands of the same proprietor at Lea Brook, "opposite to Taylor's Engine lying upon the Road leading from Ocker Hill to Wednesbury" (this abandoned engine was probably one of Newcomen's atmospheric engines, for both of those early types had been tried for pumping the Wednesbury coal mines).

It was enacted that the proprietors of all "fire engines," as they then called steam engines, should lift the water out of the pits into the canals; and the company took powers to erect their own pumping engines in the water-logged region of "Broadwaters in the parish of Wednesbury." The cut from Ryders Green (which actually was a green in those days) to the "Fire Engine Coal Mines" at Broadwaters was $4\frac{1}{2}$ miles, with a fall of 46 feet.

By way of "Lock Dues," fourpence per ton was payable on all "coal, coak, and ironstone" passing from the mines into the Birmingham canal.

From Broadwaters, which is near Moxley, a branch canal was made to Walsall, and another to Bradley; also cuts communicated with Bloomfield at Tipton, and Deep fields. A Dudley Extension Canal linked up Netherton with Windmill End, Coombes Wood, and Halesowen. And so there gradually grew up a network of navigable waterways, the value and utility of which it is difficult, in these days of railway and motor transit, to rightly estimate.

The easier and cheaper method of water-carriage, in boats holding 25 tons of coal, could not but give an impetus to the trade of the entire district, in which Oldbury failed not to reap a full share of the advantages. It is estimated that by the close of the eighteenth century the collieries between Birmingham and Wolverhampton were raising 15,000 tons of coal per week; of which it is computed 5,000 tons were used in Wednesbury, Walsall, Bilston, Tipton, Dudley, Oldbury, and West Bromwich; 2,000 tons went to Wolverhampton,

Bridgnorth, and other places on the Severn; and 8,000 passed into Birmingham and places beyond.

And not only did the new artificial waterways foster the traffic in raw minerals, but early in the nineteenth century Oldbury boasted blast-furnaces for the production of pig-iron, and steelworks, the heavy productions of which needed cheap freightage to ensure their prosperity. The canals certainly brought the barge-building yards, and probably suggested the brick and tile works.

Of the improvement of the new waterway carried out in 1789, a Birmingham newspaper in the June of that year records "that the stupendous work now carrying on by the proprietors of our navigation at the Sumnit, near Smethwick, is at this time so far advanced that we understand the water will be let in to its new course within a very few days."

The canal terminus in Birmingham was at the Old Wharf in Paradise Row. Previously coal had been carried from the Black Country pits by horse wagons, and weighed on the town machine, which stood at the bottom of Great Charles Street. With the introduction of water-carriage this heavy traffic was diverted to the new and cheaper means of transport, and coal was now sold in Birmingham as low as fourpence per hundredweight of 120lbs. The Birmingham poet, Freeth, could not refrain from celebrating this in verse:

> There never in war was for victory won,
> A cause that deserved such respects from the town;
> Then revel in gladness, let harmony flow
> From the district of Bordesley to Paradise Row,
> For true-feeling joy in each breast must be wrought
> When coals under fivepence per hundred are bought.

James Brindley's canal came to be thought nothing better than "a crooked ditch," into which the boat horses were constantly staggering from the ill-kept towing-paths. Besides which, the inconvenience of bringing boats up and down the "watery ladder," the summit of which was 460 feet above sea level, induced the company in 1824 to call in the aid of Telford to cut through the highest portion of the ground, and so reduce the number of locks. This was the last improvement before the canals were eclipsed by the railways.

But there have been incidents in the history of the local canals more noteworthy than any associated with its railways.

In connection with the erection of certain iron bridges over the canal in the Birmingham district, the great Duke of Wellington paid his only visit to this part of the country in 1830. On this occasion his carriage was stoned by a mob, owing to his opposition to the Bill for Catholic Emancipation. In company with Sir Robert Peel, he made a trip along the canal in the directors' state barge. At that time the canal company ran swift packet boats, drawn by three horses, for passenger traffic. It was by this method of locomotion the British Association, in 1839, made an excursion from Birmingham, at which place they were holding their annual conclave.

This excursion was the only one made by the Association that year. It was to the Rowley Hills and to what Professor Phillips termed "those marvellous works of art, the Dudley Caverns," which, "by the liberality of Lord Ward," were illuminated on a grand scale by 1,600 dozen candles.

The day of the excursion was wretchedly wet, and Professor Edward Forbes, who was one of the party, wrote some lines on the event, which lie described as "A light set off to the Dryness of the Report of the British Association Meeting." It began:

> Come, listen, all as members be,
>   Whether of Sections A, B, C,
> D, or else of E, F. G,
>   As go to Dudley by water!
> As how from Brummagem we set
> Upon one Friday very wet,
> To gather stones, and fossils get,
>   All at Dudley by water!

The Association was but eight years old then, and this was the way its young lions roared. They made a great joke of their "voyage" through Oldbury. On passing one of the canal locks, boats had to hand a "manifest" to the canal company's clerk, in order that the proper dues might be collected for the freight; on this occasion the document read:—"Draught, 13 inches. Weight, $3\frac{1}{4}$ tons. Cargo, Philosophers."

It was on the next occasion of the Association meeting in Birmingham, in 1849, that Sir Roderick Murchison was playfully crowned "King of Siluria" within the vast lime-stone walls of Dudley Castle Caverns, in recognition of his researches into the scientific history of the Silurian system of rocks. The development of these useful limestone deposits owed not a little to the cutting of the canal through the district.

At that time a covered "market boat," as it was called, drawn by two horses, plied three times a week between Birmingham and Wolverhampton.

The time-bills which advertised the daily service of these Swift Packets between Birmingham and Wolverhampton were as fraudulently seductive as any advertisements of the kind could be. They were ornamented by a rough woodcut, which depicted a sort of gondola ploughing its watery way between finely wooded banks, and traversing a country of extraordinary natural beauty. As a matter of fact, the barge was a sort of elongated house-boat, drawn at a jog-trot by a pair of sorry steeds rope-harnessed to it, one of them ridden bare-backed by a Black Country urchin. While as to the landscape through which the journey was made, the best that can be said of it was—well, it was the newest and therefore the lightest fringe of the dingy Black Country. The inside of the boat was accounted "first class" accommodation, and the outside top of the cabin was second class." It was a common practice for poor folk, journeying from town to town along the tow-path, to throw their loads or bundles to some friendly passenger on the outside deck, and to recover their property at the nearest lock to their destination—a cheap way of getting their luggage or marketings carried home, of which many an Oldbury man was wont to avail himself in those easy-going, simple-minded days.

A Birmingham advertisement, of which the following is a copy, explains itself.

EXCURSION TO DUDLEY CASTLE.
Admission Ticket, 1/6.
ON TUESDAY, JUNE 20TH, 1843,
the Packet starts from the
WAGON AND HORSES, FRIDAY BRIDGE,
at half-past six o'clock precisely.

These "fly-boats," as they were called, continued to ply regularly along the canal through Smethwick and Oldbury, until such time as they were superseded by the train service of the Stour Valley Railway, which line runs alongside this waterway for several miles of the distance.

It is a long cry from the days of ill-kept roads and slow, horse-drawn wagons to these days of fast railways and express goods trains; it is the difference between an output of Jews' harps and clout nails and one of anvils and ships' anchors.

Gratifying as such progress must be, it is scarcely creditable to the commercial genius of this country that it should have provided no alternative method of transport capable of relieving the scandalous congestion of traffic which generally occurs on the principal railway systems whenever exceptional industrial activity happens to prevail. The deficiency, however, is to be made good in the immediate future by the Waterways Association, whose efforts will undoubtedly benefit the Midlands. The Trent is at once to be made navigable from the Humber to Nottingham for 100-ton barges, and the time occupied by the passage reduced from 57 hours to 31 hours, or possibly to 22 hours by working double shifts. From Nottingham the canals will be made to take 30-ton barges, which will reach this midland area via Burton-on-Trent, the distance to Birmingham being 63 miles, and Wolverhampton 78 miles. The local authorities of the places en route are to participate in the control of these improved and much to be desired waterways.

XVIII.—THE OLDBURY MINING DISTRICT

Oldbury, like Dudley, is a Worcestershire town falling within the benign influences of the prosperous South Staffordshire Coalfield. And so it has grown into a Black Country manufacturing town of some importance.

The main part of the coalfield lies within the county which names it, but the fringe of it extends some four miles into the northern part of Worcestershire, where also lies the small accompanying coalfield of Rubery.

The discovery of coal in Halesowen dates back to the fourteenth century; in 1607 a tenant of the manor was getting coal at Cole Pytt Leasow, near Coombes Wood, at a profit of 40/- a week; and in 1794 good coal was still being gotten at Coombes Wood. But the mere possession of mineral resources is not in itself sufficient. Coal, for instance, must exist in workable quantities; facilities must be found for putting it on the market; and other considerations enter into the question. That good coal and plenty of it existed at Oldbury, and that the new canals found a good and ready market for it, speedily developed the place into a thriving colliery region; and by the middle of the nineteenth century Oldbury had all the industrial and social characteristics that had belonged to Wednesbury and Bilston and the older parts of the coalfield for a century or so.

What were the conditions of industrial life in such a region may best be gathered from the records of concrete happenings.

Even with the advances made in the methods of working the seam, the coal-mining of Oldbury was not free from the usual toll on the lives of the colliers, and one fatal accident in the July of 1866 raised a legal question of some importance at the time. The Mines Inspection Act of 1860 required that places which were suspected of being foul, though they were not in actual working, should be fenced off so as to prevent any person going into them. At the Bromford Colliery of Mr. W. H. Dawes was an old gate-road, which was known to contain choke damp, yet was not properly fenced off. Three pit boys walked into it, and were suffocated. Then the question of responsibility was raised. Did it lie with the owner, Mr. Dawes, or with the Charter-master? When Mr. J. Cope was proceeded against, he pleaded that he was Consulting Mining Agent, and not an agent responsible according to the provisions of the Mines Inspection Act. The Stipendiary Magistrate, however, decided that he was the responsible person under the Act. The effect of the decision was to make any Consulting Mining Agent, or Engineer, responsible for the safe working of any mine in connection with which he gave professional advice or assistance.

On November 9th, 1846, a very serious fire-damp explosion occurred at Rounds Green Colliery, concerning which Mr. Smyth was appointed by the Home Secretary to hold an inquiry. His report showed that no efficient system of ventilation had been employed at the colliery. It appeared that there were two shafts of about 180 yards deep, and 7 feet in diameter, near to each other; and that there was not sufficient difference between the weights of the columns of air in the two to produce a serviceable ventilating current. Nor, again, had the abandoned parts of the workings been shut off properly, and consequently large quantities of fire-damp accumulated in these old workings, and often found their way into the gate-roads. The outcome of this inquiry was the submission of Mr. Sinyth's report to two expert scientists, Sir H. T. De la Beche and Dr. Lyon Playfair, who had no hesitation in advising the authorities that such a condition of things called for the establishment of a Government system of mine inspection.

Strangely enough, soon after, when the first Act for the inspection of coal mines had been passed, a disastrous explosion occurred at the Ramrod Hall Colliery; this was on August 13th, 1856, and eleven lives were lost. In this case the pit had been idle for four days; again the shafts were about equal in length, and there was no furnace to assist the ventilation. The Charter-master, or "butty," being anxious to resume working as quickly as possible, and regardless of warm weather and a low barometer, sent down eight men without making any preliminary examination for the fire-damp which was almost sure to have accumulated. The men detected the gas immediately they reached the bottom, and signalled for a lighted safety lamp to be sent down. Instead of complying, the "butty" himself got into the skip, along with seven more men, taking a shovelful of fire with them, and they had not descended twenty yards before, naturally enough, a tremendous explosion occurred. All the eight men in the skip lost their lives, as well as three the others at the bottom of the shaft. The fatuity of the old-time butty-collier was responsible for countless "accidents" of this type.

Another type of accident, not infrequent in those days of the "rule of thumb," was the boiler explosion, which, in connection with colliery winding or pumping engines, was doubly disastrous. One such fatal explosion occurred to a much-worn balloon boiler at Rounds Green Colliery in the March of 1857; and another, to a cylindrical boiler of good plates, usually working at 40lbs to the square inch, occurred in the following December at Bullocks Farm Colliery, Spon Lane.

In the old colliery life of the Black Country there were often economic troubles as well as mechanical disasters. Sixty years ago, ere the police system had been properly organised, and the old parish constables were still in existence, the mining towns were ill-equipped to cope with the gangs of riotous miners who not infrequently swept through the district when strikes and trade disputes disturbed the economic serenity of the district. At that time the Earl of Dudley was the largest mining magnate hereabouts, possessing nearly 400 pits and having 5,000 miners in his employ, and these chiefly on the Dudley and Rowley side of his property. The larger coalmasters of the vicinity also included Lord Dartmouth, Messrs. Dawes, Halford, and a score of others. During a notable strike in 1860 some twenty thousand miners took part, and eventually the military had to be called out to deal with the situation.

One mob, after spreading terror and consternation in Tipton, marched to Oldbury, where one of the first acts committed by the lawless band was to burst open the cells adjoining the old Court House, in which a few prisoners for debt were confined. These were all liberated, and they immediately put their liberty to use by taking a hasty departure from the scene of their incarceration; one prisoner, an old Jew belonging to Birmingham, caused much amusement by his oriental effusiveness in calling out, "Dod bless the colliers!" On the same occasion in the Old Hill and Darby End district some very exciting scenes were witnessed; the strikers took up a position on some slag heaps at Withymoor, and when the cavalry came up to disperse them, greeted the soldiers with showers of missiles consisting of stones and lumps of cinder. Before the disturbance could be quelled a large number of men had been seriously injured.

These were some of the industrial and economic troubles in the earlier stages of Oldbury's mining industry. By this time the coal mines of Wednesbury and Bilston were largely failing, while those of West Bromwich and Oldbury were highly flourishing—the centre of gravity in the famous coalfield had moved southwards.

XIX.—MINERAL RESOURCES AND MINING ENTERPRISE

By the year 1860 signs were not wanting, in that part of the South Staffordshire Coalfield which had been longest worked, that the once vast deposits of mineral wealth were becoming rapidly exhausted. It was therefore a source of new hope and quickened enterprise to discover that there were valuable extensions of the thick coal, ironstone, associated measures, beneath the Permian strata at Sandwell and the Rowley Hills. About that period a Royal Commission,was inquiring into the nation's coal supply. In the locality mentioned expensive trial pits were sunk; for theoretical geology was now boldly endeavouring to justify its logical conclusions that the coal would probably be found beneath the Permian and Triassic rocks. The sinkings at Sandwell between 1870 and 1873 were successful in proving this; the "downthrow" here was from 80 to 120 yards. After finding several minor coal seams, the thick coal, of excellent quality and nearly seven yards through it, was pierced at a depth of 420 yards in 1874.

The famous "thick coal" of South Staffordshire is really made up of several seams, and attains to a thickness of fiftly feet in the southern part of the Black Country.

Within the limits of this coalfield the extreme depth of the coal is about 1,200 feet in the south, and less than 2,000 feet in the northern part.

The visible, or exposed, part of the South Staffordshire and East Worcestershire Coalfield extended from Brereton on the north to Frankley Beeches on the south, and from Wolverhampton and Himley Wood on the west to West Bromwich and Walsall Wood on the east. This older, or better known, area of the carboniferous field is almost surrounded by a series of red sandstones, marls, and pebblebeds, constituting part of the Permian and Triassic formations. The boundary lines between these and the coal measures were by "faults," but for years the nature of these boundary lines was very imperfectly known. The sinking of the Heath Pits near West Bromwich, and tests made at Himley, Kingswinford, and other places at this period all went to show that the boundary lines were faults having large "throws," and that the coal measures would probably be found if the Permian and Triassic rocks were pierced.

Sinkings made in 1864 by Mr. W. H. Dawes at Manor Farm, near Halesowen, a mile outside the known productive area of the coalfield,. resulted in the discovery, at a depth of 300 yards, of a three-feet coal seam, believed to be a part of the famous thick coal. A level driven out from the bottom of one of the shafts, 430 feet deep, in the direction of Old Hill, ran into the thick coal at a distance of a thousand yards from the shaft. A similar trial at Wassell Grove, near Hagley, had no better result; for the coat measures here appeared to deteriorate, thin out, and finally die away. The cost of the two experiments was no less than £30,000.

The exhaustion of the mines became more apparent as the century advanced, and in the Spon Lane district of West Bromwich and the Rood End portion of Oldbury heavy losses were incurred. The Blakeley Hall mining enterprise, started about 1880, was a conspicuous failure in the annals of the coal trade. The undertaking was initiated when the industry was in the full tide of its prosperity, and the prospects of this colossal undertaking were regarded as quite good. Two large shafts were sunk in one interesting corner of Worcestershire, but immediately adjoining the Staffordshire boundary, and also close to well-known and extensive seams of coal. Not only had adjacent mines yielded abundantly, but a portion of the Blakeley Hall estate, consisting of about 82 acres, had been procured from the Bromford Colliery, belonging to Messrs. Dawes, which for many years was a most profitable concern. Gate-roads were driven from these pits through a portion of the Blakeley area to the Birmingham and Oldbury turnpike road, and the coal all along the line was reported to be of excellent quality. The directors were thereupon emboldened to launch out on a vast scale to work what was computed to be a fifty-year supply of high-grade fuel. But after four years' operation the undertaking had to be abandoned at a sacrifice of £80,000 in consequence of the discovery of a huge "fault," the dangers attending the work, and the risk of tapping a large pound of water that was known to stretch away to Spon Lane. Strange to say, all the usual coal-bearing measures were found, but without the coal. The "fault" had falsified the high hopes of all the mining experts, and the failure of the Blakeley Hall Colliery dealt a heavy blow to coal-getting enterprise in the Black Country.

From Sedgley to Rowley Regis stretches across the Black Country, in a south-easterly direction, that low range of hills which is such a conspicuous feature in the landscape, viewed from either the Wednesbury or the Stourbridge side. Though seeming to form one range, the hills vary greatly in structure. The western portion, comprising the Sedgley Hills, Wren's Nest Hill, and Dudley Castle Hill, are formed of uplifted Silurian limestone. The eastern summits, from Cawney Hill to Rowley Regis, are formed of the coal measures, capped by an extensive sheet of basalt, locally known as Rowley ragstone.

While the coal was known to crop out against the bases of the Sedgley and Dudley Hills, it seemed to pass uninterruptedly beneath the Rowley Hills. But it remained an unsolved problem whether the coal here was workable, or worth working. Was the layer of basalt very thick? Had the coal, if it existed, been burnt or rendered worthless by the basalt when it flowed out hot from the earth's interior? When the tunnel for the Birmingham canal was cut through the base of the Rowley Hill in 1856 no basalt had been met with. This augured well; for it might be that the basalt had been poured out in a thin sheet through a small volcanic pipe that pierced the coal measures. So mining engineers determined to put the matter to the test. In 1867 pits sunk through the hills at Tividale found coal at a depth of 230 yards, without encountering the basalt. Similar successes afterwards accrued at other places in the hills, though the pits sunk by Lord Dudley in 1874 at Lye Cross passed through 65 yards of basalt, met with at a depth of 11 yards from the surface, before striking the thick coal, at a depth of 220 yards.

When the lower part of the basalt was reached, vast quantities of water poured into the shafts. To deal with the flooding of the South Staffordshire and East Worcestershire Coalfield an Act of Parliament was passed in 1873, which empowered a Commission to carry out a comprehensive system of mines drainage, and charge the expense, levied in proper proportions, upon the various mine-owners interested. The coal, situated on a table-land containing the sources of the Stour and other feeders of the Severn, and of the Tame and other tributaries of the Trent, was peculiarly liable to floods, and the first step undertaken by the Commission was to deal with the surface drainage, making good the beds of all the streams in the district. The pumping of the deep water came afterwards. The average height of the visible coalfield, stretching from Brereton to Halesowen, is 500 feet above mean sea level, while the average height of the strip of country bordering it is only 400 feet. It therefore follows that the coalfield stands up well above the surrounding country, and as it is largely bounded by gigantic "faults," and the dip of the beds appears to be away from the coalfield, the underground waters to be dealt with are mainly due to percolation from the surface. Viewed as a whole, the coalfield is self-contained as a drainage area, having to deal mainly with its own rainfall, which has been calculated at 350 million gallons per annum for every square mile.

In setting about the task of coping with this plague of underground water, it was at once decided that the part of the coalfield lying to the north of the Bentley "fault" should be exempted from the operations of the Act, leaving the remainder, stretching from Rushall to the Clent Hills, to receive the active attentions of the Drainage Commissioners. This drainage area was then divided into five subsidiary districts, of which Oldbury was one; the others being Old Hill, Kingswinford, Tipton, and Bilston. The first rate to meet the operations of the Act was levied August 4th, 1874, at 1d. per ton on all coal, slack, fireclay, etc., raised within the affected area.

The Oldbury Mines Drainage District was bounded by the Dudley Port Trough Fault, the Rowley Hills, and a line drawn in an arbitrary manner past Sandwell Park. The Old Hill District lies to the east of the Kingswinford District and the south of the Tipton and Oldbury Districts.

The surface drainage was carried out mainly by the puddling of all brooks and canals, the drainage of large pools and swags, while not a few of the natural watercourses were advantageously straightened. Still, the waters continued to rise in the various underground pounds. The troubles of the Commissioners were great, and the Act had to be amended to endow them with greater powers. The Oldbury and Kingswinford Districts promptly voted themselves out of the operations of the Act, so far as the drainage of the mines was concerned, and undertook to unload their pits of water by the employment of privately-owned pumping engines.

There is no necessity to chronicle here all the difficulties of the South Staffordshire Mines Drainage Commissioners, but it was quite twenty years before, as the result of much costly experience, the work of the Commission made any real progress. Basins had to be shut off from each other, a well-calculated concentration of pumping power had to be effected, and many expensive operations undertaken, ere tile Act could be said to be working with that material advantage to the local mining industry which its original promoters had contemplated. And yet, in 1903, it was estimated that not less than forty million tons of coal were water-logged in this midland coalfield.

The continuation of workable coal had been demonstrated at Sandwell in 1874 and at Hamstead in 1880. This led to trial sinkings at Baggeridge Woods, where the carboniferous rocks were struck in 1897—a coal seam 20 feet thick and of superior quality, 556 yards down. In 1902 the coal was struck at Himley, at a depth of 580 yards, after an expenditure of £30,000—a "come" of water exceeding 60,000 gallons per minute having necessitated the employment of powerful and costly pumping appliances.

In the Oldbury district, as in some of the others, ironstone was mined as well as the coal. So was fireclay, beds of which stretch from Bilston and Tipton towards The Lye, Cradley, and Stourbridge. As excellent fireclay is found in the Stour Valley, so is good brick clay everywhere in the Oldbury district. Bricks made from the famous blue clay are as hard as iron, and more durable. For the making of bricks, tiles, and similar products, nearly a million tons of clay is dug out annually in this locality. Also in the region of the Rowley Hills some 200,000 tons of basalt are mined or quarried every year, to be used chiefly as a paving material, than which there is no road metal in the world more serviceable.

XX.—THE BRADES WORKS

The canals had opened out the collieries, had steadily developed the mines of iron ore and limestone, and had given to the entire mineral wealth of the district that fluidity which engenders manufacturing activity and leads to commercial prosperity. The iron and steel trade took firm root here as early as anywhere in the Black Country.

The Brades Works, on the confines of Oldbury, is the oldest of its kind in the Midlands; its furnaces, kilns, and factories, its workshops, warehouses, and wharves cover several acres of land. Its original founders were George Cabel Adkins and Frank Adkins, and the firm was subsequently joined by George Heaton, of Birmingham.

On the death of the Adkins partners, the undertaking was incorporated under the Companys Act, and the business has long been carried on under the style and title of William Hunt and Sons (The Brades), Limited.

The firm is celebrated throughout England and America, if not the whole civilised world, for the quality and cheapness of its edge tools. The Brades trowel, for instance, rules the market for that class of goods, and of these wielded by American masons, it was calculated, only a few decades ago, that ninety-nine in every hundred bore the trade mark of this firm. This fact was put on record in 1868 by the American Consul then resident in Birmingham, the cultured and genial Elihu Burritt.

Burritt was known as "the learned blacksmith," who, while working at his trade, devoted his leisure to the learning of languages, acquiring in this way a thorough knowledge of Latin, Greek, Hebrew, Arabic, and most of the modern European languages. His country honoured him by making him her Consular representative in this great Midland manufacturing district; and no American — or other foreign expert, for the matter of that—ever brought to bear on his task a keener insight into the, industrial affairs of a community, or a finer appreciation of that which he found to be meritorious therein, than did this literary genius whose business it was to report all that he saw here in the way of trade, manufacture, and commerce to the Department of State at Washington.

It is therefore worth taking note of anything he has to say, in his WALKS IN THE BLACK COUNTRY, concerning any of our manufacturing towns or establishments.

Of the Brades Works he says they are "the growth of a century of accretion, each decade of the century seemingly adding its independent structure, so that the whole looks like a small village of buildings annexed to each other by narrower roads between them than the public streets of a town." This is simply vivid description; there is nothing meant to be unkindly in it; it is not a sneer of our English methods of developing a business haphazard, instead of "scrapping" old and obsolete plant, and entirely rebuilding out-of-date factories, as they do in the go-ahead States.

"It is truly a representative establishment," he continues, "embracing in itself nearly all the industries and productions of the district. I doubt if such another can be found in England or the world for this remarkable variety of enterprise." Surely this is no small praise from a Yankee, and a critic of his calibre.

Then he proceeds to illustrate the variety and commercial versatility which strikes him so forcibly. "In the first place the Company have sunk seven pairs of coal mines around their works. Most of the good coal they sell, using themselves the refuse for their furnaces and forges. They also own and work their own iron ore. Then from the furnace to the forge, from pig to bar, goes this raw material to their manufactures. The iron, now ready for its hundred uses, parts company for several stages of manipulation, then unites again in infinite shapes and relations.

"A portion is selected with great care for the carbonating kilns, or ovens, in which it is, as it were, seethed and saturated with the fire and fumes of charcoal. It now comes out blistered steel, fit for working up into tools that do not require a cutting edge; and a considerable quantity is used at this stage for such purposes.

But most of it is now broken up into short pieces for the terrible crucibles, or melting pots, of the air furnaces. If anyone has a curiosity to know how air may be made to act on combustion, or how the air-draught power has been developed, let him study the simple economy and arrangement of these furnaces. There is a large range of about twenty of them, all under draught if not blast at once.

Nebuchadnezzar's furnace, seven times heated, was a kitchen fire compared with one of these for heat.

"Each is charged with its covered pot full of blistered steel, with coal to match. Their lidded mouths dull the roaring sound of the terrible combustion, but the furnacemen show by their looks the intensity of the heat. The pouring off sight is *really* thrilling. When the lid is removed from each furnace, and the pot of molten metal lifted out by a pair of long-handled tongs with rounded jaws, even a spectator must have steady nerves to look at it. To speak of white heat, or the heat of molten gold or silver, would be like comparing the flame of a yellow tallow candle with the magnesium light. As the stalwart men, naked to their waists, remove the cover from the pot and pour the fluid into flasks for ingots, the brightness is almost blinding, even to one standing at the distance of several paces. As the whizzing stream runs into the mould, it emits a sparkling gray dashed with rainbow tints from various ignited gases. When the metal is sufficiently cooled and hardened, it is taken from the moulds in ingots or bars of cast steel about twenty inches in length and an inch and a-half square. It is then rolled, and hammered into all sizes and shapes, each operation refining and fitting it for the finest uses, to which it is converted in the smith-shops of the establishment.

"Most of the iron made into cast steel and shear steel comes from Sweden, and it is the best for the purpose yet found in the world. In fact, no really good edge-tool can be made of any other. The English makes good blistered steel for wagon springs and common tools; but does not combine toughness with hardness sufficiently for axes, cutlery, and even hoes and hammers. Still, the quality of steel made of English iron has been so much improved by the new processes lately introduced that the Swedish has been considerably reduced in price.

"The Brades Works use themselves most of the steel they make in the manufacture of their agricultural and other tools. They get better prices for the steel they sell than any other house in England, except Huntsman, of Sheffield. They supplied the pen trade of Birmingham up to about 1850, at which time the rolled cast steel was reduced to 38/- per cwt., and Sheffield took the business.

"They make their own files for economy's sake, as they last so much longer when made of such steel as they manufacture themselves.

"First on the list of the Brades manufactory, as a special distinction, are their famous trowels, which in their line of use and excellence are equal to the celebrated Toledo blades in the implemental machinery of war. They are fully as elastic as any sword-blades, and can be bent double either way without a permanent crook. Plantation hoes rank next to trowels in their celebrity. Vast quantities are sent both to the United States and Brazil; those for the latter country are full twice the weight of the former. As they axe for the cultivation of cotton in both countries, the difference in size and weight is singular.

"The union of machine labour in their production has been brought to great perfection. The rolling-mill and trip-hammer do the greatest part of the work. In the first place, the moulds or patterns are formed. The cast steel is edged, or chamfered, in the bar, then cut into lengths of three or four inches to correspond with the width of the hoe-pattern. The borax weld is often made complete at one heat, and never more than two are taken. This operation is performed by the common hand-sledge and hammer; and nothing but a firm weld of the steel to the iron is sought for. The pattern or form thus steeled goes next to the great trip-hammer, which brings it out to its required size and thickness. Thence it is taken to the anvil of the smith-shop, where the eye is formed with remarkable tact and celerity, and the blade trimmed into shape with the shears.

"It may serve to show the facility and fertility of their production, to say that four men will steel twenty dozen a day of these great hoes. The iron is worth from £8 10s. 0d. to £10 per ton, and the steel from 42/- to 45/- per cwt. It takes about three pounds of iron and six ounces of steel per hoe. The small coal, mostly used, costs on delivery about 7/- per ton.

I have dwelt (says our super-blacksmith) more fully upon trowels and hoes as the manufacture which has won for the Brades Works their especial reputation abroad. But they turn out a prodigious number of all the implements known to agricultural labour—shovels, spades, forks, garden-hoes, chaff-cutters, steel mould-boards for ploughs, and other articles of almost infinite variety and use. It may suffice to show the variety in design, shape, and size of one class of these articles to say, that the model department of the establishment contains 4,000 different patterns for straw-cutting machines, and nearly 2,000 patterns for cast steel mould-boards for ploughs!

"Now, considering that, with the exception of the iron imported from Sweden for making their cast steel, the Brades Works draw all the material they manufacture into their infinitely-varied implements from the bowels of the earth around and under them, one cannot contemplate their operations and productions without admiration. Indeed, they constitute one of the chief Lions of the Black Country.

"I said, under them; which is literally true, for the whole village of buildings comprising the establishment has sunk full eleven feet below their first level. Once their foundations stood higher than the canal that runs by their side. The top of the canal is now nearly as high as their caves, as it has been watched by rangers who have kept up its first level, while the furnace and forge buildings with all their chimneys have sunk from being undermined.

"In returning to the railway station we saw a score of houses sunk up to their knees, and we looked down from the street upon floors once above its level, but now four or five feet below it. This is a characteristic feature of the

Black Country. Everywhere you have the signs and presentiment of treacherous foundation. You see buildings that have subsided from their first levels at different angles of deflection, one end often sinking lower than the other, and making a rent in the walls.

Some go down pretty evenly, like the Brades Works. Right under these terrible furnaces the moles are at work night and day rooting out walks through deep coal seams. Under the foundations of tall-steepled churches, all a-light with the evening lamps and resounding with the voices of devotion, the pickmen are at work grubbing lanes under towns, hills, railways, and canals. Everybody seems to feel that they live, labour, eat, and sleep on a very uncertain and unsteady footing.

A house seldom, if ever, sinks so deep that its occupants have to escape through the roof. The railways and canals, which require better levels, have to be looked to with some care; but no serious disasters have ever occurred in this district in consequence of this honeycombing of its under-priming."

It is the charm and accuracy of Burritt's writing that justifies the length of this extract.

XXI.—The Chance Interest

The new activities of Oldbury found expression in other directions than in the iron trade.

If the Brades Works is the most time-honoured industrial concern, the business establishments of Messrs. Chance run it a very close second. And fortunately for the town the interests of this firm lay in an entirely different line of business.

In the earlier hall of the last century there was a popular lecturer and social worker labouring in this district, named Charles Hicks. Here is an extract from a lecture delivered locally by him in 1850—it was entitled "A Walk Through Smethwick":—

"Returning [from the London Works of Messrs. Fox, Henderson, and Co.] to the canal side we approach the French Walls, the property of Boulton and

Portrait of Sir James T. Chance, Bart.
(J. C. Horseley, R.A.)

Watt, but occupied by George Frederick Muntz, Esq., M.P. for Birmingham, eccentric as a politician—neither Tory, Whig, nor Radical—but an honest, useful, and independent member of the Senate withal, carrying on here a lucrative and extensive business, guarded by a patent, in the manufacture of zinc and copper plates for the sheathing of the, under surface of ships. So you see the 'French Walls,' the derivation of which appellation I know not, are employed in promoting the efficiency and durability of the 'Wooden Walls' of Old England.

"Pursuing our way, we at last come to the confine of the parish, whereon stands the immense establishment of Messrs. Chance. Call you this prodigious work, which includes masonry enough almost to build a town, and men, women, and children, artizans and labourers enow to people a colony; where, some time ago, nearly as much as £2,000 were weekly paid in wages alone, and which establishment, before the abolition of the glass duty, contributed to the national revenue something like £150,000 a year! Call you such a vast concern as this nothing? I am quite sure that if such a great manufactory, giving employment and support to so many hundreds of the industrious classes, could be removed to some such large town or city as Shrewsbury, Worcester, or Hereford, which are pining into atrophy for the want of some great staple manufacture, those places would deem your Spon Lane Glass Works a most valuable importation, a mighty temporal benefit. The production in several kinds of glass in this establishment is prodigious, but particularly in window glass. Latterly has been added to it a wing for that most beautiful and fascinating branch of art, the staining and painting in glass, in the processes of which there is now great improvement over the old methods. Several splendidly emblazoned windows for our churches, cathedrals, colleges, and civic halls have issued from this department of Messrs. Chance's works. In the recent Exposition of Arts and Sciences in Birmingham, Messrs. Chance exhibited some exquisite specimens of this artistic order.

Before quitting this establishment we must pay Messrs. Chance a tribute of high praise for the philanthropic spirit evinced by them in the erection of neat and commodious School Houses for the benefit of the children of the workmen in their employ and other residents in that populous vicinity. I know nothing of the condition or internal management of this educational establishment, but I do admire and commend the noble spirit of this firm, and the good purpose for which so much money has been liberally expended by them."

This is independent opinion, and as such worthy of respect.

Certainly a name pre-eminent in the commercial life of Oldbury is that of Messrs. Chance, who early in the last century established the Glass Works at Spon Lane, on the confines of the parish, and subsequently the Chemical Works a mile distant in the heart of it.

Glass-making in the Midlands is an industry which stretches at long intervals from Birmingham to Stourbridge, where several branches of it are located, Messrs. Chance Bros. and Co. being chiefly identified with the manufacture of Crown, sheet, and rolled or rough plate glass; Crown glass, however, is no longer made.

Painted glass also, reckoned among the art industries of Birmingham since the days of Francis Eginton, of Handsworth, who died in 1805, occupied an important department of the Spon Lane Works in former times.

Antique glass for decorative purposes and glass shades are manufactured at Oldbury by Messrs. W. E. Chance and Co.

The connection of the Chance family with the manufacture of glass began about the year 1790, when William Chance and Edward Homer, hardware merchants of Birmingham, became associated in partnership with their brother-in-law, John Robert Lucas of Bristol, in glass works at Wick and Nailsea, near that city. This William Chance sprang of a long line of yeoman farmers of Shepley and Burcot, in the parish of Bromsgrove, and he was the first of Birmingham, migrating thither in 1771.

His eldest son, Robert Lucas Chance, was a man of exceptional energy, ability, and industry. After managing his father's business from the age of 14, he joined (in 1811) his uncle at Nailsea, and in 1824 purchased for himself the works of the British Crown Glass Co. at Spon Lane, built some ten or twelve years before. Seven years later he was joined in that undertaking by his brother William, a leading merchant of Birmingham and High Bailiff of the town in the previous year. In 1832 they introduced into England (having with difficulty obtained the services of French and Belgian workmen) the manufacture of sheet glass, till then a closely guarded monopoly, abroad. Two rows of cottages built for these workmen, "French Row" and "Belgian Row," existed till recent times within the Spon Lane Works, whose extension has long since engulfed them. In 1851 the firm was able to supply the glass for the great Exhibition building of that year, now the Crystal Palace.

The following obituary notice of this William Chance appeared in the *Birmingham Daily Press* of 11th February, 1856:—

> In the death of William Chance, which took place on Friday last, Birmingham has lost a man who was universally respected, whose kindness endeared him to many, and whose charity was felt in all directions. He had not lately taken any part in politics, either local or general, but during the earlier part of his life lie had held many of those public offices, the election to which showed the estimation in which he was held by his fellow-townsmen . . . . He was a magistrate for the borough, and for the counties of Warwick and Worcester. . . . Mr. Chance was an earnest and zealous

member of the Church of England, the lay offices of which he often filled. His life was like that of the good men of all parties, and by the good men of all parties his loss will be deplored.

After his death the east window in Oldbury Parish Church was erected to his memory. This having been wrecked by a gale, it was replaced in 1914 by a new one, at the expense of his grandchildren.

In 1838 the two brothers were joined at Spon Lane by William Chance's eldest son, James Timmins Chance, fresh from high mathematical honours at Cambridge. He, again, was a man of extraordinary vigour and ability, a scholar of law, theology, and languages, as well as of mathematics. His first achievement was the invention of a process for grinding and polishing sheet glass, whereby a new branch of the trade was established to furnish glass peculiarly applicable to purposes for which none previously existed. This is the glass known as "patent plate."

But the highest achievement of Messrs. Chance Bros. and Co. at Spon Lane has been the establishment of the Lighthouse Works, the only one of its kind in the kingdom, a distinction won solely and purely by merit; technical skill and attention having been long and assiduously directed to a whole series of improvements in the production and equipment of lighthouse lanterns. These improvements relate to the optical agents, to the lamps and illuminants, and to the mechanical appliances employed.

The optical agents are those of the "dioptric" system, the invention of Augustin Fresnel, by which metallic reflectors were long ago superseded. Its lenses and prisms call not only for the mathematician to calculate the curvatures of their surfaces appropriate in each case, but also for highly skilled and intelligent labour to carry out his designs.

The weight of the unworked cast glass in a complete revolving light of the first order is upwards of two tons and before it is sent out every prism and lens is scientifically tested, in connection with the foci suitable to the data supplied; while the practical effect of the apparatus is ascertained by a night test with the lamp properly illuminated. A light of the first order, whose brilliance is computed in millions of candles, can be seen across the water to a distance limited only by the horizon. Light reflected by the sky has been discerned at a distance of 60 miles. A great advance this, since the days when the coast was dark and the approach perilous; or when the greatest effort was the warning signal of a wood fire in an elevated cresset.

Lighthouse lanterns of this type have been supplied from the Spon Lane Works—there are but two or three others in the world capable of producing them, and these are at Paris—not only for erection round our own stormbound coasts, but to the order of nearly every maritime power in the world. From this enterprising establishment of optical science in the heart of England have gone forth thousands of sea lights, port lights, and ship lights for the illumination of all the dark waters of all the seven seas.

It was to this work that James Timmins Chance devoted the best years of his working life, after he had been invited in 1859 to assist a Royal Commission appointed to enquire into the condition of the lighthouses of the United Kingdom.

Inspired mainly by the desire to render Great Britain independent of France in so important a matter, he devoted almost his whole attention to the correction of existing faults and the designing of improvements. Some of the lights which he erected—for example, the great one at Europa Point, Gibraltar (1864)—remain, so far as the glass is concerned, unchanged and as efficient as when new.

In recognition of the services rendered and of the large sums he expended for the public benefit, among which may be noticed his foundation of the "Chance School of Engineering" at Birmingham University and his gift of West Smethwick Park to the people of Smethwick and Oldbury, he was created a baronet in 1901.

The present Chairman of the Spon Lane Works is his second son, George Ferguson Chance.

The Alkali Works at Oldbury were founded by the Spon Lane firm about the year 1837 to supply the chemicals required for the glass manufacture. In 1890, having some years previously been separated from the parent firm, they were transformed into a limited liability company under the style of "The Oldbury Alkali Company, Limited"; and in 1898, after an amalgamation with Messrs. Hunt, of Wednesbury, became "Messrs. Chance and Hunt, Limited."

Raw material was easily accessible, and there was good canal accommodation, which shortly afterwards was supplemented by the railway. Salt was ready in any quantity at Droitwich; at that date there being also an adequate if not an abundant supply of sulphur, obtainable from the black or coaly pyrites of Staffordshire, even nearer at hand. The pyrites, however, it has long since been necessary to obtain further afield.

By roasting it, the alkali maker obtains sulphuric acid or vitriol, a commodity largely in demand for a number of local manufactures. Of the production of soda and other chemicals, it is not here necessary to speak.

In 1865 Mr. Alexander Macomb Chance was appointed manager of these works for the Spon Lane firm. He was the youngest son of George Chance, a third brother of Robert Lucas Chance and William Chance, and partner of the latter in an American merchant's business established in 1815. Having gone to manage its affairs across the Atlantic, George Chance married in 1825 the daughter of Mr. A. S. de Peyster, of New York, who, as also his wife, belonged to the oldest and best families among the early settlers in America. Mr. A. M. Chance's baptismal names are derived from his mother's great-uncle, General Alexander Macomb, who in 1841 was Commander-in-Chief of the United States Army.

Mr. A. M. Chance was born at Birmingham in 1844, educated at King Edward's School, which he left in 1859 to study in Germany; from 1860 to 1864 he attended the Technical School at Lausanne where he received a scientific training and acquired proficiency in languages. On his return, he spent a year at the Spon Lane Works, and was then transferred to Oldbury, where, in the course of nearly fifty years of able direction, he became successively managing partner, managing director, and finally Chairman of the Company. Among his many successes may be mentioned the Chance-Claus Process for the recovery of sulphur from "alkali-waste," the fruit of ten years' experimenting, and widely in use at home and abroad. For a paper on the subject, read before the Society of Arts, he was awarded the Society's silver medal.

Sufficient has been said to show that Messrs. Chance have not been mere exploiters of other men's talents. The successive members of the firm, possessing technical knowledge themselves, and taking an intimate and practical part in the actual working of the concern, have, while encouraging initiative among the men, applied their own inventive faculties to the improvement of everything they have produced.

Their industrial establishments belong to that happy class in which identity of interest has not only been discovered by employers and employed, but has been cordially acted upon from the first for their mutual benefit. Day Schools for the workpeople's children have been in existence at Spon Lane since 1845 and at Oldbury since 1851—almost a pioneer effort of its kind in elementary education. The duty of the firm towards those they employ they have never failed to keep steadily in view, with the result that there is no branch of social effort that can be industrially organised which was not in successful operation at these works long before the awakening of the national conscience had insisted upon all those legislative measures of recent enactment—ameliorative, provident, compulsorily philanthropic—on behalf of the labouring classes.

One institution only of the Alkali Works needs mention here—as a natural corollary to the medical dispensary there has been established a Convalescent Home at Quinton, within a few miles of the works, but pleasantly situated within sight of the Clent Hills. It needs only to be added that in most of these schemes a sense of personal responsibility—and also, of course, of personal proprietorship—is purposely inculcated, by working them on the easy contributory system. The taint of charitable dependence is at these establishments as repugnant to the masters as to the men.

Mr. A. M. Chance is not only head of these Oldbury establishments, but for many years he has filled a large place in the public life of the Birmingham Midlands. As Chairman of the city Licensing Bench, as a member of various governing bodies, as of hospitals and other philanthropic institutions, as the prime mover in a hundred and one beneficent enterprises, he has found full scope for that busy life of social usefulness which best becomes a man of golden opportunities. Of Mr. Chance!s beneficences which come within the present purview, mention may be made of the fact that he was largely instrumental in the erection of new vicarages at Oldbury and at St. John's, Harborne, and of the new church at Langley; also that he largely aided the movement for the purchase of Warley Woods as a public recreation ground. Of many others outside the area under notice cognizance need not here be taken.

Oldbury contains a second chemical producing establishment of the first importance in the Phosphorus Works of Messrs. Albright and Wilson. Here are manufactured highly specialised products requiring great chemical skill and carefulness of working; such as carbon tetrachloride, a powerful anæsthetic; chloride of sulphur, used as a solvent for indiarubber; potassic chlorate, used in matches, also as an explosive; several forms of phosphorus, used in the red state for tipping matches, and also largely worked up into explosives, as well as forming the active ingredient in a number of important medical preparations.

Of the personnel of the firm, something may be learnt, particularly of the social influences on the community of the Albright family, from a work recently "printed for private circulation only," entitled ARTHUR ALBRIGHT— NOTES OF HIS LIFE, the subject of which was born in 1811 and died in 1900. A member of the firm, the Rt. Hon. John W. Wilson, has been M.P. for North Worcestershire since 1895.

It will be seen that the two chemical works differ entirely in the character of their commercial products. Messrs. Chance probably have an output of more tons than the other have of pounds, dealing as they do with industrial products which are used in immense quantities, such as soda crystals—caustic soda used in soap-making, the preparation of paper pulp, and in many other industries; they also turn out a number of ammonia compounds, some used in dying, others as fertilisers, whilst caustic ammonia (liquid), by reason of the great bulk of ammonia gas it holds in solution, produces by the action of a suction pump such rapid evaporation that it turns water into ice, and so is used for refrigerating purposes. Latterly, too, they have been economically turning out a very useful cement, made from what at one time was a troublesome waste-product with them.

XXII.—IRON-WORKING AND IRON-WORKERS

"Not far from the Brades Works," said that powerful writer, Elihu Burritt, "are the Bromford Works of the Messrs. Dawes, perhaps equally celebrated for the production of the best kind of bar iron. Indeed, they may be regarded as a representative establishment for the district and I visited them one day with peculiar interest. When in full operation, with their sixty puddling furnaces in action, they present a scene which would have stirred the muse of Homer or Virgil beyond any of their vivid fancies. Puddles! Mud puddles! What rustic Saxon similes are applied to these fierce operations! To an outsider looking into one of those sixty furnaces, and seeing, if his eyes would bear it, the boiling, bubbling mass of metal, ten times more than red hot, a puddle would sound too wet and watery to describe it. The puddlers who fish in the troubled fountain are generally stripped to the waist, and flooded with perspiration. They fish out a mass at the end of the rod, of a weight which shows what athletes they are trained to be. I hardly know what figure to use to convey an idea of the appearance and consistency of this burning, frittering, fizzy mass of metal thus brought out of the furnace. Should one dip a large sponge into a mud puddle, it would fill in a moment with the impure matter, which, on compression, would all flow out again, leaving the sponge as it was before the dip. There is this difference in the simile: the meshes of the sponge are in the metal puddle itself, and they all come out together with the mass. This mass, cooling a little on its way to make it more coherent, goes under a hammer, or into a squeezing machine, which, at the first blow or turn, throws out the spray of the impure puddle-matter, such as melted stone, cinder, etc. Thus the sponge part is only the genuine iron meshes or grains, which are thus squeezed and hammered and rolled into solid bars. To see these masses at white heat running down iron slideways from every direction to the squeezers, hammers, and rollers is a stirring sight. Some of these hammers are of tremendous power, especially the Nasmyth pounder., When it falls with a ton weight upon a liquid boulder, you will see a horizontal shower of meteors, which would penetrate a suit of the best broadcloth at a considerable distance. There was a machine called the squeezer which operated to admiration in the first stages. It was a large fluted horizontal wheel which turned in a fluted semi-circular case, the receiving being twice as large as the delivering hopper. A mass of the half-liquid material was thrust in on the left, and pressed into a constantly narrowing space, until it was delivered, at the right, a compact elongated roll ready for the trip-hammer or rolling machine."

This, written nearly half a century ago, is one of the most graphic descriptions of the processes of puddling and shingling ever penned.

In the Bromford Ironworks puddling is not now carried on. Formerly, the first stage in the production of wrought iron at these famous works was conducted in a refinery; but refining has been long out of practice in the Bromford Works, and, indeed, throughout the Black Country generally.

The Bromford refinery was described, with illustrations, in Dr. Percy's classical book on IRON AND STEEL MANUFACTURE. Percy described it as consisting essentially of a rectangular hearth, with three water-cooled tuyeres on each side inclining downwards. The sides and back were formed of hollow iron castings, called "water-blocks," through which water was kept flowing; the front, of a solid cast iron plate, contained a tap hole; and the bottom, of sand, rested on a solid platform of brickwork. Coke was used as fuel, and cold-blast air was supplied at a pressure of 3lbs. per square inch. The space immediately over the hearth was enclosed on each side by cast iron plates, the back with folding wrought iron doors, and the front with a wrought iron door suspended at the end of a lever, whereby it could be raised or lowered. A short iron chimney, supported on cast iron columns, completed the whole.

In the refinery the pig iron was cleared of much silicon, and a superior white pig iron was produced for the puddler.

To-day at Bromford Ironworks a considerable quantity of steel billets, imported from the Continent, is rolled down into useful forms, much of it being bright-rolled. Without these cheap billets it is not improbable the rolling machinery would too often be idle. Messrs. W. Dawes and Sons long exported railroads to China from these works.

At Brades Steel Works the process of "cementation," as it was called, was abandoned many years ago. The firm here have now a process of heating and rolling down cemented bars-generally known as "blister steel" bars into single and double shear steel, They still continue to make first-class crucible cast steel for their renowned trowels; and among their customers are many works which they supply with tool steel of the finest quality.

By the middle of the last century iron-making in the Black Country had reached the zenith of its prosperity. From Dudley Castle Hill on the one hand, or Wednesbury Church Hill on the other, or indeed from any adjacent height overlooking the upper basin of the Tame, the night scene was that of a land of fire; flaming blast-furnaces reared their heads everywhere, and puddling furnaces could be counted by the hundred.

Oldbury blast-furnaces were carried on successfully for a long time by Captain Bennett. The site still bears the name of Furnace Yard, though all traces of the industry have now disappeared. The Albion blast-furnaces were established by Mr. Walter Williams, eldest son of Mr. Philip Williams, of Wednesbury Oak Works. The extensive Albion Ironworks were afterwards carried on by several firms; the Albion Sheet Iron Company and the Britannia Iron Company, though distinct, were almost identical in proprietary. Between

Albion and Dudley Port were the Stour Valley Furnaces, and the volcanic flare was continued through Tipton and Tipton Green to the confines of Wolverhampton. There were never less than thirty furnaces in blast in the Tipton, Wednesbury, West Bromwich, and Oldbury district in other directions they flamed to heaven from Tividale to Gold's Hill, and from Willingsworth to Crookhay.

In the third quarter of the century, the native ironstone being practically exhausted, quantities of Northamptonshire ore were smelted, the product being a second-class quality of pig iron, used chiefly for cheap bar iron, and still more largely for making castings. The coal of the district was now used raw, mixed with coke from South Wales. There were 28 furnaces in blast in 1886, each producing from 200 to 400 tons of pig per week, as against 100 tons thirty years before. The economy was effected by utilising the waste gases (which formerly escaped from the top of the furnace and served only to light up the region around) for producing steam and heating the blast. Very few furnaces still produced cold blast iron. Of the 28 furnaces in blast, the Earl of Dudley had 3; Cochranes of Dudley, 1 ; Grazebrooks, at Netherton, 1 ; Hingley, Old Hill, 1; New British Iron Co., Cradley, 3; Pearsons, Netherton, 2; Roberts, Tipton, 3; Rounds, Tividale, 1; and Philip Williams, Wednesbury Oak, 1, Of those out of blast at this period Lord Dudley had 5; Evers and Mablin, of Dudley, 2; Firmstone, of Crookhay, 4; Grazebrooks, Netherton, 1; Hingley, Old Hill, 1; Holcrofts, Dudley, 2; Jones, The Buffery, 1; Matthews and Co., Dudley, 3; Patent Shaft Co., Wednesbury, 3; Pearsons, Windmill End, 3; Roberts, Brades Hall, Oldbury, 2—altogether (ominous portent) there were no less than 85 out of blast. The historic industry of iron-smelting was gradually being driven from the Midlands to the seaboard, chiefly by the burden of excessive railway freights. The railways had killed competition in the carrying trade by buying up the canals, or by securing the controlling interest in them. The railway rate to Cardiff was 8/4, while to London it was 15/- nearly double, though the distance was the same (126 miles).

Of puddling furnaces in Oldbury there were (in 1873) 69 at Bromford, 13 at Brittains, 12 at The Brades, and 10 at the Eagle Works of Messrs. Simpson; while beyond, on one side of the town there were quite a hundred at Smethwick, and at Tipton on the other side there were the same number at one works alone (that of Messrs. Barrows).

It was indeed a region of furnaces, ovens, and kilns; of forges, factories, and iron-mills; the dull and depressing landscape varied only by heaps of cinder, slag, or miniature mountains of pit refuse, and relieved but slightly, if at all, by intersecting canals that appeared to be fed by water of the colour and consistency of pea-soup, and which indeed, near to the great furnaces, sometimes steamed like that nourishing compound.

By night, as well as by day, the pulsations of mighty engines and the monotonous "thud, thud" of heavy machines never ceased to reverberate through the busy Oldbury region. At night the sky was illuminated by the lurid glare of the countless furnaces, varying in shade from the blood-red flame of the puddling furnace to the streaked white and red of the blast-furnace, and diversified here by the yellow and blue flames of the copper works. By day dense clouds of smoke obscured the light of heaven, and kept off the vivifying rays of the sun with destructive effects to the struggling vegetation. Corroding gases emitted from chemical works in the heart of the town so completed the blight that even grass and the hardiest of plants failed not to succumb in due time. Not by incessant labour could Oldbury housewives keep fire-irons or other household utensils of bright steel in any desirable condition of cleanliness; metal tarnished in a single night, and in process of time slowly corroded away as they had been petals of a fading flower.

The smoky, grimy, manufacturing Oldbury which presents itself to us now is never, on the fairest day of Midsummer, and near as it is to a pleasant green borderland not exceeded in beauty by any other county in England, a pale semblance of what was its former self, before the age of industrialism had dawned upon it, but to blight its scenery while endowing it with material prosperity.

The servile rustic labourer of former times has given way to a present-day race of sturdy workmen and skilled artisans; the earlier of these new types were brawny colliers, who braved the dangers of gloomy mines, and the callous puddlers, accustomed to sweat in front of blazing furnaces and endure such sudden jumps of variation in temperature as would try the constitution of a steam engine.

The iron-workers of South Staffordshire are generally a well-conducted body of men, though as a class not provident in their habits. In the later decades of the nineteenth century, with the spread of elementary education, they made considerable advances; the rougher forms of sport gave way to manlier pursuits; by wider reading the intellect was cultivated; greater attention was given to home comforts; and in many directions much social progress was made. Industrially, too, many improvements were noticeable; not the least being the policy adopted for settling wages questions by means of a Conciliation Board, consisting of twelve employers and twelve operative representatives, elected annually, with an independent President as arbitrator. Satisfactory as all this is, there is still room for improvement in various directions.

XXIII.—Diversity of Employment in Oldbury

Of early traders in the towns of this country, and the local orbits of their respective trading operations, an enduring form of evidence is preserved in those old trade tokens which, in the then existing dearth of the smaller coins of the realm, had to be provided by the private enterprise of those who conducted ready-money business transactions on a scale that called daily for such a medium of currency. Boyne's well-known work on coins and tokens includes one issued in Oldbury, but, of course, gives it under the heading of Shropshire, in which county the town was then reckoned. It is thus described:

Obverse: OLIVER ROVND=St. George and the Dragon.
Reverse: IN OLDBURY. 1663. HIS HALFPENY.

No record remains of the line of business followed by the enterprising Oliver Round, but probably he was a factor—perhaps a nail factor.

Modern Oldbury has perhaps as great a variety of industries as any place of its size in the Black Country. Lying well within the coalfield, it first became a coal and iron producing centre; being also situated about midway between Birmingham and Wolverhampton, it was presented from time to time with opportunities, which it failed not to seize, of developing in other directions at the same time. Nor can it be said to have neglected any of its natural resources. In 1870 the Crosswell's Brewery of Messrs. Walter Showell and Son was established at Langley Green on the site of an ancient medicinal spring known as the Wells of the Cross. Whatever the curative properties of the water in mediæval times, it was proved by Mr. John Green, of Oldbury, to be admirably suited to the brewing of beer.

The selection of Oldbury as a suitable place for the manufacture of railway rolling stock goes back almost to the forties of last century, when the railway mania was dominating the commercial mind of this country and stimulating its engineering faculties to the utmost. In 1847 Messrs. Johnson and Kinder started a concern for the construction of railway rolling stock at Bromsgrove, on a site now occupied by the wagon repairing shop of the M.R. There they turned out wagons and coaches which fulfilled all the requirements for railway transport which the mind of man had as yet conceived; good, no doubt, but primitive things considered in the light of the present luxurious and fast-going age. That they were considered clever carriage builders is seen in the fact that the firm was entrusted with a contract—after the manner of those early years of the railway era—to "work" the Birmingham and Shrewsbury line, now part of the G.W.R. system, of course supplying all the wagons and coaches after the then manner of "road contractors."

After taking a similar contract for an Irish railway, Messrs. Johnson and Kinder thought it would be advantageous to remove their works to Oldbury, which was near to Birmingham and in the Black Country as well; and in 1854 the transfer was accordingly made. Three years later Mr. Kinder withdrew, and soon afterwards Mr. Johnson turned the concern into the Oldbury Railway Carriage and Wagon Company (Limited). Since then the direction and management have included the names of some well-known local commercial men, including Messrs. Herbert Wheeler and Percy Wheeler, as joint managing directors. The former, who is father of the latter, belonged to the early days of the concern when it was located at Bromsgrove, and brought to the guidance of the Company's affairs a ripe experience which, in the days of its infancy, contributed not a little towards the success which it ultimately attained.

The works, which cover a large area of ground, stand close to the L. & N.W. line from Birmingham to Wolverhampton, and is connected with it by a private siding. The G.W.R. is not far away, and a branch of the Stour Valley Canal connects the works with a network of waterways. Seven or eight acres are covered with substantial brick-built shopping, all of it lofty, well-lighted, and hygienic in construction. A descriptive article on these works appeared in COMMERCE of August 2nd, 1899; it was profusely illustrated, showing, among other views, both exterior and interior, the forges, foundries, smithies, and fitting shops; the timber mills and wood working shops; the steel frame machine shops, and the wagon erecting shops; the carriage body shops, and the painting shops; a pictorial catalogue which by no means exhausts the actual number of the departments, omitting as it does a large upholstery shop and a number of smaller departments devoted to those branches of industrial art (as wood-carving) so necessary to the finishing of railway carriages and saloons in that luxurious style to which the world has now become accustomed. Orders came into Oldbury for carriages and wagons, and every variety of railway rolling stock, from nearly all the railway administrations of the world, to whom the name and fame of this Company needed neither introduction nor recommendation.

At the beginning of the present century a combine was effected of a number of rolling stock undertakings, which took in this Oldbury Company, the Metropolitan Railway Carriage and Wagon Co., of Saltley; Brown, Marshall and Co., also of Saltley; the Ashbury Railway Carriage and Iron Co.; and the Lancaster Railway Carriage and Wagon Co., the main objects of which were to do away with competition, economise in the cost of management, and to avoid the duplicating of special plant. In the following year (1902) was effected a further amalgamation of other large concerns, namely, the Patent Shaft and Axletree Co., of Wednesbury; the Willingsworth Iron Co.; and Docker Bros., Limited; the whole now being known as The Metropolitan Carriage, Wagon, and Finance Company, Limited. In the new era of English "combines" this was one of the earliest essays in American commercial methods.

It was an Oldbury man who, nearly a century ago, invented the lap-welded wrought iron tube. Cornelius Whitehouse was born here July 22nd, 1795, and spent the earlier years of his working life at the gun trade. From the making of gun-barrels to the making of longer pipes for carrying gas, or water, or steam, was the line of evolution taken by Whitehouse. The use of coal-gas was, indeed, hanging fire at that time, for the want of cheap tubing. How Cornelius Whitehouse met the demand by inventing hollow furnaces for heating long lengths of strip-iron, and then welding them into strong, reliable tubes by applying his force, equally and rapidly, from outside pressure, need not be told here. The benefit of his invention, patented in 1825, was reaped chiefly by others, notably the Russells, of Wednesbury. The largest concern in the trade to-day is that of Messrs. Stewart and Lloyd, one of whose tube factories is at Coomb's Wood, Halesowen.

A great advance on the wrought iron tube is the modern weldless steel tube, which combines increased strength with a much lighter weight of metal. These tubes are drawn from hollow-blooms of mild steel. The bloom is first "tagged," that is, has one end drawn down under a pneumatic or other hammer, to form a tail, or "tag," which can be gripped in the draw-bench "dog," the tool which, by engaging an endless chain—which is sometimes actuated electrically and sometimes by steam power—pulls or draws the tube along the bench, through the dies and over the mandrel, during the repeated processes necessary to reduce the thick, lumpy-looking bloom to the thin, paper-like proportions of the finished tube. Sometimes eight or ten "draws" are necessary to attain the desired thinness, though the tube is reduced very considerably in diameter at each passage through the dies, and all these operations are made with the steel in a cold state. The blooms used are always of well-known and approved ductility, either best British, or charcoal-smelted Swedish steel.

The immense advantage of a tube which, with such astonishing lightness of metal, combines adequate and reliable strength, has contributed not a little to the vast strides made in recent years by many mechanical appliances, particularly in cycles, motors, aeroplanes, and other modern inventions. The rapid rise of Messrs. Accles and Pollock Ltd., of Oldbury, who produce weldless steel tubes of every kind and variety, may be taken as evidence of the wide and still growing demand for such material. This firm started at Perry Barr in a very modest way some seventeen years ago, the weekly wages bill amounting then only to £50, whereas now it is, with the thousand people they employ, well over £1,200.

For increased accommodation the concern was removed some fourteen years ago to Oldbury, where the new works, all well-built and equipped in the most up-to-date manner, cover an area of nearly nine acres. The output, which, besides steam piping, electric conduits, cycle, motor and aeroplane frames, and tubular work of every type, includes specialities in such number and variety that even a technical paper (THE MOTOR-CYCLE AND CYCLE TRADER of 26th February, 1915) has declared the effect on a visitor to the works to be positively "bewildering!" The Company is fortunate in possessing in and Mr. W. W. Hackett, the joint Managing Directors, men not of marked ability only (the one on the commercial side, the other on the mechanical side) but of real business enthusiasm. The concern is characteristically a progressive one, as consistently so in "the piping times of peace" as in the rush and feverish activities of war time.

The ever-increasing variety of the town's industries augurs well for the future prosperity of Oldbury. Besides the wide range of its hardware output, from edge-tools to bicycle frames, and of its chemicals, from alkali to phosphorus, it produces blue bricks and cardboard boxes, tar, jam, and pale ale, immense engine boilers and delicate surgical dressings, and a catalogue of other manufactures equally strange in their diversity, to say nothing of the railway carriages and the canal barges by which they may be expeditiously carried away. It is well that the town no longer relies on an output of heavy goods only. For if its mineral resources had not begun to fail, heavy railway freights would have handicapped it (as they have all the other Black Country towns) in its competition with the newer iron and steel districts on the seaboard.

XXIV.—OLDBURY: EARLY FORMS OF LOCAL GOVERNMENT

The municipal status of Oldbury is exceptional and in some respects anomalous. As already shown, it is an ecclesiastical parish which has been carved out of the ancient parish of Halesowen. Also, as previously disclosed, Oldbury, as. part of Halesowen, was included for centuries in the county of Salop.

When, in 1174 (p. 11), Halesowen passed to the county of Salop, Cradley, Lutley, and Warley Wigorn, not being included in the lordship, remained in Worcestershire as part of the barony of Dudley.

The passing of the revolutionising Poor Laws of 1834 drew attention to the many anomalies caused by irregular boundaries; among them to this detached fragment of Salop lying more than a dozen miles away from the geographical county. So, for the greater convenience of administration, Oldbury was transferred with other portions of Halesowen by a general Act of 1839 (2 *William IV.*) and is now situated in the cast of Worcestershire.

As a portion of Worcestershire it is included in the Hundred of Upper

Halfshire. The name Halfshire seems to possess almost a literal signification. It comprises a large slice of the north-east of the county, embracing those divisions which at the time of the Norman Conquest were known as the Hundreds of Came (Camele, Kamel, or Cham), Clent (Klint), Creslau (Cresselau, or Kerslau), and Esch (or Aesc). The union of these was effected at 1175; a map illustrative of these ancient political divisions is given in the VICTORIA HISTORY OF WORCESTERSHIRE (III., p. 2), from which it will be seen that Halfshire includes a part of Dudley parish detached from Worcestershire and lying within the boundaries of county Stafford.

In the Calendar of State Papers of the reign of Charles I. are documents of 1631-1637 relating to the measures taken for the relief of the poor within the Hundred of Halfshire. In 1635, in the Sheriff of Worcester's assessment for providing a ship of 400 tons, the Hundred of Halfshire's share is set down at £672 3s. 6¾d.

When a standing army was created and the old feudal method of charging the ownership of land with the duty of maintaining an army abandoned, a land tax was substituted for the burden of military service. Whether territorial magnates made a good or a bad bargain this is not the place to discuss. This land tax was introduced in the reign of William III., and in 1692 a new assessment or valuation was made throughout the kingdom. The method of raising the land tax was by charging a particular sum on each county. Here are the local figures for that impost:—

The allocation of the land tax for Halesowen parish was accounted for in two parts; the Worcestershire portion for the three manors of Cradley, Warley-Wigorn, and Lutley; and the Shropshire part at 4/- in the £ paid £19 2s, 8d. for the borough, and £122 0s. 6d. for Romsley quarter, which included Romsley, Hunnington, Hasbury, and Ylley; the like for Hill quarter, which included Hill, Lappal, Warley-Salop, and Ridgacre; and the same sum for Oldbury quarter, which included Oldbury, Langley, Hawn, and Cackmore, in all £385 4s. 2d., which, with £159 12s. 6d. for the Worcestershire manors, made the total sum payable £544 16s. 8d.

The anomalies of its administration did not cease with its transference to Worcestershire, for it still constitutes a portion of the Staffordshire Poor Law Union of West Bromwich. The Poor Law Act of 1834, which created the Unions, paid no respect to ancient county boundaries, a high-handed proceeding which naturally led to administrative difficulties. In 1850 an Act had to be passed for the proper collecting of the Poor Rates and other county imposts in Oldbury and West Bromwich, both these places being within the same Poor Law Union, but in different counties.

Until 1832 Halesowen was a very extensive parish, including Oldbury, Cakemoe, Cradley, Hasbury, Hawn, Hill, Hunnington, Illey, Lappal, Lutley,

Ridgacre, Romsley, and the two Warleys. In all there were some fifteen townships or parishes, which are now divided among three or four Poor Law Unions. Seven ecclesiastical parishes have since been formed, namely, Oldbury, Cradley, Quinton, Langley, Romsley, Blackheath, and Rounds Green.

Those parts of Halesowen parish which have continued to retain their rural character are now becoming alive to the advantages of a higher form of municipal life than that conferred by Parish Council government. Hill and Cakemore are proposing to amalgamate, and not improbably Hasbury and Hawne will also combine, the actuating motive being the laudable desire to exchange the rural form of government for that of an Urban District Council, with its higher powers and greater opportunities for communal development.

Our older forms of local government grew out of the authority pertaining to the manorial court, moulded and corrected in the later centuries by that vested by statute in the Vestry.

The maintenance of the highways, for instance, was a responsibility thrown on adjacent landowners or their tenants, unless the tenure were specially exempted. The farmers turned out with their labourers, equipped with carts and tools, and mended the roads; a surveyor or "waywarden" elected by the Vestry inspected the work on behalf of the parish. And so on, in other departments of local administration; the churchwardens, the beadle, and the overseers being important parochial functionaries.

But everything was chaotic and without system till the beginning of the nineteenth century, when Parliament made feeble and tentative attempts to reduce local government to some sort of order. The reforming Poor Law of 1834 is mentioned in another place (p. 2). In 1835 was passed the Highways Act, of which Oldbury was not slow to avail itself, for by the March of the following year it had formed a Board of Surveyors for the more efficient government of the town. In this early attempt at a more representative form of local government, the traditional supremacy of the Church in such matters could not be entirely ignored, for the members of the newly-constituted body had to be elected by a show of hands in open Vestry Meeting.

This form of government served Oldbury upwards of twenty years. In the meantime the country had been visited (in 1848-9) for a second time by the cholera scourge—the first visitation in 1831 had devastated the Black Country, the deaths in Dudley numbering 277, in Sedgley 290, in Tipton 404, and in Bilston 742. The chief outcome of the second plague was the Public Health Acts. At last it was recognised that the first duty of a local authority was the care of the public health.

Oldbury did not secure its first sanitary authority till 1857, when a Local Board of Health was constituted under an Order of 20th January of that year, the first meeting of the Board being held on April 22nd.

Under this body the town was well governed till it was superseded by the present authority, the Urban District Council, which held its first meeting December 31st, 1894.

XXV.—Oldbury Municipal Progress.

Oldbury at the close of the eighteenth century found itself emerging from its rurality and fast developing into a busy industrial village, one outward sign and symbol of which was the Birmingham Canal, surrounding it on three of its sides in the shape of a horse-shoe. The old manorial forms of local government were not only antiquated, but were altogether inadequate to meet the new condition of things; and as yet the law had set up no local government machinery to take the place of this out-of-date feudalism. Curious and primitive were some of the expedients devised to cope with the communal requirements of the "populous places" then springing up wherever the new industrialism was taking root.

In 1857 a Market Hall, earliest sign of municipal aspirations, was erected in Church Street; but here as elsewhere the open-air market is the more popular, and in 1895 the local authority purchased from the lord of the manor the right to the market tolls. Markets are held on Tuesdays and Saturdays.

Proper housing is the first requirement for sanitary efficiency. It was at this period our modern towns inherited the muddle of slumdom by trying to make village cottage accommodation suffice for an ever-increasing artisan population. Another necessity for the maintenance of public health is a good water supply. Many houses and cottages had private wells, and nearly all possessed cisterns or water-tubs for the storing of rain-water to be used for cleansing purposes. But it is not conducive to health or cleanliness when every drop of water has to be carried forty of fifty yards, and sometimes then only by permission of a neighbour. In the first half of the nineteenth century there were one or two public wells of good potable water in the parish.

Before the days of artificial waterworks the best supply of water open to the inhabitants of Oldbury was that of a beautiful spring on the north side of the town, known as Fountain Well, which was surrounded by a high wall, and never failed in the driest of seasons. Oldbury now takes its supply from the South Staffordshire Waterworks Co.—an account of which undertaking will be found in A History of West Bromwich, pp. 110-111, and in Olden Wednesbury, chap. XXI.

In the early days of its iron-making era the blast-furnaces of Oldbury were popularly known as "the four moons," because the glare set up by them at night-time illuminated the whole town sufficiently to enable the local governing body to dispense with street lamps. But if this form of artificial lighting was cheap to the ratepayers, it was a very wasteful industrial process; and in the progress of science the time came when the gases which flamed forth in this picturesque waste were captured on their way up the stack and applied to more useful and remunerative purposes.

When Oldbury began to grow and the need for artificial lighting began to make itself urgently felt, Messrs. Chance offered to supply the town with gas if the ratepayers would be at the expense of laying down the mains. The offer, it is not surprising to learn, was declined by the champions of "keep down the rates" policy.

Since 1880 Oldbury has possessed its own gas-works, acquired from the Birmingham Corporation after costly litigation.

The block of public offices in Market Square was erected 1890, from the designs of Messrs. Wood and Kendrick, the memorial stone being laid May 19th of that year by Mrs. Alfred Thompson, wife of the Chairman of Oldbury Local Board.

Combined with offices for the town officials, Council and Committee rooms, and all other necessary accommodation for carrying on the government of the town, is a Free Library. The Library portion was provided by voluntary contributions, amounting to £1,600, half of which was contributed by Messrs. Chance Brothers and Messrs. Albright and Wilson, in equal proportions. The total cost of the buildings and their equipment was nearly £6,000.

The Town Hall, which adjoins the public offices, is an adapted building. Originally built by the Temperance Party, it was successively known as the Peoples Hall and as the Public Hall. When first acquired as a public property it was called the Vestry Hall, and its offices are still used mainly for the administration of the Poor Laws.

Of public parks and pleasure grounds, the largest, At Barnford Hill, Langley, comprises twenty acres, recently presented to the public by Mr. W. A. Albright. One of twelve acres, situated at Bury Hill, was presented in 1897 by Mr. J. W. Wilson, M.P. Langley Park was the gift of Mr. Arthur Albright, and the Broadwell Recreation Ground of Mr. W. A. Albright. The public park at Park Lane, comprising about four acres of land, was given in 1884 by Messrs. Chance Brothers.

Oldbury is now a well-equipped town, among its municipal institutions being a Technical School, a Fire Station worked by a Volunteer Brigade, and (owned and used jointly with the County Borough of Smethwick) an Isolation Hospital. It is well-sewered, and possesses an up-to-date Sewage Farm. The Burial Board controls a well-laid-out Cemetery.

Under the Local Government Act, 1894, Oldbury (with Warley Wigorn and Warley Salop) was constituted the area of an Urban District Council, Langley forming a Ward of the said District. The Rural Sanitary District of Warley, and a part of the civil parish of Warley, have since been formally annexed by Orders of the Local Government Board. Warley Wigorn was a detached hamlet, intermixed with which were portions of another hamlet called Warley Salop.

When created the new Urban District Council was estimated to exercise jurisdiction over a population of some 24,000; in 1901 the population of Oldbury was 21,467, and of Warley 3,724; the gross population at the 1911 census 32,240. The assessable value was then £64,112.

The area governed by the Urban Council is given as 1,547 acres of land, with 51 acres of water surface in Oldbury, and 1,922 of land with 5 of water in Warley—in all a superficial area of 3,525 acres.

The Clerk to the Oldbury Authority for many years was Mr. William Shakespeare, his successor in this important administrative office being Mr. Sydney Vernon, LL.B.

For communication with the outer world Oldbury has ample facilities. The Stour Valley section of the L. and N.W. Railway, opened in 1847, passes through the east of the town, and has a station at Bromford Road, placing the town on what is practically a main line connection between London and the north. Of the Great Western Railway, the West Midland section intersects the parish, and has two stations, one in Oldbury town and one at Langley Green; thus placing Oldbury in direct communication with the county-town, Worcester, and with the entire south-west. For upwards of a quarter of a century an excellent system of street tramways has linked up the place with Birmingham on one side and with Dudley on the other; and through West Bromwich with all the other Black Country towns. Contrast these facilities for inter-communication with those disclosed by the Directory of 1855, which informs us that the Post Office was at Jacob Lowes', in Birmingham Street, and that the mails arrived twice and were despatched twice in the twenty-four hours. (Refer back to p. 3 for postal accommodation in 1769)

XXVI.—Oldbury: Administration of Justice

Not the least important chapter in the history of modern Oldbury is that relating to the local administration of justice-not police or magisterial, but civil.

In the former nothing out of the ordinary prevailed. As in every other manor and parish, a constable was appointed by the Court Leet, and a constable or two were elected in Vestry; and these amateur peace officers, who were sometimes identical by double appointment, sufficed in the days of our great-grandfathers to maintain order and preserve the King's peace.

Then, in the days of Sir Robert Peel, came the Police Acts, and the establishment of County Constabulary.

A Directory of 1855 shows how primitive were the arrangements for the peace preservation sixty years ago. We are informed that the Police Station was in Wesley Street, and that Samuel Simmonds was the police officer. This was in the early days of the police system, when a constable wore white duck trousers and a dark blue, swallow-tailed coat with stand-up collar, drawn tightly to the waist by a broad black leather belt; the whole finished off by a top hat of shiny oil-skin. The awe inspired by one policeman in this dignified uniform seems to have been sufficient to preserve the peace of a population of several thousands. Oldbury is now the head of a Petty Sessional Division, and holds Petty Sessions at the Court House every Tuesday.

In the matter of civil jurisdiction, Oldbury boasted a Court of Requests, such as then existed in most trading towns, for the recovery of debts not exceeding £5, almost from its earliest days as a commercial community.

Then came the creation of a local Court by special Act of Parliament.

In 1807 (*47 George III., Cap 36*) was passed an "Act for the more speedy and easy recovery of debts within the parishes of Halesowen, Rowley Regis, Harborne, West Bromwich, Tipton, and the manor of Bradley, in the counties of Worcester, Salop, and Stafford"; and in accordance with this enactment a Court was established at Oldbury, as the most commercial centre in the parish of Halesowen (see p. 4).

The first Court was held on May 19th, 1807. The Minutes inform us that

"Thomas Turner, Esq., was in the chair; Ellis Sutton, gent., elected Clerk of the Court, and Thomas Johnson, yeoman, was elected Sergeant of the said Court. Twenty-two gentlemen were present and signed the minutes.

It was resolved:—

"That the thanks of the Court be given Rev. L. Booker, LL.D., Vicar of Dudley, for his excellent sermon given in Oldbury Chapel on the day of opening the Court, according to Act of Parliament, and that he be requested to allow it to be printed for the restraint of dissipation and vice, the encouragement of frugality and virtue, and the universal diffusion of prosperity and happiness."

The business of organising the new institution proceeded apace, as the Minute Book discloses:—

July 28th, 1807—Resolved to acquire land for the erection of a building and prison for use of the Court."

Ordered "That Thomas Turner, Esq., Rev. David Lewis, and Mr. Arthur Gilbert, be requested to wait upon Francis Parrott, Esq., Lord of the Manor at Oldbury, in order to arrange for and purchase from him part of a piece of land situate in Oldbury."

On the same date, it was ordered "That a silver cup be purchased by us, the undersigned, according to our several subscriptions. with the arms of the Right Hon. Lord Lyttelton engraved thereon, to be used by the Court as a memorial for the services rendered by the Hon. William Henry Lyttelton in obtaining the Act for the said Court." Then follow the subscriptions, which appear to be 10s. 6d. each, some of which, apparently, were not paid.

To give effect to the first resolution it was resolved to purchase immediately a quantity of land in a convenient part of Oldbury for the erection of a commodious Court House, and a Prison for the use of the Commisioners.

Yet several years elapsed before the Court House was actually built; from the wording of a Minute the delay was not improbably caused by official circumlocution. We read:—

"April 3rd, 1815—Ordered that Mr. William Harris and Mr. Thomas Whitehouse, carpenters and builders, be requested to give a plan and estimate of the new Court House, to be erected in accordance with the directions of the Commissioners."

The Court buildings were completed in 1816. An architect had reported on the plans seven years previously, and the Commissioners had urged the execution of the work at once.

How licensed houses were used for all kinds of public business appears in the following record:

25th August, 1809—A special meeting of the Court was field at the Swan Inn, West Bromwich, to fill the vacancies in the list of Commissioners."

For the dignity of the Court its minor officers had to be fitly clothed. In the first year of its existence it was ordered:—

"That an appropriate hat, with a black band, be purchased for John Turner's attendance at the Court, and also a hat, with a gold band, for Sergeant Thomas Johnson."

A beadle without a gold band was unthinkable in those days.

Equally quaint and typical of the times are the proceedings disclosed by other Minutes:—

"29th December, 1807.—Ordered that the fees now in the hands of the Clerk for contempt of Court be applied in the following manner: The sum of £1 4s. 2d. be distributed in bread to the poor of Halesosven, £1 4s. 2d. to the poor of Harborne, £1 1s. to the poor of Oldbury, the same to be published in the respective churches and chapels."

"9th January, 1810.—Ordered that all fines and forfeitures incurred by insulting and obstructing the officers of the Court shall be forthwith paid by the Clerk to Mr. Joseph Wright, as Treasurer of the Sunday Schools established at Oldbury, and the sum be appropriated to the use and benefit of the said Sunday Schools, and which said sum amounts to £11 13s. 4d."

"9th December, 1808.—Ordered that John Turner be allowed a new pair of boots, to be paid by the Treasurer."

But public officials, not even those acting in a Court of Law, and clothed with the authority symbolised by a uniform, are not impeccable,

24th July, 1810.—On a complaint made against Sergeant Thomas Johnson, by James Walker, it is ordered that the said Thomas Johnson immediately pay to the said James Walker the sum of £1 1s. as a recompense for the injury done him, and also make confession of his conduct."

"16th October, 1810.—Other complaints were made against this same Thomas Johnson, and a special meeting of the Commissioners was held as to whether he ought to be discharged."

On the 30th April, 1811, Thomas Johnson was ultimately discharged."

John Turner, who had been officially shod in recognition of his merit, was evidently a more worthy officer of the Court. 'In 1810 he zealously reports that certain goods (presumably goods seized for debt) were being secretly removed by night.

"October 16.—John Turner deposed he was passing by the house and said to them, 'You are removing your goods in time.' The answer was made to him by a woman, who was carrying part of the goods, 'Ah, damn you, you stripped that house once of all the goods, and we will take care you shall not again.'

In May, 1820, it was very sensibly ordered that no working tools should be taken in distraint for debt if sufficient other effects for the debt and costs could be found.

These Commissioners who had the administration of the law placed in their charge, sometimes found themselves involved in litigation.

12th October, 1811.—Stephen Porter, Birmingham. basket maker, being present at the Court, did there and then make use of insulting language before the Commissioners sitting in Court, and thereby did interrupt the proceedings, and continued to do so after being admonished. That the said Commissioners order the said Stephen Porter to be taken from the Court House; whereas an action was afterwards taken by the said Stephen Porter against the Rev. David Lewis, and considerable expense being incurred by defending the said case, we, the undersigned Commissioners. judge it to be protected, and it is hereby ordered that the said expense be defrayed and discharged out of the funds of this Court."

Even if debtors should prove contumelious and obstreperous when brought before the Court, the Commissioners knew how to take care of themselves. Debtors consigned to prison needed stern treatment:

"21st July, 1820.—Ordered that in future no kinds of provisions, ale, spirits, or drinkables be allowed to be received or taken into the prisoners belonging, to this

Court for their use of any description whatever, except a loaf of bread weighing 1lb. for each person per day."

The last entry in the recorded history of this Court is:

"25th August, 1820.—Resolved that Mr. Coldicott be appointed receiver of all fees and monies due to this Court."

The prominent position given to Oldbury among the surrounding towns, by the holding of this Court, was retained later when Courts of Requests were superseded by the newer Courts instituted for the recovery of debts.

Under the County Courts Act of 1846 (which incidentally repealed the local Act of 1807) Oldbury was included in the places in which the new County Courts were to be held. The whole of England and Wales was divided into 500 districts, which again were divided into 59 circuits, with a judge to each circuit. Oldbury was included in the twenty-fifth circuit, probably because it had a good Court House, with a spacious prison attached for the confinement of debtors.

Here the new County Court Judge of the twenty-fifth circuit held his periodical Courts. At first a Court was held monthly in the Oldbury Court House, but subsequently as the amount of business necessitated.

The first officers of the new County Court were:—Sergeant Clark, judge; Mr. Joseph Heapy Watson, clerk; George Megevan, high bailiff,

A dozen years had scarcely passed ere an agitation was got up in West Bromwich to have the Court transferred to that town. Oldbury offered strong resistance, the attempt of West Bromwich failed (for the time), and Government spent about £3,000 in improving and enlarging the Court buildings.

A second attempt on the part of West Bromwich, made in 1889, succeeded in wresting from Oldbury the privilege of a County Court which it had so long enjoyed, and which had given it some little prominence for three-quarters of a century. But West Bromwich had now advanced to the position of a county borough, and was rightly regarded as a more important commercial centre.

The Court officials at that time were:—Mr. Alfred Young, judge; Mr. George Stewart Watson, registrar; Mr. Walter Holden Stuart, high bailiff; Mr. Alfred L. Davey, chief clerk.

The old buildings, used so many years for both County Court and Police Court business, are now used as a Police Court and Police Station, having been purchased by the Worcester County Council.

The present Magistrate's Clerk for Oldbury is Mr. W. F. Vernon, who has for some years represented the Broadwell Ward in Oldbury on the Worcestershire County Council, his official position no doubt lending his voice some weight on the representative body, especially in such matters as licensing, or where local interests need safeguarding from those whose knowledge of all the factors is less intimate.

XXVII.—OLDBURY: EDUCATIONAL INSTITUTIONS.

A community that is not decadent has to advance mentally and intellectually as well as materially. And it may be said that Oldbury kept itself fairly abreast of the times by the establishment of such educative and recreative institutions as were within the reach of a working-class town.

In the early Victorian era Mechanics' Institutes were highly popular in all self-respecting industrial towns, and one was established at Oldbury by Thomas Flewett, who for many years controlled its destiny by acting as its Secretary.

Then came Messrs. Chance's Institute, and the Oldbury Working Men's Club, with a membership of over 200, organising lectures and getting up good concerts every Winter season.

The Public Hall in Tabernacle Street was well used for concerts and entertainments; and the Temperance Hall in Portway Road became the centre of the temperance propaganda.

Is it anathema to mention a public-house among educational institutions? However it may be, there was at that time a capital collection of stuffed animals, open freely to the public, at the Windsor Castle Tavern, Rounds Green. In the absence of any municipally provided museum, who shall deny it a place of merit? Primitive times, primitive methods, and simple tastes soon satisfied.

Modern Oldbury is well provided with a system of efficient primary schools. One or two of the schools are of historic interest. One foundation illustrates the keen practical interest taken by early Nonconformity in the education of the people. It may not be forgotten that in 1665 a law was passed forbidding dissenters to teach in schools, under pain of extremely heavy penalties.

The Free School dates from 1780, when it was conducted in a small room 13 feet by 25 feet, afterwards enlarged to 13 feet by 40 feet. The first schoolmaster was Jarvis Booth, who lived in the cottage adjoining the schoolhouse. In 1789 Mr. Booth was succeeded by the minister of the Meeting House, and from that date to 1864 the succession of schoolmasters was the same as that of the ministers at the Meeting House. In that year, on the retirement of the Rev. William McKean, Mr. J. J. Lynam was appointed head master. For a number of years afterwards the minister continued to take part in the teaching, but subsequently the association of the two offices of minister and schoolmaster was discontinued.

Although designated a Free School from the first, it would appear that of a total of 40 scholars only half that number were educated free of expense. The distinction of free scholars and fee-paying pupils was abolished in 1845 by the

Rev. W. McKean, but was revived in 1864, when those who pleased were invited to pay a fee of 1d., or 2d., or 3d. per week, according to the standard. A good proportion continued to be accepted free, and the cost of maintenance largely exceeded the income, till such time as the Education Department removed the disability of Endowed Schools to earn Government grants without any deduction in the respect of their endowment. In 1817 the Trustees had formally required the master to admit twenty free scholars—there were actually twenty-six at the time—but this concession of grant-earning enabled the liberal-minded Trustees to abolish fees altogether.

The early efforts of these educational enthusiasts were naturally of a very primitive character. The quarter's salary paid to Mr. W. Proctor, the first minister-teacher, discloses that the amount of his annual remuneration for teaching "ye charity children" was £25. A female assistant, Mary Barnett, received the sum of £2 10s. 0d. for instructing twelve of the children. Other modest items of the master's account, duly receipted to a Mr. Lakin, were 2/6 for pens and ink, and £1 13s. 0d. for copy books, slates, and pencils. More curious is another account of 29th April, 1789, in which Jos. Gosling acknowledges the receipt from the Rev. W. Proctor, as due at Lady-day, for one year's land and jail tax, the former 3/-, the latter $4\frac{1}{2}$d., and the total 3/$4\frac{1}{2}$d.

The present school building was erected in 1851, at a cost of £700. In 1864 an accumulated debt of £800 was generously liquidated by Messrs. Samuel Hunt.

When the aggregation of an industrial population in Oldbury called loudly for a more adequate provision of elementary education, Messrs. Chance, with their usual philanthropy, were not slow to throw themselves into the breach. It was as early as 1851 that they erected their schools near the works, for the accommodation of 320 children. In 1868 the premises were enlarged by the erection of a separate school to accommodate 145 girls, and four years later another room was added for the use of 40 infants.

The Oldbury National Schools in Broadwell Road, to succeed the older ones in Birmingham Street, were erected in 1866 during the incumbency of the Rev. H. B. Bowlby, afterwards suffragan bishop of Birmingham.

It is to be accounted among the sins of omission in the public life of Oldbury that it never had a School Board. When, however, the Act of 1902 came into force, and abolished those useful *ad hoc* authorities, the town decided to provide its own primary school accommodation, apart from the control of the county.

For the work of secondary education there is an efficient Technical School under the control of the Worcestershire County Council. It was erected in 1899, at a total cost of £5,687, raised mainly by private subscriptions, with the aid of a liberal contribution from the County Council. The accommodation comprises a well-equipped chemical laboratory, with balance and store rooms, lecture room, and all the necessary provision for science teaching; there are modelling rooms and others specially fitted for teaching a number of art subjects; together with class-rooms for manual instruction. It is doing a large and useful work in the town and neighbourhood.

The Higher Education of the town is conducted under the county scheme by the aid of a Local Committee, of which the present Chairman is Mr. F. F. Simpson. The Secretary of the Oldbury Education Committee is Mr. Sydney Vernon, LL.B.

The Warley schools will be treated in a subsequent chapter.

Mention may not be omitted of those educational institutions outside Oldbury in which the town possesses an interest.

In 1644 John Pearsall, of Hawn, gave by Will £5 towards building a free school in Halesowen.

Old Swinford Blue Coat School is a commendable charity in which a number of the surrounding parishes have been given a valuable interest. It was established in 1670 by Thomas Foley, and possesses a goodly income of £4,000 a year, with which are taught, fed, and clothed 120 boys, who are afterwards apprenticed to a trade and carefully put out into the world. The original number of boys was 60, but the property has increased in value so that double that number are now benefited. Old Swinford is in Worcestershire (it is the mother parish of Stourbridge), while Kingswinford is in Staffordshire, and the benefits of the charity extend to both counties. The Old Swinford Hospital receives poor boys from Old Swinford, Stourbridge, Kidderminster, Pensnett, Wordsley, Quarry Bank, Alvechurch, Pedmore, Dudley, Witley, Kingswinford, Kinver, Clent, Holt, Harborne, Halesowen (Halesowen, St. Kenelin's, The Quinton, Oldbury, Langley, Cradley), Sedgley, Wombourne, Rowley Regis, Wednesbury, and West Bromwich.

XXVIII.—WARLY AND LANGLEY.

Although Warley and Langley are both included within the boundaries of Oldbury, each place has enjoyed a separate existence at some period in its early history.

Anciently, the barons of Dudley were the superior lords of "the manor of Warley in the county of Worcester." In 1308 it was held by Sir William, Fokerham, whose holding included lands and tenements in "Wernlegh (Warley), Ruggacre, Cakemore, Langley, and Wallaxhall, with the chantry of Brendhall belonging to the chapel of St. Katherine." This is the earliest mention of "St. Katherine's chapel" at Warley Wigorn. In 1339 a "licence was granted to John de Homesworth for Walbroke chapel at Warley Wigorn." To this day the east end of the north aisle of Halesowen church is known as the Chapel of St. Katherine.

In 1320 Warley Wigorn appears to have been identical with Brandhall (or Brendall). Brandhall is positively named as the manor house of Warley Wigorn in 1444.

In a document of 1485 the estate is called Fotheral de Wearley, and is designated a manor; in this deed the waters of the moat and fishery are reserved to the lord.

"Fotheral" may mean the Further Hall of Warley; and it has sometimes been assumed that the capital residence of the Fokerhams was nearer the site of the present Cakemore Brickworks than is Brandhall.

The manor was held upon what was known as "kitchen tenure"; that is, by a payment in money or in kind to the King's kitchen. The lord of it, therefore, had hereditary right of hawking and fowling from Warley to the gates of Shrewsbury, on the condition of supplying to the royal table "pheasants and wooden platters."

When the Dudley barony was divided in 1321 between two co-heiresses, the sisters of John de Someri, the manors of Warley and Northfield went to Joan, the wife of John de Botetort, whose chief seat was Weoley Castle, Northfield. In the following year the manor of Cradley was also assigned to her.

Very little is known of Weoley Castle, although frequent mention is made of it in ancient documents relating to the neighbourhood. All that now remains of it are a few yards of ancient wall, and a large moat which encloses the garden of a farm house.

> The lordly moat with its waters wide
> Doth mirror the armed men beside.

sings Mr. Marston Rudland, who has made Joan Botetort the subject of one of his BIRMINGHAM BALLADS.

> Heir of the Someris, Lady Joan,
> Botetort's mate, thou makest no moan.

> Botetort dead, Botetort's son
> Shall rule the lands that his sires have won.

> In Weoley Castle, thine own good hold
> Thou keepest thy state as thy sires of old.

> Lady Joan, at her castle gate
> Doth greet thee fair in her fair estate.

And so on.

Seven years after her succession, Joan Botetort, by a licence in mortmain, bestowed her manor of "Weireleye" upon the abbot and convent of Halesowen; twenty shillings of the rents arising therefrom were to be distributed to the poor every year from the abbey gate, and for the remainder of the Lady Joan's bounty prayers were to be said for ever for the health of her soul. These masses are supposed to have been said at a little chantry chapel attached to Warley Grange and dedicated to the St. Michael, the site of which is said to be indicated by the name Chapel Croft. Other place-names of interest around the grange are Moat Field and Monks' Chapel.

After the Fokerham tenure (p. 25) there is a gap of several centuries in the manorial history of Warley.

In 1772 Brandhall Farm was sold by George, lord Lyttelton, to Mr. Robert Glover.

Brand Hall Farm is a big rambling building, which local tradition says was not actually the ancient manor house, but merely the servants' hall and out-offices attached thereto. It has a large pool in front of it, and is rather picturesquely situated. Near by, the Chapel Croft is pointed out, and described to visitors as an ancient burial ground.

Years ago, when the residence was occupied by "Squire Monckton," a great Maypole Festival was held here annually, and attracted thousands of visitors.

Of the ten large granges or demesne farms belonging to Halesowen Abbey, one of the largest was at Warley.

The residence now known as Warley Abbey stands on the site of the old conventual grange. In modern times it has been held, with 150 acres of land, by the Galtons, a well-known family of Birmingham bankers. The name "Abbey" was conferred upon it by Sir Hugh Gilzean Reid, M.P. for Aston Manor, who occupied it in the eighties of last century.

Warley being here considered as a detached hamlet independent of Oldbury, it will be necessary to make mention of its schools and other institutions in which the larger member had no direct interest.

Warley Endowed School dates from 1730, when John Moore, yeoman, of Warley Wigorn, left £100 to John Partridge and Samuel Parkes, to be by them laid out in the purchase of land, the yearly profits of which were to be expended on "some man or woman skilful in literature and sufficiently qualified to teach poor children residing in Warley Wigorn in English learning." In pursuance of this bequest a school-house was erected, with an enclosed garden thereto, upon some waste land near Brisnell Hall, Warley Wigorn, and lying within the lordship of Sir Thomas Lyttelton, of Hagley. Money was also laid out in the purchase of several acres of land at Coombs, near Halesowen, the proceeds of which constituted the bulk of school endowments.

In 1801 Thomas Newby left £4 per annum, issuing out of a field at Brisnell Hall Farm; of which £2 was to be applied towards the maintenance of a Sunday School, £2 was to be distributed among the poor of Warley at Christmas-time; with the proviso that if the Sunday School was discontinued, the whole of the £4 was to go to the poor—and as this happened some years ago, the money is now divided among the poor as directed.

Another bequest was made by the late Richard Powell, of Moat Farm, who had been a school trustee, and took a profound interest in its welfare. This was a legacy of £500, which was to be applied to the thorough repair of the school buildings; which was accordingly done.

But on the formation of a School Board, and the erection of a modern elementary school in the vicinity, the old Endowed School, which had done such excellent work for a century and a-half when popular education had elsewhere been generally neglected, succumbed to the superior attractions of the new school, and had to be closed for lack of scholars. The old premises and the endowment lands were all sold, and the sum invested in Consols, which produce an income of £36 18s. 0d. a year. This money is (under the Charity Commissioners) in the hands of Trustees, who employ it in awarding prizes to meritorious school children belonging to the hamlet of Warley Wigorn and attending any of its public elementary schools; and also in providing two scholarships of £10 a year for more advanced children who wish to continue their education at some higher educational institution.

From 1876 until its absorption into the present-day "urban district of Oldbury" Warley had its own School Board, of which Mr. William Shakespeare was the first Clerk, succeeded in 1880 by his partner, Mr. W. F. Vernon.

A small Board school to provide the necessary accommodation for the hamlet was erected by this authority in 1881, as just mentioned.

Branch establishments of the Free Library have been provided for the two outlying districts of Langley and Warley. At the former place the library and newsroom are conducted in rooms rented from the Langley Institute; while at Warley a small branch library has been specially built to provide the necessary accommodation.

Langley, though an integral part of municipal Oldbury, and well within the industrial area, is by no means a smoking inferno or a howling wilderness of mining and manufacturing waste; for here the works are scattered more widely apart, leaving intervening spaces that are pleasant of aspect, where healthy shrubs and grass that is really green may be found growing quite bravely.

Anciently, Langley went by the name of "Wallexhall, alias Langley Wallexhall," and is first described as a manor in the sixteenth century. Since the dissolution of the abbey it has descended as a part of Oldbury, and it is probable that before that date it constituted a part of Oldbury—the "green" part, or common land, perhaps. It was actually, as its name implies, "a long ley."

As an ecclesiastical district Langley was taken out of Oldbury by an Order in Council, dated 23rd December, 1845. By 1852 the new church had been erected.

Portway Hall, on the way to Rowley, though wearing the appearance of an old castellated Tudor mansion, is a stuccoed house, which, at the beginning of the last century, replaced the half-timbered homestead of a substantial yeoman farmer. The date of the earlier edifice was, 1671, and it was the home of a family named Johnson. At the date of the Rowley Regis Inclosure Act and Award (1799) the occupant was named Daniel Johnson; a little later, when the alteration was made in the style of the fabric, his son, William Eayles Johnson, had succeeded to the ownership. Subsequently it passed into the hands of the Williams family, the first of whom to hold it was Philip Williams.

XXIX.—Oldbury and the Prospect Around.

Elihu Burritt was not the only writer to whom the romance of the Black Country appealed. A decade before he took his "Walks" in the murky labyrinths of this Dantesque region, another mid-Victorian had penetrated its sooty recesses, descriptive note-book in hand. This was Walter White, a writer who took long walks from one end of the country to the other, and then sat down to write up the topography of his travels with an appreciative and gossipy pen. His book, written in 1860, called ALL AROUND THE WREKIN, contains a highly readable account of a walking tour through this district. Everything that he says of this "great midland table-land" is interesting and informative.

Leaving Birmingham on one of his perambulations, he says:—"We now start for another walk, journeying the first few miles by railway. The Stour Valley line accompanies for some distance the broad canal—one of Telford's latest works, which runs the whole length of the Black Country without a lock, contrasting with the crookedness of Brindley's canal adjoining. Soon we are speeding past Soho, and great heaps of coal, coke, and clinkers, great refuse heaps that look like waste mortar; past large patches of wild camomile, and here and there potato patches, and little venturesome gardens that tempt Nature under very discouraging circumstances. The temptation is not in vain; for flowers and vegetables do grow, and station walls look gay with nasturtiums. We alight at Oldbury, in Worcestershire, a place of smother amid smother, and, on leaving the station, can count seventy-nine furnace and factory chimneys without turning round, all of which pour forth their cloudy contributions, varied by the blue and yellow smoke of copper-works, while noises resound afar. Among the chimneys rise those of a phosphorus factory, where, with some risk, and in a fierce temperature, phosphorus is extracted from bones, in such quantities that England, which used to import now exports the article, sending many tons to Vienna, and receiving it back on the ends of matches by hundreds of millions every week. One pound of phosphorus, worth about two-and-ninepence, suffices to charge a million matches.

"While we walk through the shabby-looking town, Temperans tells me, that, not till recently, when a public meeting was held to start a savings bank, could working men find a single place in Oldbury to help them to save money, although there were two hundred public-houses to entice them to spend it. He had to follow a speaker at the meeting who held up riches and greatness as the objects most worthy of pursuit; and, taking a truer view, impressed the crowd of hard-handed listeners with his conviction that goodness would prove to be a more satisfactory prize than either.

"Here, as elsewhere, are signs of plenty to eat; piles of wheaten bread, such as German artisans never see, unless a Serene Highness invites them to breakfast; and the stores of drapery are suggestive of plenty to wear. A man shows us the 'gainest way' to our destination, and corrects himself with 'You'll do't more gain; and reminds us of the dialect of Mercia. 'Hur's naish enough for a leddy,' said a miner, speaking of his wife one day to Temperans, meaning that she was very finical; and another described his wife as the 'esfosterinist woman as ever was.' What did he mean?

"Temperans," it may be explained, is a lay figure on which our gossip hangs his moralisings. As to his difficulties with the dialect, it may be accepted that Black Country folk retain much of the Anglo-Saxon of their forefathers.

Presently (he continues) we come to clay-diggings, and more patches of wild camomile and clover, and docks and coltsfoot, and here and there dead trees, and such ragged, perishing hedgerows as are pitiable to look on with the thought that they once looked beautiful and smelt sweetly with the bloom of May. Then appears an ironstone pit, with little tramways, and not far off, a characteristic sign, the Whimsey Inn. Then we see—a frequent sight in the Black Country—houses hooped with iron to keep them from tumbling to pieces. The ground is so widely undermined that sinkings continually occur, to the detriment of all that stands on the surface, and you can hardly see a perpendicular chimney or house; and in some instances the distortion is so great that fall seems imminent."

Well, all this, which as a description of the place is photographic in its truthfulness, portrays Oldbury as it was over half a century ago. And in some respect the picture would hold good of the place as it is yet, except that the number of tall chimney stacks which now pierce its gloomy sky has been vastly multiplied since that date. Black Country folk look very leniently on the chimney shaft, which, in active eruption, to them means trade prosperity. In the arms of the borough of Wednesbury the crest consists of a "tower in flames," which is the nearest heraldic device to a blast-furnace. The forge-stack has even inspired the poet. -

> Erect, in a Coronet Sable
>   A prince of the chimney-pot clan?
> A petrified giant of fable?
>   A pillar of heaven's wide span?
> Or is it a Tower of Babel,
> In Temple of Mammon—or Man?

The region of Oldbury as seen to-day from a railway carriage on the Stour Valley line does not present an inviting aspect to the stranger, notwithstanding fleeting glimpses caught of picturesque hill-ranges that limit the view and form a background. The landscape mostly presents itself as a depressing expanse of colliery waste, the desolation of which is intensified by the drearier mounds of clinker-cinder and furnace refuse. Even the atmosphere is contaminated, and the sickly verdure is blighted and withered by sulphur-laden fumes that are poured out from countless kilns, ovens, and furnace-stacks. Such in the Black Country is

> the smoke and stir of this dim spot
> Which men call Earth.

Yet to the south and west—on the map Oldbury is a tongue of Worcestershire territory standing up into Staffordshire, the true Black Country, by which it is surrounded on three of its sides,—in the direction of pleasant Worcestershire, there are discernible, almost on the verge of this smoky township, many pleasing vestiges of what was once a delightful stretch of country; an undulating country of green knolls and bosky dells, intersected by tiny, rippling streamlets. As the undulations roll away and merge into the greater heights beyond, the imagination is assisted in the attempt to visualise the landscape as it was a century or so ago. Nor does it require the gift of prophecy—nothing more, indeed, than an optimistic faith in the strivings of human progress—to realise a prospect of this corner of Worcestershire when fortune shall once again have restored to it its pristine natural beauties.

When the man of pensive mood stands upon one of the elevated walks in Oldbury public park, and looks around upon the scene on a clear Sunday evening—the only day on which the smoke pall lifts—regrets unbidden, and vain though they be, never fail to arise in his breast for all that the Black Country has lost, for all those amenities it has ruthlessly sacrificed at the sordid shrine of Industrialism.

To the north his view encounters the murky horizon of Wednesbury and Walsall; the murk of its sooty gloom somewhat relieved on the north-west by the Silurian domes of old Dudley, the Wren's Nest, and Hurst Hill; and on the north-east by the fairer heights of Barr, overtopping the myriad chimney-stacks of West Bromwich. In the haze eastward, above the thinning strata of Smethwick's smoke clouds, appear the higher parts of busy Birmingham. Next, round to the southward, first Warley and then Quinton range into view. And, lastly, as the spectator completes his revolution, on the horizon of the south-west—the only quarter in which Nature has not succumbed to the allurements of grimy arts and handicrafts—the view is bounded by Hagley Hills and Pedmore, beyond which lie the pleasant gardens, orchards, and farmlands of the Worcestershire countryside.

The area under survey in these pages, or, rather, the entire region of the Black Country, is an elevated table-land in the heart of England, and consequently the system of artificial waterways lying between Birmingham and Wolverhampton in one direction, and Brierley Hill and Cannock in the other, is a somewhat complicated one.

The maintenance of an adequate water supply is one problem which has to be solved. A supply cannot be maintained by natural drainage because of the altitude of the canal levels. Leakages caused by mining operations have also to be made good.

To meet the difficulty four great reservoirs have been provided, and powerful pumping machinery to lift the water to the highest levels, the maintenance of which entails a considerable yearly outlay. It is interesting to note in this connection that at one of the pumping stations at Ocker Hill is still carefully preserved, as an engineering curiosity, a most primitive-looking pumping engine, designed in 1776 by James Watt for the Birmingham Canal Company, and Boulton & Watt at Smethwick. It is constructed by Boulton & Watt at Smethwick. It is supposed to be the earliest pumping machine in existence made by that firm for sale. Until 1892 it was still regularly working, when it was removed to Ocker Hill. Even now it can be set in operation for the entertainment of visitors.

At Ocker Hill the highest and lowest levels meet, and there is installed the chief pumping station for lifting the water from one level to another, or from the bottom to the top flight of locks.

To minimise the difficulty in some degree, when the canals were cut, some of the greater elevations were pierced by tunnels. Among these are the Lappal tunnel, over two miles long, the Dudley tunnel, and the Netherton tunnel, each

Rowley Hailstone, 1845.

about a mile and three-quarters long; and the Gosty Hill tunnel, 557 yards long.

The Netherton tunnel, constructed about 1858, has a towing path on each side and is lighted by gas, but for the use of this tunnel a special rate of fourpence per ton is charged.

The other and earlier canals have no towing paths, A boat has to be propelled through them by two men, who, lying on their backs on the top of the cargo, or on a cross beam, one on each side of the boat, "tread" with their feet against the side of the tunnel, and so push the boat through at the rate of about half a mile an hour. That in these progressive times men should have to "leg" a boat in this laborious and primitive manner is scarcely creditable to our powers of invention.

XXX.—Rowley Regis: Its History and Industries

Rowley Regis, though immediately connected with Oldbury socially, and having much in common with it, is in another county. It is a lofty peninsulated tract of Staffordshire, which stretches into Worcestershire between Dudley and Cradley.

At the close of the eighteenth century their was found in this parish a piece of ancient pottery, global in shape, which contained 1,200 Roman coins, all silver, but of many different sorts. Some of them bore fine impressions of the Roman emperors, Galba and Otho.

Rowley Regis, otherwise King's Rowley, was an ancient Staffordshire manor which for a long time was Crown property.

There was a portion of Rowley outside the royal manor, which belonged to the barony of Dudley, and which for some time was known as Rowley Somery, so called from the Somery (or Someri) family, lords of Dudley Castle.

Henry II. granted the royal manor to Richard de Rushall; subsequently it was held by a family who called themselves de Rowley.

In the time of Edward III. the manor was granted to the Abbot and Convent of Halesowen by John de Hampton, of Dunstall, who reserved to himself and his heirs the right of nominating a canon who was to pray daily for the souls of him and his wife. The rights conveyed in this grant appear to have been legally unsound, as for many years afterwards the Abbot and Convent were subjected to harassing legal proceedings by claimants to the manor. In the twenty-third year of the same reign, the King made a grant of confirmation to the Abbot and Convent, notwithstanding which the old proceedings were revived in the reign of Henry VI. This King made a grant to the Duke of Clarence of the rent of £10 6s. 8d., which was yearly due from the Abbey to the

Rowley Regis Church in 1907

Exchequer for the manor of Rowley Regis. The manor remained in the hands of Halesowen Abbey till its dissolution in the reign of Henry VIII.

Rowley exhibits a striking singularity, being physically distinct from any other district in the neighbourhood, or in the county. It is principally composed of an insulated mountain, finishing in various peaks or summits. The highest summit, called Turner's Hill (876 feet), is the most elevated point in South Staffordshire; the next highest in the range being Oakham and Cawney Hills. Sedgley Beacon is not so high as any of these points (see p. 5).

The mass called The Hailstone, a bold feature on the south-west of the range, looks almost like a piece of castellated masonry; indeed, Dr. Plot absurdly expressed a doubt of it being a production of Nature.

The hills north of Rowley, running through Dudley and Sedgley, are composed of limestone; while those of Clent, to the south, are composed of what is sometimes called stone brash (or breccia), fragments of broken rock stone intermixed with sand and sandy loam. Rowley, insulated as it were, differs from both; being igneous rock with a surface soil of strong marly loam, retentive of moisture even in its elevated parts, and so producing a good herbage of grass (see p. 8).

The field fences on these hills were formerly nearly all made of the native ragstone, and some of them still remain. They were built of "randoms," that is, irregular pieces of stone, piled up without any binding of mortar or cement.

Some of the roads of this parish are so precipitous that till the beginning of the nineteenth century most of the heavy carriage was done on the backs of horses.

In the admirable little work, ROWLEY RAG, already alluded to on p. 8, will be found much useful information of a technical and scientific nature, connected with the geology and quarrying of this useful rock.

A range of hills, approaching 900 feet in height, are a physical feature that cannot but uplift (in more senses than one) the aspect of this industrial region, and soften some of the severities of its all-pervading dinginess. The smiling wheat-fields and flourishing hedgerows of the lower slopes may not wear the air of rusticity they presented sixty years ago, but wherever hills exist some of the open country must always remain. From the visible portion of the landscape can be easily inferred the beauty that must have pervaded the whole country before it was subjugated by the havoc of smoke, when every slope had its wood, every hollow its rill, bordered by pleasant pastures; when Dud Dudley was making experiments, and proving that iron could be smelted with coal, with manifest economy to Woods and forests. He would not recognise the landscape now; but the hills rise above it, and refresh the eye with pleasant scenes, interspersed with quarries, from which is dug the blue basalt, the Rowley Rag of builders and road surveyors.

"The higher we go (says the topographer previously quoted) the more rural is the way, till we come to the village of Rowley Regis, whose church is as conspicuous for miles around as that of Harrow; and here the click-click and thump-thump of hammers in nearly every house makes us aware of having arrived among the nail-makers. The whole village resounds with the strokes, and each cottage has its little forge occupying the place of a wash-house. We look into one after another and see none but women at work, three or four together, assisted in some instances by a boy or girl. The fire is in common; and one after another giving a pull at the bellows, each woman heats the ends of slender nail-rods, withdraws the first, and by a few strokes fashions and cuts off the nail, thrusts the end into the fire, and takes out the second rod, and gets a nail from that in the same way. So the work goes merrily on; the rods growing shorter and the heap of nails larger. 'It aint work as pays for men,' answers one of the women in reply to my inquiry, 'and 'tain't much better than clemmin' for women.' To make a pound of 'fine clout' requires three hours, for which the pay is threepence half-penny; so it is hard work to earn a shilling a day. The women being a comely body, I ask her why she had not married, to which she replies: 'I hanna seen my mate yet; and 'tis better to do 'ithout than have a bad 'un.'

"In another cottage two women are busy over 'countersunk tips,' for which the pay is two shillings a pound; but the nails are small and the heads must all be cone-shaped, hence it is good work to make a pound a day. One of the two lamented that the days were past when she could be in on Tuesday and earn thirteen shillings a week. Poor woman! she had come to the anvil the day after her baby was born, because her husband had long been out of work. She sits down to comfort herself with a pipe of tobacco while we talk, and says: 'We be poor foak here, and mun dew what we can.'"

This was written in 1860—its pathos remains to-day.

As some index to the social life of the place at that date, this locality had the doubtful honour of producing a common hangman, a man named Smith, whose portrait was published in a West Bromwich weekly paper, October 11th, 1913. He flourished about the middle of the nineteenth century, and is represented as wearing a smock frock and a tall hat. He lived in a little cottage at the top of Oakham Road, the tall tree in front of which was commonly called "the hangman's tree." Although called upon to occupy this prominent public office—he is credited with having performed more than a score of executions at Stafford or Shrewsbury gaol—he appears to have led a disreputable life in his earlier days, having been a regular haunter of the lowest type of tavern in Rowley Regis, and always an undesirable neighbour.

A story attaches to the manner in which Ramrod Hall, Rowley, obtained its peculiar name, It is to the effect that during the American War of

Independence it was found, particularly by the large numbers of British officers who were picked off by sharpshooters, that the shooting of the Americans was far superior to that of the British troops.

An investigation revealed what was accepted as the cause of this superiority. It was found that whereas the British soldiers used wooden ramrods, the Revolutionists rammed home their charges with ramrods of steel, and every discharge from their muskets was in consequence far more reliable than the shots fired from the loosely-charged British weapons. Upon this discovery the authorities in London forthwith issued orders for all British muskets to be fitted with steel ramrods in place of the old-fashioned wooden ones. Birmingham received the bulk of the orders, and the Brades Works supplied the steel for the new rods. One local contractor grew so rich out of this business that he built himself, at White Heath, Rowley, a substantial and comfortable residence, which his neighbours promptly designated Ramrod Hall.

This story, in some of its features at least, presents an aspect of probability.

The village of Rowley Regis is a sleepy and straggling collection of houses round a church; the main industry of its inhabitants is found in the quarrying of its stone.

Blackheath is the part of the parish which has developed most as an urban district, and, compared with Rowley, wears quite a town-like appearance. This development dates only from 1841, as will be noted in the next chapter. Blackheath is a long street of prosperous Shopkeepers, who depend on the custom and patronage of the surrounding population engaged in the manufacture of nuts, bolts, rivets, chains, spades, and shovels. Blackheath, the daughter, has far outstripped Rowley, the parent.

Old Hill, another part of the parish, down in the dip from Blackheath—the latter attains an elevation of about 600 feet, while the former sinks to about 400—and connected with it by tramway, has also grown rapidly. Although its coal has become nearly exhausted, its blast-furnace (belonging to Messrs. Noah Hingley & Sons) still blows, and many of its nail and chain hearths are still kept busy.

But the trend of modern methods is to provide factories, of which there is an ever-increasing number, for the better regulation of its thriving manufactures of chains, swivels, and anchors, of nuts and bolts, and of a number of other similar hardware productions. Old Hill is the busiest of the three places, though not so "towny" looking as Blackheath.

No account of Old Hill would be complete without allusion to the Bassano family, who in recent times have been resident there, and taken an active interest in all its public affairs. The late Walter Bassano was a colliery proprietor and iron-master in the place. He was on the Commission of the

Peace for the counties of Stafford and Worcester, and served as chairman of the local authority for a period of twenty years. The building of Trinity Church at Old Hill was mainly due to him. His two sons, Mr. Alfred and Mr. Charles W. Bassano, are now members of the local magistracy; the former, who takes a prominent part in all local government matters, being chairman of the bench.

The Bassano family is of Italian origin, a genealogy, with the arms and crest, collected from Herald's College and other sources, being given in Glover's HISTORY OF DERBYSHIRE (Vol. 2, part 1). This tree traces the descent from one Antony Bassano, who came to England about 1530, and whose family settled first in London, and afterwards removed to Derbyshire and the Midlands.

The Bassanos are connected by marriage with an ancient local family, the Hadens of Haden Hill. This family has no doubt given its name to Haden Cross; the old wayside cross now stands in the park at Haden Hill, where the Haden family lived for centuries. Mr. C. W. Bassano has in his possession a number of documents relating to the property, going back to the year 1100 A.D.

On the Tipton borders is Tividale, another populous hamlet. The entire region is one of ironworks and collieries, brickfields and stone quarries. Messrs. Doulton & Co. have also a pottery here.

Other industrial features and episodes will be noted when treating of the neighbouring parish of Cradley.

XXXI.—ROWLEY REGIS ECCLESIASTICAL HISTORY.

The church of Rowley Regis, perched on the summit of the hills, is a landmark for miles around. Not only is it the most prominent feature of the landscape, but it is core and centre of the place's historical associations.

Anciently, it was a chapel-of-ease attached to Clent, the vicar of Clent being also vicar of Rowley, the two places being some six miles apart, and both in the diocese of Worcester. The original fabric was built between the years 1199 and 1216. The only features of interest found in its deformed successor, which came down to the opening of last century, was a curious old font, supposed to be Norman, and some memorial brasses of the Haden family, dating from 1717.

Shaw, the historian of Staffordshire, who examined the church in 1797, says that it was the least remarkable ecclesiastical edifice he had ever seen; the order of architecture appeared to be Gothic, but that it had been so patched up and enlarged with bricks and mortar, as to have resulted in what he can only describe as "an unseemly structure." Then he adds a very curious note:— "There is," he says, "a charnel cave left open in the churchyard, containing a great number of human skulls and bones, to serve, I suppose, as a *memento mori* to the living villagers, and to tell them that to that complexion they must come at last." The charnel-hole remained unaltered for many years after these words were written.

Much inconvenience arose from the linking together of the two widely-separated parishes of Rowley and Clent. When a Vicar, for instance, insisted that Rowley couples wishing to be married should come to him at Clent, rather than he should journey to their parish to perform the ceremony, there was just cause for resentment.

Clerical neglect or indifference often leads to parochial friction: it did in this case.

In 1812 was published, in the form of a bulky pamphlet, "A Sketch of the Controversy Relative to the Rebuilding of the Parish Church of Rowley Regis," by the Rev. George Barrs, A.M., curate of Rowley Regis. It is a long-winded effusion, couched in very aggressive language against those parishioners who opposed the rebuilding of the church, and whom he declared to be in a contemptible minority. "The church is absolutely fit to stand no longer for a place of worship, and the parishioners are ardently desirous of having it rebuilt," he declares in his Preface of sixteen wearisome pages. It takes him 120 pages more to give an account of the proceedings in Vestry and elsewhere during the previous four years which had led up to the present position. It is adorned with classical phrases and well-worn tags characteristic of the old pamphleteering style of controversy.

The Rev. George Barrs was a strenuous and persistent fighter; and as he undoubtedly felt that he had right on his side, he continued the struggle for many years—and in the end triumphed, as he deserved to do. His success was embodied in a Private Act, passed 21st June, 1841, for "severing the chapelry of Rowley Regis from the vicarage of Clent in the county of Stafford, and for the sale of certain lands situate in the parish of Rowley Regis and belonging to the vicarage of Clent with the chapelry of Rowley Regis annexed, and thereby providing a residence and maintenance for the curate or officiating minister of Rowley Regis, and for other purposes."

Clent at that time, it may be noted, had just been severed from Staffordshire, and transferred to Worcestershire, to which it had anciently belonged, after a separation of about eight centuries. During its localisation in Staffordshire it had formed part of the Hundred of Seisdon; when re-united to its original county it was accounted a portion of the Hundred of Halfshire, the old Worcestershire Hundred of Clent having long disappeared, (see p. 107).

The preamble of the Act of 1841 enlightens us considerably as to the position of local affairs at that time. It states that the vicarage house of Clent was six miles from Rowley, and therefore inconvenient to the parishioners of the latter place; that while Clent was an agricultural parish with a population of 900, Rowley was a mining district with a population of 10,000. Further, that at this time there was no resident minister, nor a house for one—though it appears the Rev. George Barrs was curate there then, as he had been for many years previously.

On the other hand, the glebe of Rowley consisted of some sixty acres of land, estimated to be worth, for building purposes, £10,000, though the rental had never been more than £120 a year. It was therefore enacted that after the death of the Vicar, the Rev. Adolphus Hopkins, the parishes should be separated, the glebe sold, and a vicarage house built with part of the proceeds, while during the remainder of Mr. Hopkins' incumbency the stipend of the Curate of Rowley should be £150 a year.

Thus, says Mr. Amphlett in his HISTORY OF CLENT, a connection which had existed from the time of Roger de Someri was put an end to. Under this Act, Black Heath was sold off, and has since become a populous place.

The living of Rowley is now valued at £350, with residence, and is in the gift of the Lord Chancellor.

The old church was pulled down and a new one was built on the site. The tower was reconstructed in 1858. Mining operations had long affected the stability of the fabric, and in 1894 the nave was declared so unsafe that the church was closed for public worship. In 1904-6 the edifice was entirely rebuilt, with the exception of the tower.

The new church was of brick, faced with terra cotta, in the perpendicular style of architecture; it consisted of chancel, nave, and aisles; with a side chapel, and at the west end the embattled tower, containing a clock and eight bells. When this imposing structure rose from its foundations the parishioners might have thought its vicissitudes were at an end.

On the night of June 18th, 1913, the church, so long conspicuous as a landmark on the summit of Rowley Hill, was destroyed by fire. How the fire originated will probably never be known. It was variously attributed to some strikers engaged in an industrial dispute at Coomb's Wood; to a foreign-looking incendiary who is said to have been seen in the neighbourhood just before the catastrophe; but most people laid the blame at the feet of the suffragettes, who were just then particularly rampant in the violence of their political propaganda. Anyway, such a beacon light has seldom been seen, or watched with so much awe and sympathetic interest. The flames leaped up in mighty tongues, and tremendous were the crashes as one part of the roof and then another fell into the furnace raging below.

The building had cost more than £6,000, but unfortunately the amount insured was £1,500 less. The destruction of the fabric was complete. The ancient Norman font, the registers, and the bells, though injured, were happily saved.

The benefaction boards of St. Giles's Parish Church, Rowley Regis, used to be on the west wall, inside. They have long since disappeared, but the quaint phraseology of many of these boards call for preservation in the interests of the parishioners and the public.

The Lady Elizabeth Monins mentioned in the first Table formerly lived at Tividale Hall.

Table I.

The Lady Elizabeth Monins of this Parish by Deed 1703 Gave Ten Pounds a year for ever to teach Twenty-four poor children of the parish of Rowley Regis to read and write and be instructed in religion, and Five Pounds to buy books.

John Moore of Worley Wigorn in the Parish of Hales Owen by Will 1724 Gave £50 to be laid out in land, the profits whereof for ever are to be yearly distributed on St. Thomas's Day to the poor of the Parish of Rowley Regis.

William Turton Gent. of West Bromwich Gave 13s, 4d. a year for ever to the Poor of this Parish to be paid on Good Friday and St. Thomas's Day.

John Turton Gent. of this Parish by Will 1714 Gave £10 the interest whereof for ever is yearly to be given to the Poor on St. Thomas's Day.

JOHN BATE, JOHN PLANT,
Churchwardens 1727.

Mr. Thomas Newby of Brisnall Hall by a deed enrolled in the High Court of Chancery dated June 15th 1801 gave to Twenty-four Trustees a parcel of land, about 2 acres 1 rood 38 perches with a dwelling house and appurtenances situate at Worley Wigorn of which one half of the profits to be given by the said Trustees, in the Church at Rowley Regis, on the 26th December in every year, to such poor aged impotent persons inhabitants of Rowley Regis as shall not have received parochial relief, nor gone about receiving alms from any persons, and as shall appear to the said Trustees, the Churchwardens and Overseers of the poor to be the fittest objects of charity.

The other half to be given in like manner in the Chapel at Oldbury on the 26th December in every year.

Table II.

Mr. George Mackmillan late of this Parish by a deed enrolled in the High Court of Chancery dated 16th March 1792; Gave Twenty Pounds per annum to the charity school at Reddal Hill and also Twenty Pounds per annum to the school at the bottom of the village of Rowley Regis; chargeable for ever on an estate commonly called or known by the name of the Style House Farm, situate in this parish, now in the occupation of William Walter and William Adams, towards the support and maintenance of proper school masters and schoolmistresses, to be chosen by the respective Trustees of the said Schools "for the teaching and instructing of poor children of both sexes" in the principles of the Church of England as now established by law, and in all good proper and moral principles and useful learning.

"The boys to be taught to read write and account, the girls to read. knit and sew."

Table III.

Mr. Thomas Aynsworth of this Parish nail ironmonger left in January 1795 a £100 to the school at Reddall Hill, after the death of the Rev. Christopher Stephenson then minister of this parish, and of Mrs. Elizabeth his wife.

Nov. 1802 Mrs. Phoebe Parkes of this parish left £10 to the said school.

Nov. 1805 Mr. Ed. Chellingworth of this parish Maltster left £42 the interest to be divided between the said School and the village School.

Nov. 1814 Rev. C. Stephenson B.A. then Vicar of Olney Bucks. left £300 to the said school at Reddal Hill.

His son Rev. J. A. Stephenson M.A. Rector of Lympsham Somersetshire gave £30 the amount of Legacy tax paid on the said £300.

(There is understood to be a Subsidiary Endowment by Thomas Sidaway of the value of £46.)

Table IV.

Eliza White of this Parish by Will Gave £5 a year in land for ever to be given to the poor of this parish at "Midsummer and on St. Thomas's Day."

Mrs. Mary Payton late of Dudley widow by Will dated February 27th 1758. Gave Thirty Pounds the interest arising there from to be given yearly upon St. Thomas's Day to such poor widows or householders belonging to this Parish as do not go about begging or receiving collection of the Parish. At the discretion of certain Trustees.

                                    RICHARD BATE,
                                    BENJAMIN SIDAWAY,
                                    Churchwardens 1760.

John Turton Gent. of the Brades by deed dated March 22nd Ano Dom. 1688 Gave to Seventeen trustees the Almshouses at Old Hill in this Parish, in trust, for ye use of ye Poor.

John Thurling of this Parish by Will 1703 Gave £10 the Interest thereof for ever yearly to be given to ye Poor on St. Thomas's Day.

Alice Chambers Widow of this Parish by Will 1615 Gave £10 the Interest whereof for ever, is yearly to be given to ye Poor on St. Thomas's Day.

John Sparry of Clent by Will Gave £10 ye Interest whereof for ever is yearly to be given to ye Poor on St. Thomas's Day.

William Russell of this Parish by Will Gave £5 ye Interest whereof for ever to be given to ye Poor on St. Thomas's Day.

N.B—All the aforesaid gifts to be given to such Poor persons as receive no collection at ye discretion of the Church Wardens and Overseers of ye Poor for the time being.

                                    JAMES MACKMILLAN,
                                    SAMUEL SMART,
                                    Churchwardens 1749.

The Almshouses at Old Hill have long since disappeared. In the allusion to "Poor Persons who receive no collection at the discretion of the Churchwardens and Overseers," we have a vestige of the earliest form of Poor Law. The first attempts to cope with the difficulty of supporting the indigent and infirm were made by Statutes in 1552, in 1555, and again in 1557. First, the poor were restricted from begging, except within a certain specified district. Next, each parish was required to support its own poor, by means of charitable alms collected on Sundays, and stimulated by the appeals of the parson. Collectors were assigned, and the system, which was purely parochial, evidently lingered in Rowley to a later period than in most parishes.

The Staffordshire Parish Register Society recently issued to its members Vol. I. of the Rowley Regis Parish Registers, 1539 to 1684, with an index. The introduction contains a brief history of Rowley Regis, written by Miss Auden, whose ancestors were associated with the parish. Among some twenty others West Bromwich is the only other Parish in the southern extremity of the county which has been similarly honoured by the Register Society.

Of course, the volume contains much information concerning the old local families. The place-name of Oakham, a portion or most of which is in Rowley parish, appears to have been formerly written Holcombe, or Holcom.

The published volume contains a transcript of all the baptisms, marriages, and burials at Rowley Church which are recorded in the existing original registers. Unfortunately, there are some gaps—from July, 1558, to December, 1565, there are no records. From November, 1576 to August, 1602, no records are to be found, and from September, 1632, to April, 1639, there does not appear to have been any records kept at Rowley. These omissions may be accounted for by reason that Rowley Regis was merely a chapelry attached to Clent, the vicar of Clent being vicar of Rowley also. This connection existed from the thirteenth century to the middle of the nineteenth century—the Act of 1841, already referred to.

Reference has also been made to the vicars of former times insisting upon Rowley couples travelling to Clent for the performance of the nuptial ceremony; the grievance caused by this inconvenient arrangement was very openly expressed against the Rev. Lyttelton Perry, who was vicar of Clent and Rowley from 1776 to 1816.

Some of his predecessors in office might have held similar views as regards baptisms as well as marriages, but those could hardly apply to burials. Yet it is possible (says Mr. A. A. Rollason) that the gaps in the Rowley Registers might be made up from entries in the Clent Parish Registers.

XXXII.—The Cobbler Poet of Rowley.

When the rolling uplands of Rowley were still green, and in full verdure clad, no fitter nursery for a poet of the people could have been found in all England.

James Woodhouse, "the cobbler poet," our English Hans Sachs, was born at Rowley Regis in 1735.

He came of yeomen stock, and was brought up as a shoemaker, his poor earnings from which an early marriage compelled him to eke out with school-keeping.

His first poem to bring him into notice was a piece entitled "Ridicule."

An elegy dedicated to the poet Shenstone, whose residence, the Leasowes, at Halesowen, was not more than two miles distant from the shoemaker's cottage at Rowley, the former had printed in Dodsley's edition of his own work.

In one of his published letters—it is dated 1763—William Shenstone thus alludes to his humble neighbour, Woodhouse:—"My health, generally bad in Winter and Spring, has hitherto been tolerable. The influenza of last Spring continued to depress me half the Summer. Would you think the verses I enclosed were written on that occasion by a young journeyman shoemaker; and one that lives at the village of Rowley, near me? He considered my disorder in somewhat too grave a light, as I did not think my life endangered by it; but, allowing for this, and the partiality he shows me, you will think the lines pretty extraordinary for one of his occupation. They are not, however, the only, or perhaps the chief specimens of his genius; and yet before he came to me his principal knowledge was drawn from magazines. For these two or three years past I have lent him classics and other books in English. You see, to him, I am a great Mæcenas."

A postscript to this letter adds:—"I will send you some other of Woodhouse's verses when I can get him to transcribe them."

In 1764 a collection made by the friends of the humbler poet enabled him to publish his first volume, which appeared under the title of "Poems on Sundry Occasions." Two years later the work was re-issued, with a modest "author's apology," as "Poems on Several Occasions."

Woodhouse having now acquired some sort of celebrity as the "shoemaker poet," Dr. Johnson expressed a keen desire to meet him. In accordance with this wish, Woodhouse received an invitation from Mrs. Thrale, and on the occasion of the meeting of these two Staffordshire worthies, thus expressly arranged, "the great Cham of Literature" is said to have strongly recommended Woodhouse to "study Addison day and night." Shortly afterwards, however, Johnson is recorded to have uttered the opinion: "He may make an excellent shoemaker, but can never make a good poet. A schoolboy's exercise may be a good thing for a schoolboy, but it is no treat for a man." This harsh judgment Johnson is believed to have modified at a later period.

By this time Woodhouse had given up his trade, and become a carrier between Rowley and London. He next obtained an appointment as land bailiff on the Yorkshire estates of Edward Montague, where he remained some years, although he seems never to have been on very good terms with the wife of his patron, Mrs. Elizabeth Montague, the famous leader of literary society, and the queen of the "blue stockings." She was the "Patroness," the "Scintilla," or "Vanessa" of his autobiography, which at his death was found in MS. headed "The Life and Lucubrations of Crispinus Scriblerus, A Novel in Verse Written in the Last Century." This was a rhymed work abounding in digressions of a pious or a political nature, yet containing a few really good satirical lines. It was for his religious and political opinions he was ultimately dismissed the service of Mrs. Montague, to whom he had acted, on the 'death of her husband, as house steward.

He then for a short time acted as land steward to Lord Lyttelton. At a later period of his life, when out of employment, he suffered some privation. But help was forthcoming from James Dodsley, the brother of his former publisher, who assisted him to set up a book-selling business in London. It was from 211, Oxford Street, Woodhouse, in 1803, issued a volume, "Norbury Park and other Poems," dedicated to William Locke, the owner of Norbury, and a well-known art patron at that time.

The last publication of the poet was "Love Letters to My Wife," issued in 1804. His "Crispinus Scriblerus" is a rhymed work of many thousands of lines, giving his birth and education, the narrative of his life, and numerous strongly expressed reflections on the many subjects which interested his poetic temperament.

THE LIFE AND POETICAL WORKS OF JAMES WOODHOUSE (*The Leadenhall Press, 1896*), edited by a descendant, the Rev. R. I. Woodhouse, M.A., rector of Merstham, is a complete edition of his works in two volumes, the whole of the first and half the second being taken up by the wordy "Lucubrations of Crispinus Scriblerus." A few extracts from this autobiographical effort, such as are descriptive of local scenery, may be of interest to the reader. Here is Woodhouse's poetic survey of Dudley:—

> Close to the skirts of neighbouring northern height,
> Let Dudley's crowded domes arrest the sight;
> Where, o'er each sacred fane and social roof
> Rude feudal reliques lift their heads aloof.

Then comes reference to the adjacent Priory ruins, which he intolerantly describes as

> Once haunts of idols, base, and bigot Pride!
> Where papal Antichrist the sceptre swayed
> And Superstition plied her pagan trade.

Next, Himley is referred to; the terms of reference disclosing that the poet, born a yeoman on the Dudley estate, had partaken of his lord's hospitality there:—

> Near, on the left let Himley's woods appear;
> To Health propitious, and to Friendship dear!
> Sweet hospitable seat of Dudley Ward
> Who deigned to countenance our humble Bard!
> His feudal baron but his friendly lord
> Not shunned for tyranny, or Pride abhorred
> With whom Crispinus erst those woods explored
> And shared the honours of his noble board.

His poetic vision then takes in "the vast champaigne's expansive sweep," a comprehensive view of the entire countryside, its "peopled spots, wild wastes, and sylvan scenes and in the distance he sees

> On the broad bosom of surrounding dells,
> With sovereign pride, the conic Wrekin swells.

and anon—

> Proud, in the hollow of a dreary space
> Fair Enville rises, with peculiar grace.
>
> * * * * *
>
> With strong antithesis ascending, by,
> Kinver's long steril ridge benumbs the eye—
> Lifts its bleak steril back, for ever bare
> Embrown'd with burning heat, or freezing air.

After several hundreds of lines, treating of Stourbridge and Old Swinford, of the Leasowes (his friend Shenstone's seat at Halesowen) and Hagley, with passing allusions to the territorial magnates, Lords Ward, Lyttelton, and Dartmouth, the district between Birmingham and Wolverhampton comes in for poetic treatment:—

> Now, see the Sun, in day's declining race
> Each object brightens in Earth's Eastern space.
> * * * * *
> His evening legacies of light imparts
> To crowded schools of Industry and Arts.
> Exhibits bustling Birmingham to sight

In multiplying streets and villas bright—
Delineates, rear'd aloft, in russet hue
Barr-beacon's barren heights, in obvious view

Shews Wednesbury's and Walsall's blazing spires
Like metals, fused, before the melting fires;
And Wolverhampton's turrets, fair, unfold
Near Northern boundaries, tipt with burnished gold.

As it is seldom, indeed, that a coalfield inspires the poet, Woodhouse's lines on the Black Country cannot fail to interest:—

Coal's black bitumen deeper still retires,
Like sable clouds concealing latent fires;
Which, when extracted from the hollow'd rocks
To birth, obstetric, brought in solid blocks,
It shines, bless'd substitute for solar powers,
To cheer the heart, to cheat dull evening hours,
And cherish chilly man, with gladdening glow,
When Earth lies shrouded in her sheets of snow.

James Woodhouse died in 1820, and was buried in St. George's Chapel graveyard, near the Marble Arch. He was a man of stately bearing, six feet six inches in height, and in old age wore a patriarchal aspect. The 1896 edition of his complete works contains an engraving by Henry Cook of a painting of him by Hobday. Another portrait of the poet is believed to be extant. One of his sons realised a fortune as a linen draper in Oxford Street, London.

XXXIII.—Netherton, Brierley Hill, and Pensnett

It is not within the scope of this volume to describe Dudley, but passing mention may be made of Netherton on the near side of it, and of the Wren's Nest Hill on the farther side. The former is a smoky region, a place of heavy work, where in the very heart of England anchors are forged and cable-chains are made for ships that plough the waters of every ocean on the face of the globe. Relief for the eye is obtained by lifting it above the clouds of smoke, that seem to be for ever drifting over this "lower town," to the range of limestone hills upon which stands Dudley proper. For the companion hill of the Wren's Nest does offer diversity of scene, exhibiting combinations of wood and rock among its industrial features of smoky kilns and gaunt mining gear.

To the prosaic, workaday aspect of "the Nether-town" a contrast is provided in the sentimental associations that cluster around the romantic ruins of the high town.

Dudley (J. M. W. Turner, R.A.)

The great English landscape painter, J. M. W. Turner, R.A., was struck by the peculiar situation and surroundings of Dudley Castle, the anachronism of an ancient feudal fortalice in the midst of modern forges, furnaces, and iron-mills.

Turner—whose favourite poet, by the way, was Thomson, specially gifted as a word-painter of landscape, and who is mentioned at large elsewhere in these pages—also exhibited a drawing of "Woolverhampton, Staffordshire," at the Royal Academy show of 1796.

These drawings of local landscape belong to what is technically known as the great painter's First, or Schoolday Group, 1775-1800.

John Ruskin, in his voluminous notes upon the works of this great British artist, in discussing the drawings with black skies, calls particular attention to "how the distant Castle is painted in the Dudley" landscape.

"The hasty execution of the sky," says Ruskin in another note, "almost with a few radiating sweeps of the brush, is most notable. . . . I have no doubt that at least twice the time given to this whole drawing of Dudley was spent on the sky of the Heysham [another fine landscape] alone."

"As an example," he goes on, "of rapid execution, however, the drawing is greatly admirable; and quite faultless to the point he intends."

In another passage our incomparable art critic interprets the mind of the artist as expressed in the Dudley landscape:—

"One of Turner's first expressions of his full understanding of what England was to become. Compare the ruined castle on the hill, and the church spire scarcely discernible among the moon-lighted clouds, as emblems of the passing away of the baron and the monk," etc.

The Dudley picture is also referred to in "Lectures on Landscape"; it has been finely engraved by R. Wallis; reproduced by photogravure in TURNER AND RUSKIN (Vol. II., p. 324), and in colours in THE WORKS OF RUSKIN.

Some 150 years ago Parliament passed the Pensnett Enclosure Act, which gave the Earls of Dudley the right to get coal without fully or adequately compensating the surface owners; consequently houses which have been built on land of which the owners failed to purchase "the ungotten minerals" below are liable to be undermined. Indeed, great numbers of well-built houses and trim cottages throughout this region have been undermined, and remorselessly wrecked; many have fallen to pieces, and of those that have not actually collapsed in ruins there are hundreds that, in subsiding below the street level, have cracked and bulged and "settled" into all sorts of tilted angles, till the place looks as if an earthquake had struck it, and left it to endure as it may in pitiable desolation.

Brierley Hill, a similar district adjoining Netherton, though in Staffordshire, is a part of the civil parish of Kingswinford, in which coal and iron were dug in very early times, and which has now become a thriving iron-working town.

A chapel-of-ease was erected to meet the requirements of the growing population of the place in 1767, and the first curate was a man of some little note.

This was the Rev. Thomas Moss, B.A., author of "The Beggar's Petition," and afterwards domestic chaplain to the Marquis of Stafford, at Trentham.

He was born at Bilston and educated at Wolverhampton Grammar School. His poems are not numerous, but he will long be remembered for his well-known lines:—

> Pity the sorrows of a poor old man!
>   Whose trembling limbs have borne him to your door,
> Whose days are dwindled to the shortest span;
>   Oh! give relief and heaven will bless your store.

A fuller account of this clerical poet, who died at Stourbridge in 1808, will be found in STAFFORDSHIRE WORTHIES, pp. 95-98.

In the folklore of the locality, Brierley Hill is one of those places at which the jokers, in the conceit of their own superiority, have made much mock.

It is the place where Satan is said to have made his will; after which—

> He staggered on to Dudley Wood soide
> Wheer he laid him down and very soon doide.

And what was it that brought the Devil to despair and death in this tragic manner? It was, say the sage and self-satisfied gobemouches, that he thought his burning Gehenna below was likely soon to be eclipsed and entirely outdone by the blazing furnaces that poured out their myriad flames nightly from the busy ironworks of Brierley Hill.

> When Satan stood on Brierley Hill, and far around it gazed,
> He said, I never more shall feel at hell's fierce flames amazed.

All round Cradley, Netherton, Round Oak, Pensnett, and Brierley Hill the streets and highways are disfigured by crazy-looking dwellings, "pulled" about in every direction by the adjacent mining operations.

The Enclosure Act of 1784, referred to, did contain a sort of compensation clause. But it was framed when social conditions, extent of population, and many other factors in life were very different from what they are to-day. It was enacted that in the event of any damage done to property by mining operations, the whole of the landowners in the area covered by the Act should be jointly responsible, and each could be called upon to pay his proportionate share. At that time the Earl of Dudley was the chief landowner, the population was sparse, the amount of mining was small, and it was a comparatively easy matter to settle claims.

The Act was accompanied by maps which showed which properties enjoyed the rights of freehold; but these valuable documents have since unaccountably disappeared, both from the Local Registry and from the Record Office in London.

Enormous mineral wealth lay beneath the surface of Pensnett Chase, where in feudal times the barons of Dudley had taken their lordly pleasure; there were rich deposits of iron, fire-clay, and limestone, the winning of which has brought to this one-time sylvan solitude a large industrial population.

When claims for compensation are made now—generally by the thriftiest members of the community, aim is to own their dwellings, and who are therefore deserving of encouragement—the difficulty is, owing to the ambiguity of the Act, to bring home the responsibility to anyone in particular.

As the claimants are usually men of small financial resources, the question of compensation is seldom or never fought to an issue, with the consequence that in some cases at least gross injustice must prevail.

Political agitators have not failed to make capital out of this state of affairs in the Pensnett area, pointing out the necessity for a reform in the land laws, and particularly for the nationalisation of mining royalties.

XXXIV.—Cradley: Its Early History

At the time of the Domesday Book Cradley was a part of Fitzanculph's barony of Dudley, and was then in the holding of one Payn, who had succeeded the Saxon holder, Wigar. Subsequently it followed the descent of the manor of Northfield, and in 1419 was purchased by John Beauchamp. A few years later Cradley, Clent, Hagley, and Old Swinford passed into the possession of the Earl of Wiltshire (whose mother was a Beauchamp), and when that nobleman was beheaded in 1460 Cradley was granted to Fulke Stafford, passing two years later into the hands of one Prout. The two latter holders were doubtless partisans of the House of York, in whose favour the tide of war turned in 1460—for at this time the country was torn by the disastrous civil contentions known as the Wars of the Roses.

James Butler, created Earl of Wiltshire in 1449 by Henry VI., was a powerful Irish baron, being fifth Earl of Ormond. He was Commissioner of Calais, Rysbank, and the Marches of Picardy; was a Knight of the Garter, and held the office of Lord High Treasurer of England for five years. He was one of the most prominent and powerful members of the Lancastrian faction in Ireland; yet in 1449, when Richard, Duke of York, was sent to the sister isle in a sort of honorary exile, Ormond at once made gracious overtures to him, and on the Duke's departure from Ireland in 1451 was appointed his deputy and representative. At the decisive Battle of Towton (1460), which brought Edward, Duke of York, to the throne, he fought on the Lancastrian side and was taken prisoner there by an esquire named Richard Salkeld, who conveyed him to Newcastle, where he was beheaded. His estates were forfeited, and in 1473 Cradley was at the disposal of Elizabeth, wife of Edward IV., who in 1477 made a grant of the "chapel of St. Erasmus at Cradley" to the Abbot of Westminster.

Since that period Cradley has followed the descent of Hagley, now belonging to Viscount Cobham.

The manorial mill of Cradley is frequently mentioned in ancient documents. In Elizabeth's reign Thomas Birch claimed liberty of a fish-pond, which is called Birches Mill Pond. Just before the Dissolution of the monasteries the Abbot of Halesowen had altered the course of the boundary stream between Cradley and Rowley (it was also the boundary between the counties of Stafford and Worcester), for which concession he paid to the lord of Cradley an acknowledgment of twelve pence and a pound of wax yearly.

The park of Cradley was in existence in the time of Henry VIII., but had disappeared by Elizabeth's time. The essential feature of a "park" was that it was an enclosed area; it was a forest franchise granted to noblest whose territorial holdings were large, but not so vast as those who ranked themselves, as did the barons of Dudley, next to royalty. The barons of Dudley held the higher franchise, called a "Chase." Thus Pensnett Chase was a privileged place for the preservation of deer and other beasts of the forest.

According to the county historian, Nash, the ruins of the manor house were in existence in his time (close of the eighteenth century) "though much overgrown." Near the ruins, he says, was the site of the "Chapel Leasow." This chapel may have been part of the abbey estate, for it evidently disappeared very shortly after the Dissolution.

Cradley is mentioned as a separate manor in 1556, but apparently it became incorporated with Halesowen shortly afterwards.

Modern records state that a Court Baron and Court Leet were held at Cradley during the last century, on the last Tuesday in October of each year, at which the Steward of the Manor presided as judge, and was assisted by "a jury of respectable inhabitants."

Cradley is on the Stourbridge side of Halesowen, and is officially described as "a chapelry in the lower division of the Hundred of Halfshire, in the county of Worcester." On its north and west it is divided from Cradley Heath, which is in Staffordshire, by the river Stour.

How the "chapelry" came into existence is a piece of ecclesiastical history almost as interesting as that of Oldbury—it is not an exact parallel, though again it is a record of Nonconformity and free religious effort having to give way to established Episcopalianism.

From the latter end of the seventeenth century there appears to have been a Presbyterian church in Cradley, which is supposed to have been removed from King Swinford. Land was purchased in that part of the parish called Pensnett Chase in 1704, and in 1707 a place of worship was erected.

In the early years of this church, the Dissenters of King Swinford village and of several parts of the parish formed a congregation. A place called the Bower was particularly known in those times as one where they met for worship. There were probably also many resident at the same time at Cradley. From the time of the building of the Pensnett chapel they became better known. A Charity School was founded in 1746, and a parsonage house built in 1759.

From 1705 to 1736 Mr. Josiah Bassett (a youth educated at the expense of Mr. Henry Hickman, of Old Swinford) was minister. He was succeeded by the Rev. Joseph Fownes, who was author of a piece on Toleration, and published a few of his sermons. The Rev. Noah Jones succeeded to the pastorate in 1748; he was a very active minister, labouring incessantly in this place till his removal to Walsall in 1762. A brief memoir of his own life, with papers containing various accounts of Dissenters' Academies, formed part of his collection of MSS. The period of Mr. Jones' ministry in Cradley was remarkable for the flourishing state to which he brought the church. Soon afterwards a considerable increase of places of worship took place in this vicinity. The Rev. Joseph Baker followed him, and he was succeeded in 1789 by the Rev. James Scott.

In 1796 Pensnett Meeting-house was sold to a Society of Wesleyan Methodists, and a new place of worship, known as Park Lane Chapel, was erected. In 1807 Mr. Scott had, as co-pastor, the Rev. Benjamin Carpenter; other ministers in succession were Alexander Paterson and William Bowen.

Going back to the earlier records of this Presbyterian church, other details concerning the Bower in the parish of King Swinford have been found. It appears that a Mr. John Parkes, of that place, had worship performed in his house, and gave shelter there to the congregation of Cradley in 1715 and 1716, when their chapel was destroyed by the Sacheverell rioters.

Among the names honourably recorded for steadfastness in those trying times are John Davis, Rowley, Joseph Whitehouse Dalton, and Mrs. Hipkins. The ancestors of the family of Hunt, of Birmingham and The Brades, resided then at Homer Hill.

The first minister, Mr. Bassett, was an indefatigable worker, and much esteemed by his congregation. Resident in Birmingham, he officiated at Cradley for thirty years, though his salary was small, and the roads at that time extremely bad. His death occurred on a Sunday after his return from Cradley, in consequence of an apoplectic seizure.

The village of Cradley (sometimes called Cradley Town to distinguish it from Netherend—in which Park Lane is situated) also set up an Independent church. The congregation originally consisted of Churchmen, Baptists, and Independents, who founded a church and provided (1789) a place of worship for the Rev. Thomas Best to officiate in. After the lapse of a few years the building proved too small for the congregation, and a project was formed to provide a larger one. A good site was secured, and a large and handsome chapel was erected upon it. In accomplishing this a heavy debt was contracted, which no appeals to the public for subscriptions ever enabled the promoters to liquidate; the property had to be sold, and even then the sum realised failed to satisfy all the creditors.

On 12th September, 1798, the building was consecrated according to the rites of the Established Church, by Dr. Hurd, bishop of Worcester.

Shortly afterwards Mr. Best—a godly man and a strenuous worker, who, as a Dissenter, had opened the first Sunday School in Halesowen, in 1773—was ordained by the bishop of Llandaff, and Lord Lyttelton gave up the patronage to him (as perpetual curate) and his heirs for three turns, provided they happened in 99 years. This was accomplished by means of an Act of Parliament "for settling the right of presentation to the new chapelry of Cradley" (1799).

Out of the dissolved Independent church grew up a Baptist Society, which in 1803 provided itself with a place of worship.

Strange, indeed, have been the struggles and vicissitudes of the self-supporting "free churches." But freedom is always a precious boon.

In the early decades of the nineteenth century the population of Cradley began to increase steadily with the accession of new industries. The census of 1841 showed that there were 2,686 inhabitants in the village. Then came the constitution of an ecclesiastical parish, and in 1850 the Post Office authorities set up a "receiving house" here. At that time Cradley was not only extensively making nails, hammers, files, and rasps, but included sword blades and bayonets among its hardware productions, with which the manufacture of bellows was not unfitly associated. But the making of felt hats, which was also practised, seems quite outside the category of trades likely to take root in this locality.

Yet, with accession of population and the introduction of a number of hardware industries, Cradley retained some of its ancient amenities as a place of pleasant aspect.

A DIRECTORY of the year 1836 says:—

> Beautifully situated in a woody district, amid pleasing walks, and on the banks of a large pool or artificial lakes, is Cradley Spa, where warm and cold baths have been erected; the water is impregnated with

sulphate of soda, magnesia, etc., and is much used by invalids during the Summer. An attempt was made at one period to manufacture salt here, but with very inconsiderable success.

Even as late as 1850 we find this in a DIRECTORY that date:—

A mile from the northern extremity of Cradley, in a romantic vale, agreeably diversified with plantations of firs, was a spring of salt water, called the Lady Well, highly esteemed on account of its medicinal qualities. Up till the middle of last century the well was much frequented in the Summer season.

XXXV.—CRADLEY: ITS INDUSTRIAL RECORD

Cradley is historically identified with the earliest era of the local iron trade, with the very beginnings of the Black Country. It was here that Dud Dudley made his earliest attempts at smelting iron with pit coal.

Dud Dudley, the famous pioneer of the iron trade, was an illegitimate or "half-son" of one of the lords of Dudley Castle. He was the fourth son of the prodigal Edward Sutton-Dudley, by Elizabeth Tomlinson, "his lordship's concubine." He was born about 1599, educated at Balliol College, Oxford, and early in life developed into a speculative and inventive genius. In his family pedigree the herald describes him as "of Tipton."

Noting that the woods and forests of the country were disappearing fast before the heavy demands of the ironsmelters and blacksmiths; and looking upon the charcoaling of sound British oak as a grievous waste of the nation's strength—those were the days of the "wooden walls of old England," and when as yet the memory of the Spanish Armada had scarcely faded from the public mind—he proposed to abandon vegetable fuel, and to take up the use of that mineral fuel which lay in such vast abundance all round about him.

Having some previous knowledge of his father's ironworks, he was fetched home from college, in 1619, to take up the management of them at the early age of 20.

These ironworks consisted of one furnace, and "cast-iron works of sundry sorts," on Pensnett Chase (the timber of which was being rapidly depleted to keep them going); besides two forges or iron-mills, called Cradley Forges, where the product of the furnace was "fined into good merchantable bar-iron."

He soon availed himself of his position to test the practicability of his theory. His first trial meeting with a slight success, he was animated to pursue the experiment farther. The quality of the iron produced by using coal was good and "profitable," but the output did not exceed "3 tons per week."

Accounting himself a patriot in thus trying to save the nation's supply of ship timber, so essential to the country's defence, he invoked the favour of the king, and James I. granted him a "pattent," dated at Newmarket, March, 1619.

Our inventor, with admirable candour, admitted that others had previously made efforts in the same direction, his forerunners being " Simon Sturtevant, Iohn Rovenson, Esq., and one —— Gimbleton, Esq.," all of whom had failed in a greater or less degree, while he had met with some measure of success.

Unfortunately, in the year following the grant of the patent for making iron with pit coal, a great flood of rain on the May-day not only "ruinated" Dud Dudley's ironworks and inventions, but many other men's ironworks; and at the neighbouring market-town called Sturbridge in comitatu Wigorniæ," although the inventor sent with speed to preserve the people from drowning, "one resolute man was carried from the bridge there in the day time, and the nether part of the town was so deep in water that the people had much ado to preserve their lives in the uppermost rooms in their houses."

The destruction of Dud Dudley's inventions was a source of intense delight to all the rival iron-masters of the district. But he speedily set to work and restored his plant; produced more "merchantable good iron" by his patent process, of which he sent specimens to the Tower, by King James's command, exhibiting "all sorts of bar iron fit for making musquets, and iron for great bolts fit for shipping"; which iron, being thoroughly tested, he silenced his jealous trade rivals, who had lost no opportunity to disparage his inventions at Court. Yet even with the aid of his noble father he was able to obtain only a fourteen years' patent. Parliament was setting its face against the grant of trade monopolies by the king. Still, our indomitable inventor went on cheerfully with his experiments, each year making a good store of iron which realised twelve pounds per ton; "also all kinds of cast-iron wares as brewing-cysterns, pots, morters, and better and cheaper than any yet made in these nations with charcoals."

The opposition offered to the new system by his rivals of the old charcoal order was fierce and unrelenting. When he erected a new furnace at Hasco Bridge, Sedgley, 27 feet square, and fitted with larger bellows to turn out 7 tons per week, they spitefully incited a riot, and instigated a lawless mob to cut the obnoxious bellows to pieces and demolish the works.

With accidents, riotings, and costly lawsuits—a succession of dispiriting drawbacks—our unfortunate inventor became utterly wearied and disabled. Then, as a climax, he was wrongfully imprisoned in the Counter, in London, for a debt of several thousands of pounds.

All these troubles brought him worldly wisdom, as was manifest when he succeeded (2 *May 14 Charles I.*) in obtaining a new patent. But how? By including in partnership with himself four others—a Courtier, a Member of

Parliament, a Counsellor at the Temple, and an Ironmaster—one of his neighbours! For mark why! His invention was "so much opposed formerly at Court, at the Parliament, and at the law."

But fate still buffeted the unlucky inventor. Others claimed a previous grant of the patent; and then, to crown all his troubles, the Civil Wars broke out.

Dud Dudley became a colonel in the Royalist army, and in the cause of loyalty lost his works, his estate, two mansions, and 500 timber trees. Still, he did not lose his life, and though the war dragged on, and the years rolled by, his inventive spirit never flagged, nor did his determination fail.

On the Restoration of Charles II. (1660) Colonel Dud Dudley did not lose a day in repeating his application for a monopoly patent, urging his well-proved loyalty to the throne, and arguing the importance of his invention to the interests of the nation.

All these facts of his life's labours and grievous disappointments are set forth at great length in a little book he published in 1665, to which, after the fashion of the times, he gave a fanciful Latin name. He called it METTALUM MARTIS, which signifies the "Metal of Mars," or translated more freely, "The Materials of War." A reprint of this curious little work, in *facsimile*, was produced in 1851 by John Nock Bagnall, an iron-master, and author of the first History of Wednesbury.

It remains only to note, first, that it took that generous monarch, Charles II., five years to consider the justice and admit the reasonableness of his unfortunate supporter's petition. And, secondly, that in his little treatise the ingenious Dud states that "near the author's dwelling, called Greens-lodge, there are four forges, namely, Greens-forge, Swin-forge, Heath-forge, and Cradley-forge."

As we have seen (p. 75) the great problem of creating sufficient draught in a furnace to burn the coal at smelting heat was not really solved till a century or so afterwards, when the steam-blown blast-furnace was invented.

Cradley as an industrial area in modern times has acquired an unenviable reputation; and in this category must be included with that group of small towns and villages that hereabouts stretch across both sides the borders of Worcestershire and Staffordshire. The name of Lye Waste seems to suggest a modern significance which its origin does not justify; for in early English it merely signified the Ley (or field) that was waste, that is, untilled.

The previously quoted topographer of 1860, approaching the place from Rowley, says he got "a view of a broad smoky valley," and there was "the populous district of Lye Waste, which a few years ago was a part of heathendom, with a population brutally vicious and ignorant; but is now, by means of schools and itinerant preachers, showing signs of morality and civilisation."

The population might possibly have been more ignorant than their neighbours, but the viciousness, which exemplified itself in cock-fighting, bull-baiting, and other brutal sports, was common to every part of the Black Country in those days.

Progress was more marked in the second than in the first half of last century; there are not wanting signs that it will be much more rapid in the future.

For local government purposes Lye, with Wollescote, containing a working-class population of some twelve thousand, now constitutes an Urban District.

Though mostly a region of squalor, dirt, and desolation, there are still remaining a few faint evidences which show that once it was a delightful country of charming miniature valleys; but all the loveliness has long since been hammered, stamped, and smashed out of it by the greed of modern commercialism.

There is little of the beauty of life left to the nail and chain-makers of this depressing region. Cradley proper is even worse than Cradley Heath. The domiciliary workshops are (or were) generally situated in close, airless yards. They were purposely built on to the houses, so that the occupants could step at once from the kitchen to the anvil. And the reward for this desecration of the sanctities of the domestic hearth was a pittance that scarcely provided the necessaries of life, and failed altogether to secure any of its decencies. But nail-making by hand, if not already dead, is a doomed industry. It is, therefore, unnecessary here to repeat or supplement what has already been said of the nail trade and its iniquitous traffickings (see p. 130).

The bulk of the chain-making is done by women, who heat the rod in a little smith's hearth, then cut a length and weld it into a link with a hand hammer, finally shaping it with a heavy machine hammer, called an "oliver," brought down by a foot-treadle. Not a limb but is called upon to exert itself!

It is by no means uncommon for three generations of women and girls to work together in the same shop; and occasionally an improvised cradle may be there containing a future nail-maker, whose lullaby is the clink of busy hammers—a chorus of industrial activity that resounds through the village all the long and wearisome working hours of the day.

In one workshop there perhaps will be a young woman engaged in the work of making three-sixteenth inch chain, while her child, a few months old, sleeps soundly on the bellows, undisturbed either by its motion or its stoppage, and for which at the end of a laborious week she will be paid four shillings: and in the next shop, maybe, an old man nearing the end of life, making three-eighths inch chain, for which he will get three shillings and sixpence a hundredweight, finding his own shop, tools, and fuel—his utmost endeavour will not result in an output of two hundredweights in the week.

It was no uncommon thing for women to work seventeen and eighteen hours a day at the chain, nail, and rivet-making trades in Cradley, Old Hill, Rowley, and Halesowen, with what physical degeneration of the race as the resultant may be imagined—-emaciated forms and worn faces characterised the entire working population.

Though men were employed on the larger sizes of work, so large a proportion of women workers were engaged in these industries that trades unionism seemed paralysed before them. In times of slackness and competition, these ill-paid toilers often undersold each other; and so gross became the scandal that at last a public outcry was raised against its iniquities. Agitation in the newspapers and in Parliament demanded the appointment of a Royal Commission to inquire into the underpaying, or "sweating" of these victimised toilers. Happily, the agitation proved successful; the Royal Commission on Sweating got to work in 1889, which date may be reckoned the turning point in the history of these enslaving industries.

An outcome of the Commission's inquiry was the Trades Board Act, and one of the few industries scheduled to come within the range of its beneficent operations was that of chain-making. As of old the "Nail Foggers" had been accustomed to fleece the poor unsophisticated nailmakers, so now the employers made a last over-reaching effort to evade the provisions of the new Act fixing the minimum rate of wages in the chain trade. In the August of 1910 the women chain-makers of Cradley Heath were constrained to set up a determined opposition to those employers who had induced them to sign agreements to continue their work at the old rates during the "buffer period" allowed by the Act before the new scale ($2\frac{1}{2}$d. an hour) came into force.

The women took alarm when they found that under their foolish agreement the masters were working them all at great pressure in order to accumulate heavy stocks, so that when the time came for the payment of the new rate of wages they would either be locked-out or put on short time. The workers declined to be exploited any longer.

The dispute was carried on by the women with great spirit. In the appeal which they made to the public for support, the banner carried in a street procession by one old woman was worded:

ENGLAND'S DISGRACE!
LOCKED OUT AFTER
67 YEARS CHAIN MAKING!
HELP THE FIGHT
FOR $2\frac{1}{2}$d. AN HOUR!

This summed up the situation very tersely and yet very eloquently.

Comparatively few females are now employed, and those only on the lightest work and under better conditions. The male operatives are more able to safeguard their trade interests.

As already said the wrought nail-making has been practically swept away by the inexorable competition of up-to-date machinery. The domestic workshop is rapidly disappearing; and even in this backward and neglected part of the Black Country the rights of labour are at last being vindicated, and a new era of progress inaugurated.

The manufacture within the same area of anvils and vices, anchors and cables, articles too heavy for female or child manipulation, will be found to have a cleaner and a briefer history, if a less interesting one.

Still, it is a curious fact to be noted that ships' cables and great anchors should be produced in the very centre of England, and as far as is physically possible from the seaboard, at inland places like Tipton, Netherton, and Old Hill.

When it is borne in mind that Nelson's fleet knew nothing of chain cables, but encumbered its decks with immense coils of hempen rope, the modernity of this industry as compared with the ancient nail-making trade will be recognised.

It was about 1808, or very soon after Trafalgar, that the making of chains for use on board ship was set up along the Tyne.

In 1820 Mr. Noah Hingley, who was then carrying on the business of a nail master and dealer in small chains at Cradley, introduced the cable trade into this locality. In his travels to Liverpool and other ports he had seen and noticed the chain cables in use amongst the shipping; he resolved to attempt the manufacture in the Midlands, and took an order.

This was a bold venture, as no workman in this locality had ever seen a chain of such proportions; but after a few trials one hefty workman, with the assistance of two strikers and two boys to blow the bellows, succeeded in turning out an excellent chain cable, which was sent to Liverpool, approved, and accepted. Such a wonder was the making of these first cables that people came from far and wide to see the forging of them.

Mr. Hingley afterwards introduced the making of anchors, bringing workmen from Liverpool with a knowledge of the trade, and subsequently erecting the first Nasmyth's steam hammer in the Midlands for the purpose.

This enterprising manufacturer lived to see the chain cable and anchor trade developed here to a large extent—indeed, the manufacture of them is now almost exclusively located in this district. He also took part in the establishment of proper testing machines at Netherton (where he had made his first trials) and at Tipton, under the authority of an Act of Parliament, making compulsory the testing of all cables and anchors intended for British ships.

The making of cables and anchors is carried on in factories by men and boys, with the aid of machinery, and it consumes 100,000 tons of iron in a year. The work is laborious, but well-paid.

See also HISTORY OF TIPTON, p. 48.

Messrs. Noah Hingley & Sons are extensively engaged in the manufacture of anvils, anchors, and chain-cables, having their own pits, furnaces, and other sources for producing the raw material they so largely use.

XXXVI.—A GREEN BORDERLAND OF MUCH ROMANTIC INTEREST.

Standing on the rolling upland of Rowley, in Staffordshire, to which the Worcestershire heights have here subsided, and turning his back on the sable-plumed chimney-stacks of the Black Country, it is a very pleasant borderland over which the spectator gazes when he turns his eyes towards the distant valley of gracious Sabrina and the Wigornian gardens of fair Pomona. Here, in front of the Clent and Lickey Hills, which lift themselves in the distance, are Quinton and Frankley, a green margin-land to Birmingham as well as to the Black Country.

Howley (or Owley), on the brow of the hill near Quinton, is the site of one of the ancient abbey granges. As a manor, known by the name of Owley Grange, it was granted in 1533 on a thirty-four years' lease to William Geste and Elizabeth his wife, by William Taylor, the last Abbot of Halesowen.

Howley is generally supposed to be the place of the famous horse-shoeing episode in the adventures of Charles II. after his flight from Worcester field in 1651. The fugitive monarch, after being hidden in the Royal Oak at Boscobel, was sheltered by the Lanes at Bentley Hall, which lies between Darlaston and Walsall. He left Bentley, disguised as a groom, with Mistress Jane Lane riding on a pillion behind him, on September 10th, and passed through Inkberrow, on the 11th staying at Thorne Farm, the residence of the Bushell family; and thence on towards Long Marston. There is no possibility of Charles having traversed the road north of Birmingham on that occasion, and therefore the romantic episode could not have taken place at the old smithy which stood at the junction of the old Chester and Lichfield roads, as has sometimes been claimed by Sutton and Erdington folk.

The story goes that the horse cast a shoe, and the fugitive stopped to have a new one put on. While it was being fitted, the pretended serving-man asked the brawny smith, "What news?" "None, since the beating of those rogues, the Scots. I can't hear o' that rogue, Charles Stuart, being taken yet. An' I come across him, I'll ding him o'er the yed wi' my hammer!" Charles much applauded the honest smith's opinion, and sententiously observed that when caught the rascal ought to be hanged. Such is the romantic old tale told of Howley smithy.

In the kitchen of Howley Grange Farm, suspended from the great beam in front of the fireplace, hangs a long pike or spear some fifteen feet long, with an iron head two and a-half feet in length. The story told of this old weapon is that, on the occasion of his memorable flight, King Charles found a hiding-place in this capacious chimney; and that when the Parliamentary soldiers went towards it to search for him, a great owl flew out, whereupon the officer in command observed that there could be no one hidden there, and the troopers forthwith took their departure. In token of his gratitude for the succour he had received, the King is said to have left this lance behind him as a memento of his escape; and also as a more substantial boon he is said to have granted the occupiers of the house perpetual immunity "from tythe and taxation."

Howsoever that may be, it is a fact that the house has been rebuilt since 1651, and that the pike has been most carefully re-inserted. There is very little probability in this story, which seems to have been inspired by the derivation of the name Owley from owl (see p. 14). That the royal fugitive found himself in the vicinity of Quinton and Frankley on that occasion is more than probable.

As if in corroboration of the foregoing traditions, there is at Hunnington, towards Frankley, an old house known as Good Rest Farm, a name said to have been acquired at the time of, and as part of another incident in, the same romantic episode.

The tale which pretends to account for this uncommon name says that the thinly-disguised monarch slept at this house on the night in question. The next morning, when the King arose and came downstairs, his honoured and loyal hosts respectfully inquired how his Majesty had slept; to which he graciously replied, "Good rest, thank you!" From which memorable and happy reply the house acquired the very comfortable name by which it has ever since been known.

At Frankley is the source of the Stour, which takes its course hence through Halesowen and Stourbridge to the Severn. The river Rea also rises near by, at Egg Hill, but taking its way through Northfield and Birmingham, runs its course to the sea in the very opposite direction, paying its tributary waters into the Trent.

At Frankley formerly stood the seat of the Lyttletons, which was burnt down during the Civil Wars that it might not fall into the hands of the Parliamentary forces.

Frankley Beeches is a landmark on a commanding hill to the west of the church. The largest of the famous beeches was cut down some years ago—it is said by the axe of the late Rt. Hon. W. E. Gladstone, who was closely connected with the Lyttletons by marriage. Other trees have been carefully re-planted, and are growing up.

Mr. E. Marston Rudland, in the BALADS OF OLD BIRMINGHAM, on the assumption that the original name of the place was Franchelie ("the place of free men") has a stirring poem on the subject, which begins:—

> When men shall ask where men are free
> O proudly tell of Franchelie.

Whether its freedom arose from the existence of a doubt as to the authority in whose jurisdiction it rightly lay, cannot be guessed; but it is a curious fact that in 1296 Frankley was acknowledged to be in Halesowen parish, a fact that had been litigiously disputed by the prior and convent of Dudley.

Frankley was the home of the Lytteltons from the Norman period till the reign of Queen Elizabeth, when Sir John Lyttelton, of Frankley, purchased the neighbouring estate of Hagley. The family has left its record on the history of Worcestershire in almost every age. Of its many distinguished sons perhaps the most conspicuously outstanding was the great lawyer, Sir Thomas Lyttelton (or Littleton, for at different periods the name has been variously spelt), who has been called "the English Justinian," whose profound knowledge of the law enabled him to write in Norman-French the celebrated treatise on Tenures for the use of his son Richard, who was also a distinguished lawyer. Sir Edward Coke's commentary on this famous work is well-known.

Sir Thomas was not really a Lyttelton; he was the son of Thomas Westcote, of co. Devon, by Elizabeth, daughter of Thomas Littleton, of Frankley, who, in the wishes of his grandfather, adopted the maternal name and arms. He became a judge under Henry VI., and was honoured equally by that King's rival successors on the throne; indeed, his great knowledge of the law won him the confidence of both the House of York and the House of Lancaster during the Civil Wars of the Roses. One county historian, Habington, whose MS. notes for a survey of Worcestershire have been edited by Mr. John Amphlett, and published by the Worcestershire Historical Society, wrote of him that he was "the greatest ornament of our shyre, the oracle of the lawe, the glory of judges, whose memory will never peryshe whylst our Englyshe Commonwealthe endurethe."

The lawlessness of the old feudal seigniors is well illustrated by a quarrel between the neighbouring lords of Dudley and Hagley, even in Elizabeth's reign, when feudalism was rapidly decaying. The dispute arose concerning the ownership of Prestwood House (now the property of the Foley family), and it lasted for several years.

John Lyttelton, of that date, who had married Mariel, daughter of Sir

Thomas Bromley, Lord Chancellor, was a man of arts and high character—he is sometimes called the second founder of the fortunes of the Lyttelton family —but he had a very serious dispute with his father, who had so mismanaged the large estates left to him that the son was obliged to interfere. His father lodged a bill of complaint against him in the Court of Star Chamber, alleging that he, with others, went to his house at Prestwood, all fully armed, and uttering the most violent threats, swearing that they would cut down the doors and work great destruction, unless the alleged grievances were redressed. In consequence of these violent disorders a Star Chamber Commission sat at Wolverhampton for the adjustment of the quarrel, when it is believed that Queen Elizabeth herself intervened to bring about a settlement. It was certainly proved that John was in the right.

How the lord of Dudley was drawn into the quarrel is not quite clear, but in the October of 1592 he took a very active part in an episode which reminds one very much of a Scottish border raid. In the night-time Lord Dudley roused up a hundred and forty of his men, "weaponed them all with bows and arrows, forest bills or long staves, and marched them to Ashwood, where he seized 341 sheep, the property of Sir John Lyttelton's executors, and had them driven off towards Dudley under the charge of thirty of his armed retainers. With the other hundred and ten of his men he then proceeded to Prestwood, forced his way into Mr. Lyttelton's enclosed grounds, and "with great violence chased fourteen kyne, one bull, and eight fat oxen, took them to Dudley Castle and kept them within the walls."

Mr. Lyttelton at once set the law in motion against his aggressive neighbour, but when the bailiff appeared at Dudley four days afterwards his lordship's servants threatened to cut the officer and his men to pieces, and drove them away. Part of the raided cattle, it appears, were slaughtered and eaten in the castle, but the bulk of them were sent towards Coventry, where it was intended to sell them. Although they were accompanied by a guard of sixty men, "strongly armed with calyvers, or with bows and arrows, some on horseback with chasing staves, and others on foot with forest bills," there was evidently some misgiving as to the possibility of their safe arrival at Coventry. Indeed, the convoy could not have proceeded more than ten miles on its way before this titled freebooter deemed it expedient to run no further risks. He suddenly roused up his tenants in Dudley, Sedgley, Kingswinford, and Rowley, to the number of six or seven hundred, weaponed them all, and although it was in the middle of the night, set off in great haste to overtake the stolen drove. He caught up the slow-moving beasts and their armed guard, and brought them all safely back to the protection of his Castle walls, where (we are told) he wilfully "wasted" the entire lot.

Such was life in this neighbourhood "in the days of old romance." The lord of Dudley who thus distinguished himself as a marauding chieftain was the last of the Suttons, and the father of the famous Dud Dudley, a man of violent passions and reckless extravagance.

As to John Lyttelton, notwithstanding his habitual worthiness, his life was terminated in tragic circumstances and under a cloud. He was one of the retinue of the Earl of Essex, who in 1600 rashly attempted to remove by force several members of the Queen's Council, of whom the Earl, so long the Queen's prime favourite, was fiercely jealous. The attempt failed and Lyttelton was put on trial, found guilty, and condemned. His attainder involved the forfeiture of his estate. In his defence he declared that he had no design against the Queen's person, or the Government, but merely a personal feeling against some members of the Council. He died in prison, but in 1603 his widow obtained from James I. a grant of the restitution of his confiscated estates. She lived a retired and exemplary life at Hagley, and brought up her children in the Protestant religion, which the family had not before adopted. After a life of good works, she was, at her own request, buried in Hagley churchyard amongst the graves of the poor.

The family history is indeed full of romance. Notwithstanding the change of religion just mentioned, and the evident well-disposed attitude of James I., one of the family lost his head for being concerned in the Catholic Gunpowder Plot. How Stephen Lyttelton (with his neighbour, Robert Wintour) escaped from the former's house at Holbeach, when the conspirators were being hunted, bribed one of his tenant farmers at Rowley Regis to hide him in his barn, from which after several weeks they were compelled to remove to a new hiding-place at Hagley, at which place they were eventually captured—how all this happened is too long a story to detail here.

Later on the Lyttelton family suffered considerably for its attachment to the Royalist cause in the Civil War. Sir Thomas Lyttelton assisted to raise a "trayned band of volunteers" for the King's service, who were to receive "five shillings a weeke" so long as they remained in the county, and afterwards such pay if they were drawn forth from the county as the King gave." Sir Thomas was taken prisoner by the Parliamentary forces, and kept in the Tower for two years. Sir Edward Lyttelton was among the gentlemen who marched out of Worcester after the surrender of the city in 1646. It was with a large sum he compounded for his estates.

Sir Henry Lyttelton was also a sufferer, being incarcerated in the Tower for nearly two years. After his restoration the King offered him a peerage, which he declined.

Further distinctions of the family, and more particularly the literary associations of Hagley, will be given in the next chapter but one.

The Leasowes in 1830 (Calvert)

XXXVII.—THE LEASOWES AND THE POET SHENSTONE

At the Leasowes, in the parish of Halesowen, was born, in 1714, William Shenstone, the son of a well-to-do farmer, his mother, a Penn, "being of good family."

The dame school of the village, in which he received the rudiments of his education, and the mistress of which he afterwards immortalised, is pictured in some of the illustrated editions of his works. He went later to Solihull Grammar School, and thence in 1732 to Pembroke College, Oxford. In 1745 the paternal estate, valued at about £300 a year, fell to him.

Descriptions of the Leasowes have been written by Goldsmith, and by Dodsley, the well-known publisher of the time. Dr. Johnson characteristically says of it, that from the first Shenstone began "to point his prospects, to diversify his surface, to entangle his walks, and to wind his waters; which he did with such judgment and fancy as made his little domain the envy of the great, and the admiration of the skilful; a place to be visited by travellers and copied by designers."

The place possessed natural beauties which the poet's taste manipulated in the construction of shady lawns, sequestered glades, murmuring brooklets, sparkling cascades, and "ruinated" walls. Beneath one of the walls were these lines from Virgil:—

> We dwell in shady woods
> And seek the groves with cooling streams refresh'd
> And trace the verdant banks.

It was in "Virgil's Grove" he erected an urn to the memory of his brother poet, Thomson, who had once honoured the place with a very languid sort of visit.

As a cultivated farm the estate, though small, had yielded his father a fair living. But adorned with fountains and statues, Grecian alcoves and summer-houses, lavished with all the prevailing elegance of eighteenth century classicalism, the income was soon reduced to vanishing point. The poet spent so much money on the embellishment of his grounds that he became comparatively poor, and compelled to live in a "dilapidated house not fit to receive polite friends." Yet undoubtedly the happiest hours of the poet's life were spent in planning these artificial landscapes; and when engaged in skilfully disposing his woodlands along the course of the pretty stream which threaded its way down the dingle bounding his estate, he was oblivious of every other care in the world.

He must indeed, at times, have experienced exquisite pleasure in his romantic retreat, to which every year would give fresh beauty, and develop more distinctly the creations of his taste and labour. But disappointments, various and depressing, embittered his life; the neglect of political patrons, and an unfortunate attachment to a young lady, combined to make of him, who by nature was benevolent and kindly in disposition, a querulous and an unhappy man.

There is an anecdote of him which discloses the man's real nature, and at the same time throws a flood of light on the social and economic condition of this poverty-stricken, nail-making district in the middle of the eighteenth century.

Shenstone was one day walking in his romantic retreat in company with his Delia—her real name was Wilmot—when a man rushed out of a thicket, and, presenting a pistol at his breast, demanded his money. Shenstone was surprised, and Delia fainted. "Money," said he, "is not worth struggling for. You cannot be poorer than I am; therefore, unhappy man, take it"—throwing him his purse—"and fly as quickly as possible."

The man did so. He threw his pistol into the water, and in a moment disappeared. Shenstone ordered his footboy, who followed behind them, to pursue the robber at a distance, and observe whither he went.

In a short time the boy returned, and informed his master that he had followed the man into Halesowen, where he lived; that he went to the very door of his house, and peeped through the keyhole; that as soon as the man entered he threw the purse on the table, and, addressing his wife, passionately exclaimed, "Take the dear-bought price of my honesty." Then taking two of his children, one on each knee, he said to them, "To keep you from starving I have ruined my soul," and immediately burst into a flood of tears.

Shenstone made inquiries after the man's character and circumstances; found that he was a labourer reputed to be honest and industrious, but driven to desperation by his poverty and the wants of a numerous family. When the poet sought him in his cottage, the man fell on his knees at his feet and implored mercy. Shenstone, true to his nature, not only forgave the unfortunate man, but gave him employment as long as he lived. It is a pretty story, and an instructive one.

Shenstone, with his love of the beautiful, and his gift of verse, should have been a happy man. But he built his happiness on the applause of others, and died in solitude a votary of the world. His death took place at the Leasowes, February 11th, 1763.

For some years Shenstone lived in comparative seclusion, but was always on visiting terms with Lord Lyttelton at Hagley—the "poor Lyttelton" whose "Dialogues of the Dead" or "History of Henry II.," or even his political achievements as Chancellor of the Exchequer have hardly served to keep his name alive. By the poet's advice his lordship not only introduced "artificial ruins" into Hagley Park, but actually erected a sham cromlech on the highest point of Clent Hills. It was in truth a tasteless age.

The grounds of Great Barr Hall also bore the impress of Shenstone's genius for landscape gardening: in one of the beautiful flower gardens there was a graceful marble urn to the memory of Miss Mary Dolman, who was a cousin of the poet; a medallion of the lady appearing on the centre of the urn, and an elegant Latin inscription by him on the pedestal beneath.

Dr. Percy, who paid more than one visit to "the wailing poet of the Leasowes," has left it on record that he thought Shenstone a man of unhappy temper. "In his taste for rural pleasures he was finical to a ludicrous degree of excess. In the purchase of a cow he regarded nothing but the spots on her hide—if they were beautiful, all other requisites were disregarded. His man servant, whose office it was to show his grounds, had made a grotto which Shenstone approved. This was always made the test of the visitor's judgment; if he admired William's grotto, his master thought him worth accompanying round the place, and, on a signal from the man, appeared; but if it was passed with little notice, he kept out of the way."

The poet died broken-spirited at the age of forty-nine.

"He was a lamp," said Johnson, "that spent its oil in blazing." He wrote pastoral poetry for fame, which was not awarded him by his contemporaries; he received promises of political patronage which were not fulfilled; he retired to the country, though he could not bear seclusion, there to ruin himself by his passion for landscape gardening, and always lamenting that his establishment was too mean to receive his polite friends in. He lived a life of disappointment, if not of discontent.

The final judgment of his work has been that "he should have burnt most of what he wrote; and printed most of what he spoke." From the sacrificial fire, however, Charles Lamb would have snatched the MS. of "The Schoolmistress," which is indeed one of the minor gems of English poetry. It is somewhat singular that Shenstone should have preferred to base his fame upon his epistolary writings instead of upon his "Schoolmistress." His letters are as affected as a Court lady mincing in Court attire, his "Schoolmistress" as natural as a rustic girl clad in simple gown.

Horace Walpole dubbed Shenstone a "water-gruel bard"; on the other hand, Robert Burns awarded him a measure of praise where, in "The Vision," Duan Second, he wrote:—

Thou canst not learn, nor can I show,
To paint with Thomson's landscape glow;
Or wake the bosom-melting throe with Shenstone's art,
Or pour, with Gray, the moving flow warm on the heart.

Shenstone's works were part of Burns' small library when a youth, finding a place there along with those of Thomson and Gray.

From the poems and published letters of Shenstone we obtain a few brief and fleeting glimpses of life on the Worcestershire border of Staffordshire in the middle of the eighteenth century.

From a recorded conversation with his housekeeper, we gather how pleasantly he might have interpreted his impressions of local life; he certainly would have been more extensively read nowadays had he done so.

It must be confessed few people now read Shenstone, for though his poems are models of classical grace and elegance, they do not appeal so directly to the heart as if they dealt with the more practical and ordinary phases of everyday life. There is always a feeling that, although he wrote in the country, it was for an audience in London. Yet he always posed as a pastoral poet, and his taste was supposed to be idyllic.

Writing in 1747, Shenstone laments that he has but few critical acquaintances come near his home, as he says he "lives amongst the makers and the wearers of hobnails." This is not the only insight we get into the industrial condition of the locality. In a letter dated 1762, he is suggesting that the ornamental brooklet which ran through his beautiful grounds would be a fitting subject for a poem. He says that the stream with its cascades as an ornament to his pleasaunce, skips along in playfulness with a thousand antic motions, and then a few hundred yards further along its course proceeds to roll and slit iron for manufactures of all kinds.

He explains that the pretty rills of his parklands are the principal sources of the river Stour, which supplies power to numerous works for the casting, forging, and shaping of iron for every civil and military purpose—that this particular river, in fact, has more ironworks on its banks than any other single river in the kingdom. The Stour valley, dividing South Staffordshire from East Worcestershire, marks the heart of the old Black Country.

The prototype of "The Schoolmistress"—Shenstone's highest poetical effort—was "My Old Schooldame, Sarah Lloyd, whose house is to be seen as thou travellest towards the native home of thy faithful servant. But she sleepeth with her fathers, and is buried with her fathers; and Thomas, her son, reigneth in her stead."

Of the humbler life of the locality we are not likely to glean very many details from a man of Shenstone's habits; he moved too exclusively in the higher social circles, both at home and in London.

Thus, in October, 1759, he writes:—"I have passed four of five days betwixt this week and last at my Lord Ward's at Hinley" (Himley).

Another local allusion occurs in a letter written from Halesowen:—"I drove him (a friend) to Dudley Castle, which I long to show you; I never saw it since

I was the size of my pen before; it has great romantic beauty, though perhaps Derbyshire may render it of small note in your eye.

Although to-day the popular memory scarcely ever recalls Shenstone for anything beyond his lines on an inn—

> Who'er has travelled life's dull round,
>   Where'er his stages may have been,
> May sigh to think he still has found,
>   The warmest welcome at an inn.

the poet of the Leasowes was not without his influence on the literary life of the district in which he lived.

His friendship with Dr. Johnson, and his patronage of James Woodhouse, have been alluded to. He also lent his countenance and encouragement to Miss Whateley, afterwards wife of the Vicar of Walsall. Of this lady he writes in one of his letters:—"There has been deposited in my hands a large collection of poetry, by a Miss Whateley, of Walsall; many of the pieces written in an excellent and truly classical style; simple, sentimental, and more harmonious than I almost ever saw written by a lady." Mrs. Darwall. (*nee* Whateley) published her volume of poems in 1794, years after Shenstone's death. A sketch of the poetess appears in STAFFODSHIRE STORIES, by the present writer.

Gray rather uncharitably remarks of Shenstone's correspondence that it is "about nothing else but the Leasowes, and his writings with two or three neighbouring clergymen, who wrote verses too."

Writing in 1761, Shenstone says:—"I have assisted my friend, Hull, the comedian, in altering the tragedy of 'Rosamond'; had it brought upon the stage to a full house at Birmingham, where it was well received; put Hull into a way of making an indirect compliment to the present King in the ten last lines of epilogue, which was followed by 'God save King George,' etc., in a full chorus of the audience and actors drawn out abreast upon the stage."

The Leasowes, popularly known in the locality as "The Lezzers," which, with its classic groves, still stands, like an oasis in the Black Country desert, remained for a long time one of the show place of the Midlands.

John Wesley paid it a visit in 1782 (p. 69).

It was a dictum of Shenstone that the man who planted a tree was a greater benefactor of his species than he who built a house. And he planted freely, with the result that the Leasowes remains a beauty spot to this day. Yet while the reafforestation of the Black Country is being urged on the one hand, this beauty spot is now being threatened on the other by the speculating builder— the first act of vandalism would be to cut down some 500 of the stately trees which are the crowning glory of the place.

The residence is a plain, white-painted house, on the western slope of Mucklow Hill, overlooking a valley which still retains some of its natural charm. At the foot of the hill lie the ruins of Halesowen Abbey, and the fine old parish church, in which is Shenstone's monument. Beyond, rise the two peaks of the Clent Hills, in a veil of misty blue, forming a striking background, while in the purple distance are the highlands of the Wyre Forest.

A portrait of the poet is to be seen in the National Portrait Gallery, London. In Chambers' CYCLOPÆDIA OF ENGLISH LITERATURE will be found woodcuts of three local scenes—The Leasowes (as it was), Hagley Hall, and the Cottage of "The Schoolmistress."

XXXVIII.—HAGLEY, CLENT, AND ST. KENELM'S.

Rising boldly against the sky in the south-west appear the Clent Hills, a range whose broad green slopes and breezy summits do much to compensate the adjacent Worcestershire Black Country for the gloom of its broody smokiness.

At one extremity is the village of Clent, and at the other, St. Kenelm's chapel, the burial-place of the boy-prince whose murder was made known by a miracle at Rome. Near by is Hagley Park, that "fair, majestic paradise" where Lord Lyttelton entertained the poet Thomson and a goodly company of other celebrities.

Here, for years in the courtly Georgian days, warm welcome was extended to men of light and leading by the cultured and hospitable host.

> Thou wilt be glad to seek the rural shade,
> There to indulge the Muse, and Nature mark;
> We then a lodge for thee will rear in Hagley Park.

Hagley, the present seat of the Lyttelton family (of whom the head is Viscount Cobham) is a stone structure pleasantly situated in a beautifully undulating park. It is truly a noble view which greets the eye of the visitor advancing from the park entrance towards the church. Fine trees, either sweeping round in crescent form, or clumped in happy situations, adorn the lawny slopes, and are backed by the dark firs of Wychbury Hill. The woodland beauties of the park are enhanced by a number of monuments in the classic style, which have been set to grace the various points of interest—temple, obelisk, and column, all in keeping with the mansion and its surroundings.

For this, indeed, is classic ground, having been frequently visited in the eighteenth century by Pope, Shenstone, Gray, Thomson, and Addison. There is an urn dedicated to the poet Shenstone, placed in the heart of the delightful scenes he probably took a large share in planning. Another graceful urn commemorates Pope. But of all the literary lights who visited Hagley in its palmy days, the greatest interest attaches to James Thomson, whose intimacy with his host was of the closest, and whose associations with the place have left the most compelling memories.

The master of Hagley at that time was Mr. George Lyttelton, son of Sir Thomas Lyttelton, baronet. He entered Parliament in 1730, where he acquired some experience as a speaker, came to fill a number of high political offices, and was raised to the peerage in 1759. He was a writer of considerable talent, and published a notable work, entitled DIALOGUES OF THE DEAD. He has even been identified by one critic as the elusive "Junius," and his poetry gained for him a place in Dr. Johnson's LIVES OF THE POETS. He has sometimes been called "the good Lord Lyttelton," perhaps to distinguish him from his son and successor, Thomas, the second Lord Lyttelton, whose moral character was the reverse of his father's, and who died mysteriously (1779) three days after a wonderful dream of a dove that changed into a white lady.

It was Mr. Lyttelton who introduced Thomson to the Prince of Wales; and whose earliest exercise of patronage, on coming into office in 1744, was to bestow on him the post of Surveyor-General of the Leeward Isles, the duties of which the poet contrived to perform by deputy—"the gentle tenant of the place," Thomson calls him—at a profit of £300 a year for himself.

A portion of his famous poem, "The Seasons," is said to have been composed at Hagley; at any rate, it was under final revision during one of his visits.

The poet first visited Hagley in August, 1743, and in a letter to a friend on the 29th of that month writes thus of the place.

> After a disagreeable stage-coach journey . . . I came to the most agreeable place and company in the world. The park, where we pass a great part of our time, is thoroughly delightful, quite enchanting. It consists of several little hills, finely tufted with wood, and rising softly one above another; from which are seen a great variety of at once beautiful and grand extensive prospects; but I am most charmed with its sweet embowered retirements, and particularly with a winding dale that runs through the middle of it. This dale is overhung with deep woods, and enlivened by a stream, that, now gushing from mossy rocks, now falling in cascades, and now spreading into a calm length of water, forms the most natural and pleasing scene imaginable. At the source of this water, composed of some pretty rills, that purl from beneath the roots of oaks, there is as fine a retired scat as lover's heart could wish. There I often sit.

The interest which George Lyttelton took in his poet friend extended to his spiritual as well as to his temporal welfare. There are remarkable passages in letters published after Thomson's death (Phillimore's MEMOIRS AND CORRESPONDENCE OF GEORGE, LORD LYTTELTON) which plainly show that the poet was a better Christian in heart and practice than in faith, and that Lyttelton's OBSERVATIONS ON THE CONVERSION AND APOSTLESHIP OF ST. PAUL were written mainly with a view to the poet's conviction.

In one of his poems (" Spring") Thomson exhibits a very high appreciation of his noble host:—

> These are the sacred feelings of thy heart,
> Thy heart inform'd by Reason's purer ray,
> O Lyttelton, the friend! thy passions thus,
> And meditations vary, as at large,
> Courting the Muse, through Hagley Park you stray.

The closeness of the intimacy existing between Thomson and Lord Lyttelton, and the literary nature of the sympathy which bound them together, may be judged from the fact that the latter was permitted to interpolate the following stanza into one of Thomson's works ("The Castle of Indolence") descriptive of the poet's own personality: -

> A bard there dwelt, more fat than bard beseems;
>   Who, void of envy, guile, and lust of gain,
> On Virtue still, and Nature's pleasing themes,
>   Pour'd forth his unpremeditated strain.
>
> The world forsaking with a calm disdain,
>   Here laugh'd he careless in his easy seat;
> Here quaff'd encircled with the joyous train,
>   Oft moralising sage : his ditty sweet
> He loathed much to write, ne cared to repeat.

The company at Hagley in September, 1747, included the great Pitt; writing on the 20th of that month the poet Shenstone says:—

> As I was returning from church on Sunday last, whom should I meet in a chaise, with two horses lengthways, but that right friendly bard, Mr. Thomson. I complimented him on his arrival in this country, and asked him to accompany Mr. Lyttelton to the Leasowes, which he said he would do with abundance of pleasure.

As already mentioned, Thomson paid the promised visit to the Leasowes, and the circumstance was commemorated by his host and brother poet setting up (in what he called Virgil's grove, at the Leasowes) a memorial bearing a Latin inscription, a translation of which is:

To the most celebrated Poet
JAMES THOMSON
This seat was placed
Near his favourite springs
by
W. S.

> How shall I thank thy Muse, so formed to please?
> For not the whisperings of the Southern breeze,
> Nor banks still beaten by the breaking wave,
> Nor limpid rills that pebbly valleys lave,
>   Yield such delights.

The best portrait of the author of "The Seasons" is that painted in 1725 by William Aikman, long preserved at Hagley, but now at Edinburgh. As Pitt said, it was "beastly like" the original, and is the one which has been mostly engraved. Aikman was a personal friend of Thomson, and when he died a few years later the poet wrote his epitaph.

Thomson's death occurred very unexpectedly in 1748, and writing on September 3rd of that year, William Shenstone says:—

> Poor Mr. Thomson, Mr. Pitt tells me, is dead. He was to have been at Hagley Park this week, and then I should probably have seen him here. As it is, I will erect an urn in Virgil's grove to his memory. I was really much shocked to hear of his death.

James Thomson, who "sang the Seasons and their change," was buried at Richmond, and shortly after a monument was erected to him in Westminster Abbey. Had he written nothing more than "Rule Britannia," his fame and his name must have endured so long as the British Empire shall exist. But all his poetry is full of charm particularly in his descriptions of scenery; also of the softer, pleasing traits of Nature, as in

> Come, gentle Spring—ethereal mildness, come!

His keen appreciation of the felicities of the simple life is disclosed in the lines:—

> I hate the clamours of the smoky towns,
> But much admire the bliss of rural clowns.

And it is James Thomson's pen—the pen of "that sweet descriptive writer," as Shenstone admiringly names it—that has painted for us the charms of Hagley Park. Which elysian delights, be it remembered, are removed from unsightly Oldbury by little more than half a dozen short miles.

Hagley Hall is rich in pictures, and in the possession of valuable MSS. relating to the county of Worcester. Among them are charters and grants from the time of King John, some relating to the church and abbey at Halesowen, with a Cartulary (Edward III.) and Bailiff Acts for the abbey, and many others having reference to private properties and individuals. There is a Hundred Roll of the borough of Halesowen and a Roll of the temporalities of the Archdeaconry of Worcester (*29 Edward III.):* an MS. volume on the reign of

Elizabeth, by the literary Lord Lyttelton of Thomson's days, who had written a rather famous history of Henry II.; and another large MS. volume supposed to be Habington's collection of notes for a history of Worcestershire.

All these treasures have been largely drawn on, from time to time, by county historians and other writers. There is also a large number of letters of the 16th, 17th, and 18th centuries, including letters, or copies of letters, of Queen Elizabeth, Queen Anne (the wife of James I.), Charles I., Charles II., the Duchess of Marlborough (1733), and many other notabilities—as letters from Swift, Pope, Thomson, Fielding, Garrick, Voltaire, Phelps, and Dr. Johnson. Hagley is loudly reminiscent of the Augustan days of English literature, of the romantic ages in our country's history.

At the head of a little valley between Clent and Walton Hills stands St. Kenelm's church, a quaint, twelfth century building with grotesque gargoyles, and having a rude effigy of the boy saint affixed to the outside wall just to the east of the doorway. The crude carving of the figure is said to be pre-Norman work; that the shrine of St. Kenelm here was much frequented by pilgrims in Saxon times is indeed a well-established fact.

The monkish fable of St-Kenelm of Clent is the classic legend of the locality. It is an eighth century story of which the reliable facts are very few.

Kenulph, who founded Winchcombe Abbey, was King of Mercia after the death of Offa. When Kenulph died the crown is said to have passed by will to his son Kenelm, a boy of eight. This would certainly have been contrary to custom, as the Saxons elected their King, and never chose a mere child to rule over them. At the best Kenelm's reign must, therefore, have been a nominal one. The boy had a sister, Quendreda, who was jealous of her little brother, and wished herself to be Queen. So she prompted her lover, Askobert, who was the boy's guardian, to slay him. Yielding to her importunities, Askobert took the child from the palace (tradition says there was a royal palace at Clent in early Saxon times) on the pretext of a hunting expedition; and while in a lonely wood killed him and hid his body under a thorn-tree. Soon after the murder a white dove flew to St. Peter's at Rome, and dropped a scroll upon the high altar at which mass was being said. The scroll, upon examination, was found to bear an inscription, of which a translation is:—

> In Clent, in Cowbach, lieth under a thorn,
> His head off-shorn, Kenelm, King-born.

The Pope sent his messengers to England to make inquiries. The body, found by the direction of a white cow, was exhumed and buried in the abbey at Winchcombe. From the spot on which the body had lain a spring of water gushed out, over which the church was built and dedicated to the martyr-king.

Although no spring is found there now, the church strides across a gully,

St. Kenelm's Church, Romsley

which appears to have been the bed of a stream, the water of which was conducted beneath the length of the building, and had its outlet through an archway at the eastern end. An ancient arch, rebuilt in the fifteenth century, now serves as an entrance to the heating chamber. At Spring Farm, five hundred yards away, there is still a magnificent spring of water, which may have had some connection with the miraculous spring of the story.

Such is a brief outline of the legend which has clung to the church for more than a thousand years. To his SHORT HISTORY OF CLENT, Mr. John Amphlett, M.A, S.C.L., adds an Appendix dealing very fully with the subject, and giving valuable references to a number of ancient manuscripts containing various versions of the old tale.

Chaucer includes the legend in the CANTERBURY TALES, as a portion of the "Nonnes Preestes Tale":—

> Lo, in the lif of seint Kenelm, I rede,
> That was Kenulphus sone, the noble King
> Of Mercenrike, how Kenelm mette a thing,
> A litel or he were mordred on a day,
> His mordre in his avision he say,
> His norice him expounded every del
> His sweven, and bade him for to kepe him wel
> Fro treason; but he n'as but seven yere old,
> And therefore litel tale he told
> Of any dreme, so holy was his herte.
> By God I hadde lever than my sherte
> That ye had red his legend, so have I.

This is doubtless the oldest version in rhyme; the latest is that of Mr. E. M. Rudland, in his BALLADS OF OLD BIRMINGHAM, whose "Death of King Kenelm" re-tells it with much picturesque detail; as thus:—

> False was the love of Askobert,
>   False to the King, and false to me,
> And false to the Lady Gwendreda. God!
>   What should the speeding be?
>
>   *   *   *   *   *
>
> Men say that holy waters flow
>   O'er Kenelm slain; that men are healed
> By might of his pure soul, who pray
>   Beside the slaughter field.

And so on. The interest of the story is undying.

XXXIX.—Some Old Families and Notable Personages.

In the mediæval records of Oldbury the name of Marmium, is of frequent occurrence. The Marmiums held land both in Romsley and in Oldbury, and the possible connection of this local family with the historic Marmions, "lords of Tamworth tower and town," is discussed by Mr. Amphlett in his introduction to the published Court Rolls of Halesowen, pp. cx–cxiii. Another prominent family of ancient Hales was "de Volatu, otherwise Zouche."

The Pastons were a local family of some note. George Paston, B.A., of Merton College, 1585, was perhaps rector of Kingswinford, 1622-6. Nicholas Paston, B.A., of Magdalen Hall, held that living 1626. Edward Paston, son of John, of Kingswinford, served the rectory of Sollyhull, co. Warwick, 1646, by the direction of the Westminster Assembly, and was ejected from the vicarage of Halesowen in 1660. Another John Paston held the rectory of Himley in 1669. A number of Paston Wills were proved at Worcester between 1584 and 1646. The Halesowen Registers from 1561 to 1725 contain many entries relating to the Pastons: as also do the Kingswinford Registers between 1603 and 1697. These local Pastons were a branch of the famous Norfolk family of the historic "Paston Letters."

Tandy was another old family name in Halesowen. A volume appeared in 1912 on the GROVE FAMILY OF HALESOWEN. It is a full and exhaustive work, mainly of interest to the family treated, though occasionally local history is illuminated by a fitful sidelight from it. Originally located at Wassell, in Hagley, the earliest mention of the family occurs in a deed of 1370, by which a grant is made to one Philip, son of Roger, "at Grove de Hagley"—Wassell Grove. By 1538 the Grove family, by its various branches, were well established in Halesowen, Hagley, and Rowley Regis; and presently collateral branches were to be found at Hawn, Hasbury, Ludley, Romsley, and other parts of the district. An Appendix treats of the Pearsall or Peshall family.

The family of Rider, or Ryder, who gave their name to Ryder's Green, in West Bromwich, originated in Oldbury, or at least in Halesowen. (See A HISTORY OF WEST BROMWICH, Chapter L). There are other local families associated territorially with the history of this neighbourhood; but the function of the modern topographer is not so much to enshrine family greatness, as to record the distinctive achievements of individuals of note. Right worthy of our attention are the names of inventors, artists, musicians and others whose memory adds some lustre to the history of the locality.

Peter Ward, who describes himself as a chemical manager of Oldbury, took out a patent (No. 11,279) on 6th July, 1846, for an "improvements in the manufacture of certain salts of soda and magnesia." Ward had a prior patent (No. 10,089), dated 4th March, 1844, for an "improvement in combining matters for washing and Cleansing," but at that time he described himself as "a practical chemist, of West Bromwich." Nothing further is known of him.

Another inventor locally noteworthy is Henry Adcock.

About 1851 Messrs. Chance Bros. manufactured fused blocks of Rowley rag. Air. Henry Adcock, C.E., had conceived the idea of fusing basaltic rock and casting it in moulds for building purposes and a variety of uses. Mr. James Chance placed at his disposal a reverberatory furnace, and a patent was taken out. Works were erected and a number of articles were manufactured; as slabs for steps, window heads and sills, string courses, mantelpieces, columns and capitals, table and sideboard slabs, door-plates and knobs, etc., etc. They were admirable in their way, but the cost of production was found too high, and the basaltic stone-ware is known no more. Specimens of these remarkable architectural features are still to be traced in some parts of the locality, the best perhaps being found at Edgbaston Vestry Hall, of which the ornamental steps, columns, and doorways are of this moulded Rowley rag.

The art of typography owes not a little to the genius of William Caslon, who anticipated some of the achievements of Baskerville, and has been called the Elzevir of England. This worthy was born at Cradley, in the parish of Halesowen, in the year 1692. He served an apprenticeship to the engraving of gun-locks. The gun trade had just then been introduced into Birmingham, and branches of the industry extended themselves to Wednesbury and Darlaston in one direction, and to Halesowen in another, iron-mills and iron-working being firmly located in both these districts.

The art of engraving, which had been previously applied to the ornamentation of door or cabinet locks, could only be properly learnt in a town like Birmingham, and thither young Caslon was sent. He became his own master in 1716, and began to make punches for tooling the covers of books. John Watts, a printer of some note, happened to notice the beauty of these tools, and employed him to make type-punches. Presently he devoted himself entirely to this line of business, set up as a type-founder, with his brother Samuel working with him as a mould-maker. Managing to accumulate sufficient capital to establish a type-foundry, he sought a wider sphere in London, where he elevated the cutting of type and the production of matrices to the highest form of industrial art, and became the leading type-cutter in England.

Till the appearance of the Caslon type English letters were generally rude and clumsy, and a disgrace to the printer's art as practised here. The revolution effected by this artistic Englishman was really immense; the gun-lock engraver of Halesowen gave to the world a grade of type which made it no longer necessary to go to Rotterdam or Amsterdam, as had hitherto been the custom, when superior work was to be produced. Holland was superseded, and the English market conquered.

Portrait of William Caslon

It was in 1735 William Caslon set up his foundry in Chiswell Street, London; and there the "House of Caslon" still flourishes, the founder being known as Caslon I., and his present-day representative as Caslon VII.

No firm in any line of business occupies a prouder position, or boasts a more interesting history. The family of Caslon was of Spanish origin, and came from the Netherlands to settle in England. They were Catholics, and William Caslon kept in touch with the great ecclesiastical printers on the Continent. The most famous Belgian producers of missals and brevaries still use the Caslon type, as do also the English Benedictines at Douai. Yet this artistic craftsman was on the most friendly terms with John Wesley, and it would be interesting to know the influence these two men had on each other.

William Caslon was extremely fond of music, and at the Chiswell Street House there was a concert once a month. It used to be held on the Thursday nearest full moon, in order that the guests might have a light night for walking home. A wag of the party dubbed them, on this account, the lunatics, a name they appear to have cheerfully adopted. The music performed was chiefly that of Corelli, and sometimes overtures of half-forgotten operas, such as Clotilda, Hydaspes, and Camilla, were played. Handel was often a guest; and his compositions, then, of course, the last note in modern music, were given. After the concert Caslon I. used to give his friends a bottle of wine, and ale of his own brewing. The entertainment usually ended about midnight, and before the company separated one or two songs of Purcell's were sung to a harpischord, or sometimes the party sang a few catches.

Caslon's hospitality and musical entertainments have been commented upon by several writers of the period—they appear in Dibden's DECAMERON (7th Day). He was on the Commission of the Peace for Middlesex, and died a widely-known and esteemed citizen.

John Baskerville—who, by the way, was a native of Wolverley, in Worcestershire—said in 1758:—"The ingenuity of Mr. Caslon has left a fairer copy for my emulation than any other master. Among others who bore contemporaneous testimony to this illustrious son of Halesowen were the poet Shenstone, Dodsley, his publisher, Benjamin Franklin, and Nichols, of THE GENTLEMAN'S MAGAZINE—all men of special knowledge in the art of typography, and all capable of giving an authoritative opinion on the subject.

Another local worthy, also an engraver, cannot be claimed as a native, though it was at some place not far away in the adjoining county of Stafford that he first saw the light in 1730.

Robert Hancock's early life is shrouded in obscurity, but at the age of 20 we find him an apprentice to the copper-plate engraving in Sir Stephen Janssen's Enamel Works at Battersea. The enamel trade, it may be noted, was located also in Staffordshire at that time, flourishing as an artistic industry at

Wednesbury and Bilston. Hancock is the name of an old Wednesbury family of note.

Hancock removed to Worcester, where he was engaged in the well-known works of the Porcelain Company. By his artistic powers he contributed not a little to the fame of that manufactory, and achieved a high reputation as an engraver.

One of the designs executed by Hancock at Worcester has come in for some very unkindly criticism at the hands of no less a personage than Thomas Carlyle. In 1757 the important invention of transfer-printed impressions from copper-plates was introduced at the Porcelain Works, but whether the invention originated there, or at Battersea, is not known. Anyway, in that year the Worcester works produced a piece of pottery characteristic of the period, and for the ornamentation of which Hancock was responsible. It was a china mug to contain a pint, and was decorated with a portrait of Frederick the Great, the Protestant King of Prussia being just then the hero of Europe. It is for what the critic considers such preposterously misplaced hero-worship that the biographer of Frederick and the historian of the French Revolution falls foul of this unfortunate specimen of Worcester ware.

He calls it "a diligent potter's apotheosis of Friedrich," and complains that the portrait "is twenty years too young for the time," being copied from one by Pesne; he animadverts on the artist's supplementary designs, pointing out in detail the many inaccuracies that occur in the Trophy on the other side of the handle, and calling the figure of Fame, which is depicted between the other two drawings, a sort of a Cupid who has forgotten his bow and carries a wreath of a ridiculously disproportionate size. What the rugged philosopher really means is that the mug may be good china, but as history it is very poor stuff indeed.

Unfortunately, Hancock, after becoming a partner in the concern, had a disagreement with his co-proprietors, and withdrew from the business. He then settled in Staffordshire, as a printer, and lost all his savings through the failure of a bank. It was at this critical juncture in his life that he took up his residence at Oldbury (1780). Here he developed his art, devoting himself to engraving in mezzotint. Hancock was not merely a copyist like most mezzotinters, though he engraved after Sir Joshua Reynolds the portraits of a number of celebrities; and he also did the 1790 portrait of John Wesley after Miller. But while at Oldbury he executed in stipple quite a number of portraits, and encouraged by his success in this line migrated to Bristol, where he set up as a portrait painter.

Whether Hancock invented the art of transfer-printing on china cannot be said with certainty, but he contributed largely to the success of the Company, notwithstanding Carlyle's sneers at his efforts, much of his work being exquisitely fine, and doing justice to the delicacy of the porcelain produced at Worcester. One well-known transfer design of Hancock's is the Tea Party; others are portraits of George II., George III., Queen Charlotte, the Marquis of Granby, and William Pitt. The full signature of Robert Hancock is often found on garden scenes and Watteau-like subjects. The King of Prussia mug bears only his initials "R.H." It is believed that at one time he went to do work at the Staffordshire Potteries, and his engraved plates have recently been found at Coalport.

At Bristol, between 1796 and 1798, he drew for a bookseller the portraits of Coleridge and Southey, of Wordsworth and Lamb. A number of his portraits are in the National Gallery. Among the various pupils he instructed was Valentine Green, afterwards the most famous of English mezzotint engravers; and the author of the HISTORY OF WORCESTER, James Ross, the line engraver, was another pupil.

One of his best known designs is a drawing of Shakespeare, represented as standing with one elbow resting upon some books on a pedestal. He engraved a portrait of the poet Freeth, a Birmingham worthy; and for a Bible published in that city by Pearson & Rollason he (as did also Moses Haughton, a Wednesbury enamel painter) produced a number of engraved illustrations.

In 1885 was published ROBERT HANCOCK, HIS LIFE AND WORKS, by A. Randal Ballantyne, with portrait. He died in 1817, probably at Bristol; and to those who know the present-day Oldbury it will afford a pleasant mental exercise to try to visualise that place when it was picturesque enough to attract an artist to take up his residence within its amenities.

Of living celebrities, the eminent musician, Sir Frederick Bridge, the well-known organist of Westminster Abbey, is a native of Oldbury. His family pedigree is given in Crisp's VISITATION OF ENGLAND AND WALES, Vol. 18; from which it appears that John Bridge, born at Oldbury in 1791, married an Oldbury lady; and that their son, John Bridge, afterwards of Rochester, was born at Portway, Oldbury, in 1819.

Sir John Frederick Bridge is the son of the last-named, and was born at Oldbury, 5th December, 1844. He was educated at Rochester Cathedral Choir School, and matriculated at Queen's College, Oxford, in 1868. He was a pupil of Sir John Goss, and in 1865 he became organist of Holy Trinity, Windsor, and four years later of Manchester Cathedral. In 1875 he achieved the still higher position of Organist and Master of the Choristers at Westminster Abbey.

Dr. Bridge was appointed Gresham Professor of Music in 1890, and King Edward Professor of Music at London University in 1892. The honour of knighthood was conferred upon him in 1897, and Sir Frederick was Director of Music at the Coronations of both King Edward and King George. In 1902 he achieved the further distinction of M.V.O., and in 1911 of C.V.O.

Portrait of Sir Frederick Bridge, Knt., C.V.O., M.V.O.

His "Hymn to the Creator" was produced at the Worcester Festival of 1884, and his "Rock of Ages" at the Birmingham Festival the following year. At the next Birmingham Festival (1888) his "Callirhoë" was produced, and to the Worcester Festival of 1890 he contributed a new oratorio, "The Repentance of Nineveh." For Tennyson's funeral in Westminster Abbey (October, 1892) he set to music the laureate's poem, "Crossing the Bar." One of his most successful works was "The Cradle of Christ," a translation of "Stabat Mater Speciosa," produced at the Hereford Festival, 1894.

Professor Bridge is the author of the "Shakespeare and Music Birthday Book," and has set to music Judge Parry's fairy book, Katawampus," under the title of "Katawampus Kanticles composing some quaintly melodious numbers according well with the fantastic spirit of the lines. He has written numerous hymns, anthems, and cantatas; is the author of several of Novello's Primers—as on Counterpoint, Organ Accompaniment, and Musical Gestures, the last-named being a novel system of teaching the rudiments of music by physical exercises. Which is the greater, his popularity as a musician, or his eminence in the art, it would be difficult to determine; but Oldbury certainly has cause to be proud of her distinguished son.

XL.—Habits and Customs; Lore and Bibliography.

A glimpse at some of the habits and customs of our forefathers is obtained from a perusal of three minor records which have been preserved. In 1565 Henry Billingsley was fined at Warley Wigorn for catching pheasants with springs. To destroy game by setting snares, gins, or other engines of destruction, was a serious offence even in those primitive times.

In 1572 an order was issued at Halesowen against Sunday trading during divine service, and a further order was promulgated restricting the custom of Brides Ales. A Bride Ale, or Bredale, as it was generally called, was an ancient form of marriage feast celebrated by the consumption of specially provided ale. For family gatherings they were attended by unusually large numbers of guests—

> No man may telle yn tale
> The people that was at that bredale.

Further Puritan effort was manifested in a proclamation issued by the bailiffs and burgesses in 1608, objecting to Sunday markets, and ordering that they should be held on Monday, as heretofore.

Wakes were instituted as fairs and markets to be held on the patronal festivals of the respective parishes. The chapel-of-ease to Halesowen, which was first erected in Oldbury in 1529, was dedicated to St. Nicholas, whose day in the calendar is December 6th. This saint was a patron of all schoolboys, who once upon a time honoured him by processioning on that day; but at Eton, for some unexplained reason, the boys there always performed this ceremonial march *ad montem* on June 25th; and for some equally inscrutable reason Oldbury wake was kept towards the end of August. The modern church of Oldbury, erected in 1840, is called Christ Church, and the patronal festival might be expected somewhere about Corpus Christi day, which is the second Thursday after Whitsuntide, and a long way off August, the month in which Oldbury people were wont to celebrate their wake.

Oldbury had also two annual fairs, one held 6th June, and the other on 3rd October.

Of the ancient seasonal customs, most of which were associated with religious observances, there are but few records of their observance in this outlying corner of Worcestershire.

In a number of NOTES AND QUERIES for the year 1851 it is recorded that, in the Oldbury region of Worcestershire, the ancient custom of children going round on St. Clement's Day to beg for apples, and on St. Thomas' Day to beg for money, was still in vogue. It has entirely died out since that date.

The vestige of an ancient burial custom remains. In a less refined age it was customary to bury suicides, whenever a verdict of *felo-de-se* had been returned by a coroner's jury, at the dead of midnight, and always without that last act of Christian charity, the reading of a religious burial service. An older practice was to refuse interment in a churchyard, and to bury the body at cross-roads, with a stake driven through it. If local tradition is to be credited, the centre of Oldbury market place is the site of a suicide's sepulture.

Of the old sports and pastimes of the locality but few traces are discoverable now. Bull-baiting prevailed in Oldbury as late as in any of the surrounding towns, and dog-fighting long afterwards. Indeed, it was no uncommon occurrence in the late "forties" of last century for dogfights, on the result of which heavy wagers depended, to take place in the public streets by actual arrangement of the owners and backers. Which discloses the inadequacy with which the town was policed. In 1850 a man named Bashford, of Oldbury, matched his dog against a similar champion from Darlaston; the fight came off near West Bromwich, but all the principals were arrested and heavily fined at a magisterial court held at the New Inns, Handsworth.

Rat-killing was another sport which enjoyed great popularity in Oldbury, and was practised till a much later period. The following notice posted in tavern windows is of a type which is well-remembered by many persons to-day:—

At the —— Inn, Oldbury, a Rat-killing Leger will take place on Saturday, November 1, when the Proprietor will give £1 10s. if there are ten dogs at 2/6 each. If over ten dogs all money added. Heats, the best of three; final, the best of five.

The smaller the dog that could kill the greatest number of rats in the shortest time, the more highly-prized was the canine conqueror. The usual conditions of a match were "rats for pounds," as it was expressed; that is to say, a dog weighing nine pounds might be taken as a standard, with the set task of killing three rats in one minute. The dog accomplishing his task in the shortest time was adjudged the winner. A tiny terrier might literally be worth its weight in gold, amongst the sportsmen of this "fancy." The contests took place in a rat pit constructed of thin iron bars, three or four feet in diameter and about the same in height. There were many of these rat-killing arenas in and around Oldbury sixty years ago.

Now to leave the hard paths of historic fact, and to wander for a few brief moments in the more enchanting realms of legendary fancy.

A Reformation jibe derived the name Halesowen from Hell's Own, where the devil kept his hounds, and whence, with his huntsman, Harry-ca-nab (both mounted on wild horses snorting fire and brimstone) he set forth to hunt the boars of Feckenham Forest and the great wild bulls which infested the Bromsgrove Lickeys.

In the vernacular Halesowen is often called "Yelts" by the natives of the surrounding parishes—but why this nickname was applied to the place is not known. The word "ale" is pronounced "yel" in some parts of England, and "Yelts" may possibly be the ancient pronunciation of Hales.

The bibliography of the locality is much too extensive to catalogue here. First and foremost must be noted COLLECTIONS FOR A HISTORY OF WORCESTERSHIRE, published in three volumes by Dr. Treadway Russel Nash, 1789–1799.

In 1887 was published a BIBLIOGRAPHY AND CHRONOLOGY OF HALESOWEN, issued by the Index Society; it contained much useful information which was originally brought together with a view to compiling a history of the place, based on that of Dr. Charles Lyttelton, bishop of Carlisle, and President of the Society of Antiquaries.

The locality has an extensive literature, because it is rich in literary associations. The connection of the Leasowes with the poet Shenstone, and of Rowley Regis with the minor poet Woodhouse, has been dealt with to the fullest extent permitted in these pages. Ample allusion has also been made to Hagley, so beloved of Pope, Shenstone, and Thomson, as to have been called the Poets' Retreat. The presence of an important mediæval abbey at

Halesowen made the place a subject for the avid attention of a host of ecclesiastical scribes and chroniclers; while the famous legend of St. Kenelm has adorned the annals of religious romanticism from Saxon times to the present day.

That vast storehouse of bygone and half-forgotten lore, THE GENTLEMAN'S MAGAZINE, contains a number of plates illustrative of this locality. To the local historian they are, of considerable value; and those delineating architectural features will present some startling surprises. Here is a list of the plates:—

Year.	View.	Vol.	Page.
1791.	Lid of Stone Coffin at Halesowen	61	1097
1795.	Cottage at Halesowen, called Shenstone's School	65	905
1795:	Priory (?) in Grounds of Leasowes	65	457
1797.	View of St. Kenelin's Chapel	67	738
1797.	View of West Bromwich Church	67	185
1799.	Remains of Halesowen Abbey	69	113
1801.	Hagley Park, picturesque object in	71	593
1802.	St. Kenelin's Chapel, view of	72	1177
1802.	St. Kenelin's Chapel, sculpture in	72	1177
1803.	Halesowen Church	73	613
1807.	Leasows, the Urn for Somerville	77	809
1807.	Sculpture at St. Margaret's Well	77	809
1808.	Token of William Bodeley in Halesowen, 1667	78	1057
1808.	Remains of Halesowen Abbey	78	577
1811.	Leasows, Birthplace of Shenstone	81	505
1812).	Clent Church	82	417
1812.	A Quarry of Rowley Stone	82	513
1813.	View of Chapel at Frankley	83	417

The "Priory" at the Leasowes was, of course, one of Shenstone's bogus antiquities. The sculpture at St. Margaret's Well, Hasbury, was genuine; it quaintly illustrated the legend of this ancient holy well, where crippled men arrived on crutches, and, after drinking of its miraculous waters, were able to walk hastily away without any assistance whatever.

A large private collection of drawings, prints, etchings, and views of all kinds, illustrative of the entire district, has been made b Mr. Harry E. Palfrey, of Stourbridge. The author and producers of this work have gladly availed themselves of the collector's permission to reproduce a few of them for the illumination of these pages, and they here acknowledge his courtesy and tender him their most sincere thanks.

AN INDEX

Abbeley 27
Abney 76
Accles & Pollock 105
Adcock 174
Addington 49, 53
Adkins 87
Aethelward 24
Albion 100, 101
Albright 98, 110
Alelm 24
Allan-Frazer 54
Amphlett 21, 22, 134, 157, 171, 173
Ansculph 24, 25
Auden 137

Baggeridge 87
Barbara, St. [Shrine] 35, 42
Barlow 106
Barr 45, 52, 141, 163
Bassano 131, 132
Baxter, Richard 57, 63, 72
Belbroughton 5, 13
Bentley 155
Best 30, 148
Bilston 4, 30, 72, 75-77, 81, 86, 87, 108, 177
Bird's Mill 27
Blackheath 5, 66, 108, 131
Blakeley, Blackley 13, 27, 36, 49, 50-53, 84, 85
Blount 29, 41, 48
Bloxwich 45, 47

Blue Gates 76, 77
Botetort 119, 120
Boundaries, divisions etc 2, 4, 6, 13, 22, 107, 146
Brades 5, 11, 57, 62, 64, 66, 87-91, 100, 101, 131, 147
Bradley 75, 77, 112
Broadwell 49, 110, 115
Brendhall, Brand Hall, etc 119, 120
Brettel Lane 73
Bridge, Sir F 178, 180
Brierley Hill 125, 143, 144
Brisnell Hall 121, 135
Broadwaters 77
Brockmore 73
Bromsgrove 5, 19, 38, 103
Bury Hill 9, 11, 110

Caddick 54, 77
Cakemore 6, 14, 31, 107, 108, 119
Calmore 52
Came 107
Cannock 5, 6, 11, 60, 125
Carne Hundred 24
Carriage Works 49
Carter's Green 4
Caslon 174, 176
Castle Leasow 9, 47
Causeway 47, 66
Cawnney Hill 85, 129
Chain Trade 152, 153
Chance, Chaunce 19, 93-98, 110, 116, 174

Chance and Hunt 7
Chapel, Chapelry 45, 55-57, 61, 132, 133, 146
Chapel, Private 50, 118, 120, 146
Clent 5, 7, 8, 13, 23, 35, 38, 57, 60, 67, 86, 118, 129, 132-134, 136, 137, 145, 163, 166, 170, 183
Coalfield 6, 8, 81-87
Colley Gate 22
Combs Wood 77, 105, 134
Combow 29, 43
Cornwallis 52, 53
Coseley 12, 61, 73
Courts, 4, 112-115
Cowbatch 14, 170
Cradley 12, 20, 21, 31, 33, 57, 61, 64, 73, 87, 106, 107, 118, 145-149, 151-153
Cradley Forge 22, 73, 149, 151
Creslau 25, 107
Crookhay 101
Crosswells 11, 103
Customs etc 19, 27, 28, 49, 180, 181

Darby End 83
Darlaston 47, 59, 60, 65, 73, 155, 181
Dawes 81, 83, 84, 99, 100
Deepfields 77
Dodford 3 8
Downing 49
Droitwich 12, 23, 46, 96
Dudley 3, 4, 6, 8, 12, 43, 45, 47, 48, 61, 67, 77, 106, 108, 139-141, 145
Dudley Castle 3-5, 11, 79, 85, 100, 143, 158, 164

Dudley, Dud 73, 75, 129, 149-151, 159
Dudley [family] 3, 18, 25, 29, 41, 48, 50, 71, 85, 101, 140
Dudley Port 86, 101

Eccleshall 59
Edgbaston 18, 19, 174
Eginton 94
Ell Wood 24
Enamels 176
Esch 107
Evans, Eyre 58

Fairs 28
Farley 24, 3 6
Featherstone 49, 53
Fokerham 25, 118-120
Foley 18, 57, 63, 67, 70-72, 118, 157
Fox, Henderson & Co 91
Frankley 12-14, 17, 24, 31, 41, 56, 155-157, 183
Frankley Beeches 84, 156
French Walls 76, 91

Galton 120
Gibbons 54
Gold's Hill 101
Gornal 73
Granges, etc 29, 36, 155
Great Bridge 4
Green 18, 103
Greet 27
Greet's Green 76

Grimshaw 53
Grove 21, 53, 173

Hackett 106
Haden 21, 13 2
Hagley 5, 43, 69, 120, 125, 140, 145, 157, 159, 162, 166-170, 182, 183
Hailstone 129
Halfshire 107
Hampstead 25, 36, 86
Hancock 176-178
Handsworth 2, 181
Harborne 45, 52, 98, 112, 118
Hasbury 14, 25, 31, 107, 108
Hawn, Halen 12, 25, 31, 107, 108, 118
Hill 25, 31, 107, 108
Himley 84, 87, 140, 164
Hingley 101, 154, 155
Holbeach 159
Holloways 3, 76
Hospitals 2, 98, 110
Howley, Owley 14, 36, 155
Hundred 23-25, 106, 107
Hunnington 13, 25, 57, 107
Hunt, Wm., and Sons 5, 87, 117

Icknield Street 47
Illey 12, 25, 31, 107
Izon 49

Johnson, Dr 22, 13 8, 161, 163, 165
Johnson 122

Katherine, St. [Chapel] 19, 119
Kenelm's, St., 21, 31, 35, 41, 57, 118, 166, 170, 183
King's Norton 53
Kingswinford 73, 84, 86, 143, 147, 158
Kinver 38, 140

Langley 2, 13, 25, 49, 53-55, 66, 98, 103, 107, 110, 111, 118, 121
Lappal 13, 25, 31, 107, 125
Lea, Lea-Smith 22, 29
Leasowes 12, 17, 69, 138, 161-163, 168, 183
Legends 64, 155, 156, 170, 182
Lickey Hills 5
Lifford 13
Lightwoods 13
Lutley 13, 24, 25, 36J06, 107
Lye Waste 12, 87, 151, 152
Lyttelton 17-19, 23, 29, 41, 43, 48, 51, 57, 112, 120, 139, 148, 156-158, 162, 166-168, 170, 182

McKean 62, 116
Mainwaring 54
Markets 28, 43, 48, 80, 109, 180
Marmium 173
Melley 13
Mills 26, 27, 49, 77
Mingey 53
Moxley 77
Mucklow Hill 13, 21, 165
Muntz 91
Nail Trade 71-73, 103, 130

Nash 9, 146, 182
Netherton 8, 77, 101, 125, 141, 154
Newby 121, 135
Norbert, St., 31
Northfield 13, 145, 156

Oakham 3, 129, 130, 137
Ocker Hill 76, 125
Offffloor 13, 24, 3 6
Old Hill 83, 84, 86, 101, 131, 132, 137, 153, 154
Oldswinford 36, 72, 118, 140
Olwine 23
Organs 20, 42
Owen 11, 23
Owley [see Howley]

Paganel 25
Palfrey 183
Parrot 54, 112
Paston 53, 57, 173
Pearsall, Peshall 18, 21, 118, 173
Pedmore 125
Penncricket 13
Pensnett 144-147, 149
Piddock 49
Pircote 36
Pools, Wells, etc., 5, 28, 49, 146, 148, 183
Population 23-25, 29, 111, 145, 148, 152
Portway 46, 47, 122
Powell 18, 121
Premonstratem 31, 37, 38

Presbyterians 56, 57-61
Prestwood 157, 158
Puppy Green 76

Quarry Bank 118
Quinton 13, 25, 67, 68, 69, 97, 108, 118, 125, 155

Railways 6, 8, 80, 91, 96, 101, 103, 104, 111
Ramrod Hall 82, 130
Reddall, Radwell 14, 36, 136
Registers 20, 22, 57, 137
Ridgacre 14, 25, 31, 36, 107
Riots 60, 147, 150
Robsart 50-52, 55-56
Roger, Earl, 23
Roger the Huntsman 24
Rollason 137
Romsley 13, 24-27, 31, 36, 57
Rood End 11, 14, 54, 84
Round 103
Round's Green 81, 82, 108, 116
Roway 49
Rowley Hills 4, 5, 71, 79, 83, 85-87
Rowley Regis 2, 3, 5, 14, 33, 36, 55, 58-60, 66, 73, 75, 83, 85, 112, 118, 122, 127, 129-135, 137-139, 158, 159
Rubery 81
Rudland 119, 157, 171
Rushall 45, 86, 127
Ryder's Green 77, 173
Salt 12, 23, 46, 149

Sandwell 3, 4, 28, 45, 83, 86, 8T

Schools 57, 62, 63, 65, 96, 113, 116-118, 120, 121, 135, 136, 147, 148, 161

Sedgley 4, 5, 8, 52, 59, 73, 85, 108, 118, 129, 150, 158

Sheldon 65

Shenstone 17, 21, 22, 30, 138, 161, 169, 176, 183

Shirlet 25

Showell 103

Smethwick 2-4, 14, 52, 76-78, 80, 96, 125

Soho 69, 75, 122

Somery 25, 119, 127

Southcott 70, 71

Spon Lane 11, 76, 82, 85, 93-97

Stour 9, 13, 31, 33, 85, 146, 156, 164

Stourbridge 71, 72, 85, 86, 118, 140 150

Stour, Citra 26

Stour, Ultra 26

Stour Valley 80, 87, 101, 122, 124

Sutton 47, 155

Swan Village 46

Tame 5, 48, 85, 100

Tandy 173

Taylor, Abbot 20, 41, 65, 155

Taxes, dues, etc 107, 111, 117, 146, 156

Thimble Mill 77

Thompson 110

Thomson, poet 166-170

Three Shire Oak 13

Tinker's Farm 14

Tipton 45, 57, 66

Tividale 14, 66, 85, 101, 132, 135

Toll End 76, 77

Trent 5, 28

Tuckey 29, 41, 48, 52

Turner's Hill 129

Turton 49, 52, 57, 59, 6064, 135

Uffmoor [see Offmoor]

Underhill 18

Vernon 111, 115, 118, 121

Vestry 108, 110, 111

Walloxhill 13, 25, 26, 28, 36, 49, 53, 54, 121

Walsall 35, 38, 40-42, 45, 53, 57, 77, 84, 125, 141

Walton 13

Walwick 27

Ward 3 0, 173

Warley, Salop 2, 23, 24, 3 1,

Warley, Wigorn 1, 14, 23-25, 36, 48, 106, 107, 110, 118-120, 135, 180

Warley Woods 98

Warstone 13

Wassal Grove 13, 84, 173,

Wednesbury 2, 3, 27, 30, 35, 38-40, 42, 45, 46, 57, 61, 65, 67, 71, 75-77, 85, 100, 101, 104, 105, 118, 124, 125, 141, 174

Wells, Springs 103, 109, 148, 183

Weolegh 13, 119
Wesley 18, 64-69, 165, 176, 177
West Bromwich 2, 3, 6, 8, 26, 57 61, 73, 77, 83, 84, 107, 112, 115, 183
Wheeler 104
White Heath 5, 6, 131
Whitley 3 6
Williams 122
Willingsworth 77, 101, 104
Wilmot 21, 30, 162
Wilson 98, 110
Windmill End 77, 101
Withymoor 83
Wollescote 152

Wolverhampton 3, 5, 57, 61, 77, 79, 80, 84, 101, 125, 140, 143, 158
Wombourne 45, 118
Woodhouse, poet 138-141
Wood and Kendrick 110
Wood 77
Wordsley 73
Wren's Nest 5, 85, 125, 141
Wright 53, 54
Wulfine 24
Wyrley 52

Zouche 173